CAMBRIDGE TEXTS IN THE
HISTORY OF PHILOSOPHY

LESSING

Philosophical and Theological Writings

D1603383

CAMBRIDGE TEXTS IN THE HISTORY OF PHILOSOPHY

Series editors

KARL AMERIKS
Professor of Philosophy, University of Notre Dame

DESMOND M. CLARKE
Professor of Philosophy, University College Cork

The main objective of Cambridge Texts in the History of Philosophy is to expand the range, variety and quality of texts in the history of philosophy which are available in English. The series includes texts by familiar names (such as Descartes and Kant) and also by less well-known authors. Wherever possible, texts are published in complete and unabridged form, and translations are specially commissioned for the series. Each volume contains a critical introduction together with a guide to further reading and any necessary glossaries and textual apparatus. The volumes are designed for student use at undergraduate and postgraduate level and will be of interest not only to students of philosophy but also to a wider audience of readers in the history of science, the history of theology and the history of ideas.

For a list of titles published in the series, please see end of book.

GOTTHOLD EPHRAIM LESSING

Philosophical and Theological Writings

TRANSLATED AND EDITED BY

H. B. NISBET

Sidney Sussex College, Cambridge

CAMBRIDGE
UNIVERSITY PRESS

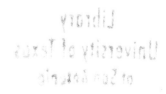

PUBLISHED BY THE PRESS SYNDICATE OF THE UNIVERSITY OF CAMBRIDGE
The Pitt Building, Trumpington Street, Cambridge, United Kingdom

CAMBRIDGE UNIVERSITY PRESS
The Edinburgh Building, Cambridge CB2 2RU, UK
40 West 20th Street, New York, NY 10011-4211, USA
10 Stamford Road, Oakleigh, VIC 3166, Australia
Ruiz de Alarcón 13, 28014 Madrid, Spain
Dock House, The Waterfront, Cape Town 8001, South Africa

http://www.cambridge.org

First published 2005

Printed in the United Kingdom at the University Press, Cambridge

Typeface Ehrhardt 11/13 pt   *System* LATEX 2ε   [TB]

A catalogue record for this book is available from the British Library

ISBN 0 521 83120 2 hardback
ISBN 0 521 53847 5 paperback

Contents

Contents

Acknowledgements

For permission to quote Michael Hamburger's translation of Goethe's poem 'Prometheus', I am grateful to John Calder (London) and Suhrkamp/Insel Publishers Boston Inc. I should also like to thank Karl S. Guthke for valuable help in resolving some problems of translation in 'The Challenge' (pp. 116–19), and Karl S. Guthke and Nicholas Boyle for many stimulating conversations on Lessing and the Enlightenment.

Chronology

1767	*Minna von Barnhelm*, comedy promoting Saxon and Prussian reconciliation, seals Lessing's reputation as Germany's leading dramatist
1767–9	Official critic and dramatic theorist at new 'National Theatre' in Hamburg, which soon collapses through mismanagement and lack of public support
1768–9	*Antiquarian Letters* and associated conflict with C. A. Klotz
1770	Meeting with J. G. Herder; appointed Librarian to the Duke of Brunswick-Lüneburg at Wolfenbüttel
1771	Engagement to Eva König, widow of a Hamburg merchant; joins Freemasons
1772	Tragedy *Emilia Galotti*, implicitly critical of courtly absolutism; studies of Leibniz
1773	*Leibniz on Eternal Punishment*
1774	Publishes first (relatively innocuous) 'Fragment' of Reimarus's critique of the Bible and Christianity
1775	Journey to Leipzig, Berlin, Dresden, Vienna; audience with Emperor Joseph II and performances of Lessing's plays in honour of his visit; joins Prince Leopold of Brunswick on a tour of Italy; audience with Pope Pius VI
1776	Audience in Dresden with Elector Frederick Augustus III of Saxony; marries Eva König and returns to Wolfenbüttel
1777	Declines post of Director of Mannheim theatre; publishes five more 'Fragments' of Reimarus's work, together with first half of *The Education of the Human Race*; on 25 December, Eva gives birth to a son, who dies soon afterwards
1778	Eva dies on 10 January; Lessing finds distraction in theological polemics against Goeze and others (*A Rejoinder, Axioms, Anti-Goeze*, etc.); publishes first three dialogues of *Ernst and Falk*; prohibition (July) of further writings on religion without advance approval of Brunswick censorship
1779	Furthers his theological campaign by indirect means through the drama *Nathan the Wise*

1780 Publishes complete text of *The Education of the Human Race*;
    A. F. von Knigge obtains a copy of the last two dialogues of
    Ernst and Falk and publishes them without Lessing's
    permission; conversations on Spinoza with Jacobi; Lessing's
    health deteriorates rapidly

1781 Dies on 15 February

Further reading

The most comprehensive edition of Lessing's works is Gotthold Ephraim Lessing, *Sämtliche Schriften*, edited by Karl Lachmann and Franz Muncker, 23 vols. (Stuttgart, 1886–1924). The new edition of Gotthold Ephraim Lessing, *Werke und Briefe*, edited by Wilfried Barner and others, 12 vols. (Frankfurt-on-Main, 1985–2003), is particularly useful for its detailed commentaries and notes, which I have found most helpful in compiling this volume; it also contains the most complete collection of Lessing's surviving correspondence.

There is no full and up-to-date biographical study of Lessing in English. H. B. Garland, *Lessing: The Founder of Modern German Literature* (Cambridge, 1937; revised edition, London and New York, 1962, reprinted Folcroft, PA, 1973), and F. Andrew Brown, *Gotthold Ephraim Lessing* (New York, 1971), contain useful basic information. The best general introduction currently available in English, with essays on most aspects of Lessing's life and works, is *A Companion to the Works of Lessing*, edited by Barbara Fischer and Thomas C. Fox (Rochester, NY and Woodbridge, 2005); a more detailed equivalent in German is Monika Fick's *Lessing-Handbuch. Leben – Werk – Wirkung* (Stuttgart and Weimar, 2000).

The best analysis in English of Lessing's philosophical and religious thought, with particular emphasis on the influence of Leibniz, is Henry E. Allison, *Lessing and the Enlightenment: His Philosophy of Religion and its Relation to Eighteenth-Century Thought* (Ann Arbor, 1966). Leonard P. Wessell, *Lessing's Theology: A Reinterpretation* (The Hague and Paris, 1977), offers an alternative reading of the theological writings; but Georges Pons, *Gotthold Ephraim Lessing et le Christianisme* (Paris, 1964), remains by far the most comprehensive study of Lessing's religious thought as a whole. Klaus Epstein, *The Genesis of German Conservatism* (Princeton, 1966) contains a judicious account of Lessing's conflict with Goeze. Lessing's relationship with Moses Mendelssohn is well documented in Alexander Altmann, *Moses Mendelssohn: A Biographical Study* (University of Alabama Press, 1973).

The reception of Spinoza in Germany is extensively covered in David Bell, *Spinoza in Germany from 1670 to the Age of Goethe* (London, 1984), and his influence on the radical thought of the early Enlightenment is explored at length by Jonathan I. Israel, *Radical Enlightenment: Philosophy and the Making of Modernity 1650–1750* (Oxford, 2001). The pantheism controversy initiated by Jacobi's publication of his conversations with Lessing is fully documented in *The Spinoza Conversations between Lessing and Jacobi: Text with Excerpts from the Ensuing Controversy*, introduced by Gérard Vallée and translated by Gérard Vallée, J. B. Lawson, and C. G. Chapple (Lanham, NY and London, 1988), with a long and useful introduction. English translations of further works by Jacobi, again with a useful introduction, are available in Friedrich Heinrich Jacobi, *The Main Philosophical Writings and the Novel 'Allwill'*, edited and translated by George di Giovanni (Montreal and Kingston, 1994). A short account of the Spinoza controversy can also be found in Frederick C. Beiser, *The Fate of Reason: German Philosophy from Kant to Fichte* (Cambridge, MA and London, 1987).

Theories of metempsychosis, palingenesis, reincarnation, and the transmigration of souls in later eighteenth-century Germany are discussed in detail in Lieselotte E. Kurth-Voigt, *Continued Existence, Reincarnation, and the Power of Sympathy in Classical Weimar* (Rochester, NY and Woodbridge, 1999). The Masonic background to Lessing's dialogues *Ernst and Falk* can be followed up in J. M. Roberts, The *Mythology of the Secret Societies* (London, 1972) and Margaret C. Jacob, *The Radical Enlightenment: Pantheists, Freemasons and Republicans* (London, 1981). I have not dealt in this volume with Lessing's ethical thought, since most of his relevant writings deal neither with philosophy nor religion but with the theory of tragedy; it is, however, examined in detail in H. B. Nisbet, 'Lessing's Ethics', *Lessing Yearbook*, 25 (1993), 1–40.

Note on texts and translations

The texts in this volume include works which Lessing himself published (nos. 5–11, 13, 16, and 17), fragmentary works published after his death (nos. 1–4, 12, 14, and 15), and the recollections of Friedrich Heinrich Jacobi of conversations with Lessing in 1780 (no. 18). Their sequence is chronological – by date of completed publication in the case of works published by Lessing or Jacobi, and by approximate date of composition in the case of posthumous works. Thematically, the texts fall into four distinct groups: early fragments on the philosophy of religion, informed by studies of Leibniz, Wolff, and Spinoza (nos. 1–4), an essay on Leibniz based on intensive engagement with that philosopher in the early 1770s (no. 5), works associated with Lessing's publication, in 1777, of 'Fragments' from Hermann Samuel Reimarus's radical critique of the Bible and with the ensuing theological controversy (nos. 6–14), and a group of late works and conversations on speculative philosophy, the last of which (the conversations on Spinoza) generated a further controversy after Lessing's death (nos. 15–18).

All of the texts by Lessing are translated from what is still the most comprehensive edition of his writings, the *Sämtliche Schriften*, edited by Karl Lachmann and Franz Muncker (referred to as LM), 23 vols. (Stuttgart, 1886–1924). Locations of the German originals, by volume and page numbers in LM, are as follows: 1 (XIV, 175–8); 2 (XIV, 292–3); 3 (XIV, 294–6); 4 (XIV, 312–13); 5 (XI, 461–87); 6 (XII, 303–4 and 428–50); 7 (XIII, 1–8); 8 (XIII, 9–17); 9 (XIII, 19–35); 10 (XIII, 91–103); 11 (XIII, 105–37); 12 (XVI, 370–91); 13 (XIII, 329–6); 14 (XVI, 518–19); 15 (XVI, 522–5); 16 (XIII, 339–68 and 389–411); 17 (XIII, 413–36). Jacobi's recollections (no. 18) are translated from the critical edition of his *Über die Lehre des Spinoza*, *in Briefen an Herrn Moses Mendelssohn* [*On the Doctrine of Spinoza, in Letters to Mr Moses Mendelssohn*] (Breslau, 1785) in *Die Hauptschriften zum Pantheismusstreit zwischen Jacobi und Mendelssohn*, edited by Heinrich Scholz (Berlin, 1916), pp. 74–103.

All but two of the texts are complete in themselves. The two exceptions are Jacobi's recollections, which form a self-contained section in the larger work referred to above, and no. 9 (*A Rejoinder*), which includes only Lessing's general, introductory section on Scriptural exegesis and omits the second, more detailed section in which he refutes the attempts of his adversary, Johann Heinrich Ress, to harmonise or explain away the ten contradictions identified by Reimarus in the gospel narratives of Christ's resurrection.

The complete text of Reimarus's 'Fragments', as published by Lessing, can be found in LM xii, 304–428 and xiii, 221–327; the final, integral version of Reimarus's work was not published until nearly two centuries later, as *Apologie oder Schutzschrift für die vernünftigen Verehrer Gottes*, edited by Gerhard Alexander (Frankfurt-on-Main, 1972). Relevant writings by Lessing's adversaries can be found in the new edition of Lessing's works, namely Gotthold Ephraim Lessing, *Werke und Briefe*, edited by Wilfried Barner and others (referred to as B), 12 vols. (Frankfurt-on-Main, 1985–2003). Their location, by volume and page numbers in B, are as follows: viii, 355–435 (Johann Daniel Schumann); viii, 475–503 (Johann Heinrich Ress); ix, 11–37, 117–45, 163–84, 357–94, 447–69 (Johann Melchior Goeze); where appropriate, references to these works will be supplied in the footnotes to Lessing's texts.

Although most of Lessing's works on philosophical and theological topics are included in this volume, three important texts are for good reason omitted. The first is *Laocoön*, his famous treatise on aesthetics, which has already appeared in *Classic and Romantic German Aesthetics*, edited by J. M. Bernstein (Cambridge, 2003), pp. 25–129, in the same series as the present volume; its subject-matter is in any case quite distinct from that of the texts included here. The second is the drama *Nathan the Wise* of 1779, whose reflections on religion (especially the famous parable of the three rings in Act III) enlarge, in poetic form, on Lessing's scepticism concerning historical proofs of religious truth and on his belief in the primacy of the ethical, both of which are conspicuous in several texts in the present collection; this lengthy drama would plainly be out of place in a series devoted to works of a theoretical and discursive character. The third major omission is his *Anti-Goeze*, a series of eleven polemical pamphlets published between April and July 1778 (just after the *Axioms* and immediately before the *Necessary Answer*) and directed at Lessing's principal adversary in the controversy over Reimarus's 'Fragments'; although this work is, in literary terms, a masterpiece of polemical writing, its main purpose is to ridicule Goeze rather than to add substantively to the theological points expounded more clearly and dispassionately in the *Axioms* and other related works included here.

English translations of some of the works by Lessing in this volume have appeared in the past, but none of them are now in print. The most complete collection, *Lessing's Theological Writings*, edited and translated by Henry Chadwick (London, 1956), contains just over a quarter of the material included here (nos. 1, 2, 4, 7, 8, 12, 13, 14, and 17); while I have found some of Chadwick's renderings helpful, I have also been able to correct a number of errors and omissions in his text. Several translations of *The Education of the Human Race* appeared between 1806 and 1908, but all are inferior to Chadwick's version. Part of *A Parable* and most of the *Axioms*, together with the *Anti-Goeze*, were published under the title *Cambridge Free Thoughts and Letters on Bibliolatry*, translated from the German of G. E. Lessing by H. Bernard (London, 1862), and a translation of the *Masonic Dialogues* by A. Cohen was published in London in 1927. All of these translations are antiquated or in other respects unsatisfactory. Two modern translations of Jacobi's conversations with Lessing are available, by Gérard Vallée and collaborators and by George di Giovanni respectively (see Further Reading above for details). I consulted these after translating the piece myself, but saw no need to alter my own version. To the best of my knowledge, the remaining texts in this volume have not previously appeared in English.

Except where otherwise stated, translations from languages other than German are my own. Where any ambiguity is possible in my English renderings of German terms, the original German term is supplied in brackets after the translation. Square brackets are used throughout to enclose editorial interpolations. Editorial footnotes are keyed by numbers, author's footnotes by letters of the alphabet.

Introduction

At the wish of his father, a devout Lutheran clergyman, the young Lessing matriculated at Leipzig University in 1746 as a student of theology. But with that independent-mindedness – not to say rebelliousness – which would characterise his behaviour throughout his life, he soon abandoned theology for secular subjects and the writing of comedies. This does not mean that he had no interest in religion. He in fact returned to it again and again, with the same mixture of respect and criticism which defined his relationship with his father; and when he eventually completed his studies a few years later at Wittenberg – nominally in the medical faculty – he spent much of his time writing 'vindications' or defences of Catholic and Protestant heretics of the Reformation period.

Even in his early years, Lessing identified himself with progressive Enlightenment thought, in particular with the rationalism of Leibniz and Wolff. He shared their view of the universe as the harmonious creation of a wise and beneficent designer, in which the tendency of all things is to strive towards ever higher levels of consciousness and perfection, while such evils as do exist are ultimately conducive to the good of the whole. In Lessing's case, this rationalism was soon modified and supplemented by the scepticism of Pierre Bayle, author of the massive *Historical and Critical Dictionary*, whose biographical articles included numerous philosophers and religious thinkers of the past.[1] Bayle's meticulous historical scholarship and destructive scrutiny of apparently established facts

---

[1] See Henry E. Allison, *Lessing and the Enlightenment: His Philosophy of Religion and its Relation to Eighteenth-Century Thought* (Ann Arbor, 1966), pp. 16–24; also H. B. Nisbet, 'Lessing and Pierre Bayle', in C. P. Magill, Brian A. Rowley, and Christopher J. Smith (eds.), *Tradition and Creation: Essays in Honour of Elizabeth Mary Wilkinson* (Leeds, 1978), pp. 13–29.

and supposedly rational certainties left lasting marks on Lessing's own writings, and encouraged him to regard all doctrines, including those which he himself put forward, as no more than provisional. In addition, Bayle's powerful advocacy of tolerance, of what he called 'the rights of the erring conscience' (that is, of all sincerely held, though possibly erroneous beliefs, including those of atheists), reinforced Lessing's lifelong sympathy with persecuted individuals and religious or social minorities.

Intellectual development

Lessing's earliest philosophical writings, all of which remained fragments unpublished in his lifetime, are heavily indebted to rationalism. *The Christianity of Reason*, probably written in 1753, depicts a recognisably Leibnizian universe, with its scale of being, universal harmony, perfectibility, and cosmic optimism. But it goes beyond Leibniz in a decisive respect which testifies to the young Lessing's intellectual autonomy: for he constructs not only the universe, but also the Holy Trinity, by a process of rational deduction, and presents the universe itself as a necessary emanation rather than a freely chosen creation of the rational deity.[2] These ideas were not new. But they were certainly heretical. And the concept of necessary creation was uncomfortably close – too close for the work to be published – to the ideas of another rationalist philosopher, namely Spinoza, whose pantheism was at that time widely held to be indistinguishable from atheism.

The next three fragments in the present collection were written around ten years later, at a time when Lessing's work as secretary to a Prussian general in Breslau (1760–5) left him ample time for private study. During those years, he acquired an intimate knowledge of the patristic writers and of the early history of Christianity, thereby preparing the way for his theological polemics of the following decade. His interest in philosophy was also reawakened at this time when his friend Moses Mendelssohn sent him his collected *Philosophical Writings*, published in 1761, in which Spinoza (to whom, as a Jewish philosopher like himself, Mendelssohn felt a certain

---

[2] For further discussion of this question, see H. B. Nisbet, 'The Rationalisation of the Holy Trinity from Lessing to Hegel', *Lessing Yearbook*, 31 (1999), 65–89.

affinity) featured prominently along with the German rationalists.[3] But whereas Mendelssohn, in keeping with his own Jewish faith, clung firmly to the transcendental God of Leibniz, Wolff, and the Torah, Lessing's two fragments *On the Reality of Things outside God* and *Spinoza only Put Leibniz on the Track of Pre-established Harmony* are, at least by implication, more sympathetic towards Spinoza's monism. The third fragment of Lessing's Breslau years, *On the Origin of Revealed Religion*, is explicitly critical of all revealed religion, which it treats as a necessary evil, an unavoidable accretion on the universal natural religion prescribed by reason. This short fragment, more reminiscent of the Savoyard vicar of Rousseau's *Emile* (1762) than of Leibniz and Wolff, marks the high point of Lessing's religious radicalism. Though he regularly criticises and questions the revealed religions – especially Christianity – in his later writings, he is never again quite so unequivocally hostile to revelation as in the concluding paragraph of this Breslau fragment (p. 36).[4]

A marked change in his attitude towards revealed religion can indeed be detected in the early 1770s, a change for which a number of factors were responsible. The death of his father in 1770 lent a new gravity to his thoughts on religion, which he had associated since his childhood with the parent whose stern piety he had simultaneously respected and resisted in the name of reason and enlightenment. His encounter, at around the same time, with a natural religion more extreme than his own in the work of H. S. Reimarus, whose consistent reduction of revealed religion to bad faith and priestcraft he found less than plausible, disposed him to look again, as he told Mendelssohn, at some of the prejudices – or truths – which he now feared he might have discarded prematurely.[5]

His change of attitude was, however, due above all to intensive studies of Leibniz, many of whose posthumous writings, including the *New Essays on Human Understanding*, had recently come to light in editions of his works published in 1765 and 1768; these editions revealed a more complex

[3] See Moses Mendelssohn, *Philosophical Writings*, edited by Daniel O. Dahlstrom (Cambridge, 1997), pp. 100-11; also Alexander Altmann, *Moses Mendelssohn: A Biographical Study* (University of Alabama Press, 1973), pp. 33–40 and 50–3.

[4] This and all subsequent page-references in the text, unless identified by an additional prefix, are to the present volume.

[5] Lessing to Mendelssohn, 9 January 1771, in Gotthold Ephraim Lessing, *Werke und Briefe*, edited by Wilfried Barner and others, 12 vols. (Frankfurt-on-Main, 1985–2003), XI/2, pp. 144f. Subsequent references to this edition, identified by the prefix B, are included in the text.

and diversified thinker than the author of the familiar *Theodicy*, with its systematic rational optimism. (Lessing's interest was also whetted by the knowledge that Leibniz had once held the same post as librarian to the dukes of Brunswick to which he was himself appointed in 1770.) What he now found most congenial in Leibniz was not so much his particular opinions, as the whole style and manner of his thinking, especially his readiness to recognise an element of truth in the most diverse philosophical and theological positions: since each monad views the universe from a different perspective, each will form a different, and inevitably partial, image of the whole. Lessing defines this strategy as follows in *Leibniz on Eternal Punishment* (p. 46):

> In his quest for truth, Leibniz never took any notice of accepted opinions; but in the firm belief that no opinion can be accepted unless it is in a certain respect, or in a certain sense true, he was often so accommodating as to turn the opinion over and over until he was able to bring that certain respect to light, and to make that certain sense comprehensible [. . .] He willingly set his own system aside, and tried to lead each individual along the path to truth on which he found him.

Applied to the question of religious truth, this approach rules out the possibility that, for example, the doctrines of revelation are comprehensively false and those of rational religion exclusively true: all of them will embody a greater or lesser element of truth, expressed in more or less rational ways. Significantly, the unfamiliar works of Leibniz which appeared in Louis Dutens's edition (Geneva, 1768) of the *Opera omnia* [*Complete Works*] included defences of several Christian mysteries such as transubstantiation and original sin.[6] In a similar spirit, Lessing now added his support, in the essay just quoted, to another Christian doctrine which Leibniz had defended, namely that of eternal punishment, extracting a rational sense from a dogma which rationalists such as J. A. Eberhard had dismissed as irrational: since the consequences of every action in a causally determined universe must be infinite and therefore eternal, the punishment which every sin incurs, in the shape of diminished perfection on the part of the sinner, must also be eternal.

---

[6] See Georges Pons, *Gotthold Ephraim Lessing et le Christianisme* (Paris, 1964), p. 231; this work remains the most comprehensive study to date on Lessing's views on religion.

There is, however, a fundamental difference between Lessing's and Leibniz's procedure. Leibniz, ever anxious not to offend Christian orthodoxy, had never claimed to demonstrate the truth of Christian doctrines, but only to defend them against rational attempts to disprove them. Lessing had no such inhibitions, contending in *The Education of the Human Race* that the rational content of revealed truths becomes progressively manifest over time, thereby superseding the original revelation; he then proceeds to extract a rational sense not only from the doctrine of the Trinity (as he had already done in *The Christianity of Reason* over twenty years earlier), but also from those of original sin and the atonement (pp. 234–5).

Lessing's philosophical position here is not one of relativism, for it does assume that there is such a thing as ultimate truth, even if complete knowledge of this truth, as he says in *A Rejoinder* (p. 98), is reserved for God alone, whereas human insights can never do more than approximate to it. But in so far as all of these insights are approximations, the truths we claim to possess are only relative truths, and in this qualified sense, Lessing is indeed a relativist. This attitude lends support to his lifelong belief in tolerance, and to the religious pluralism of his drama *Nathan the Wise* (1779), according to which each of the great monotheistic religions has an equally legitimate claim to truth, the precise extent of which can be determined only after an indefinite, and perhaps infinite, period of time. His open epistemology is likewise compatible with the qualified scepticism to which he had subscribed ever since his early studies of Bayle, and which is again evident in his polemics of 1778 against J. M. Goeze, whom he reminds that, since few passages in the Bible are ever interpreted in the same way by everyone, such credibility as the science of hermeneutics possesses can never be more than subjective (p. 141):

> Which are the right concepts to which they [the biblical passages] *should* give rise? Who is to decide this? Hermeneutics? Everyone has his own hermeneutics. Which of them is true? Are they all true? Or is none of them true? And this thing, this wretched, irksome thing, is to be the test of inner truth? Then what would be the test of *it*?

The later Lessing accordingly discerns at least a heuristic value in numerous distinct positions, while declining to commit himself exclusively to any of them.

Reimarus and the religious controversy

Towards the end of his years in Hamburg (1767–70), Lessing became friendly with the son and daughter of Hermann Samuel Reimarus, a respected orientalist and author of several works on philosophy and natural religion who had died early in 1768. Convinced that natural religion was alone sufficient, Reimarus had also proceeded, in a clandestine treatise entitled *Apology or Defence of the Rational Worshippers of God*, to attack the Bible in detail as a collection of lies and absurdities, accusing the apostles of secretly reinterring the body of Christ and inventing the story of his resurrection and divinity in order to increase their own worldly influence. Lessing at once realised, when shown the treatise in confidence, that it surpassed all earlier attacks on revealed religion, including those of the English deists, in virulence and exhaustiveness, and he prevailed on Elise Reimarus, when he left Hamburg for Wolfenbüttel, to let him retain an early draft of her father's work.

He was already determined to publish it, but even in Berlin, where Frederick the Great tolerated religious dissent so long as it did not disturb the public peace, Lessing's publisher Voss refused to take the project on after the censor, while stopping short of banning it, declined to approve it explicitly.[7] But when, in 1772, Lessing received permission from Brunswick to publish rare and learned materials from the Wolfenbüttel library without submitting them to the censor, he tested the water in 1774 by including a relatively innocuous fragment from Reimarus's work – a plea for the toleration of deists – in the periodical which he had meanwhile established in his capacity as librarian; he falsely claimed to have discovered the anonymous work in the library's holdings.[8] Emboldened by the lack of public protests, he followed this up in 1777 with five more fragments, culminating in Reimarus's critique of the resurrection story as a tissue of contradiction and deception (LM XII, 303–428).

The crucial question all this raises is what exactly Lessing hoped to achieve by releasing such explosive material, whose author had himself declared that it should be withheld until the advent of a more enlightened age. It is certain at least that he did not simply endorse Reimarus's

---

[7] Richard Daunicht, *Lessing im Gespräch* (Munich, 1971), p. 308.
[8] Gotthold Ephraim Lessing, *Sämtliche Schriften*, edited by Karl Lachmann and Franz Muncker, 23 vols. (Stuttgart, 1886–1924), XII, 254–71. Subsequent references to this edition, identified by the prefix LM, are included in the text.

position, for Reimarus's static vision of rational truth was incompatible with Lessing's dynamic view of truth and knowledge. His historical sense also told him that superstition and priestcraft do not fully account for the appeal of revealed religion to so many different ages and societies. His reservations on these and other accounts are plainly enough expressed in his editorial comments to the extracts from Reimarus which he published in 1777 (pp. 62–82). What he did agree with, however, was Reimarus's contention that the literal truth of the Bible is neither a tenable assumption nor a necessary article of religious belief.

It is nevertheless clear from Lessing's challenge to believers to rally to the defence of Christianity, and from the extended metaphors of combat to which he resorts on more than one occasion (see pp. 64 and 95–6), that he both expected and intended to provoke a major controversy. But with few exceptions, those who responded to his challenge were not those at whom it was primarily directed. For his private utterances plainly indicate that he hoped above all to provoke the so-called 'neologists', representatives of a liberal theological tendency which arose in the middle years of the century and included such eminent clerics as A. F. W. Sack, J. G. Töllner, J. J. Spalding, and W. A. Teller.[9] While not explicitly rejecting revelation, the neologists compromised with rationalism to the extent of glossing over or ignoring those revealed doctrines which could not readily be rationalised, such as original sin, the Trinity, and (as in Eberhard's case) eternal punishment. They in fact believed, as one commentator aptly puts it, that Christianity is true precisely to the extent that it is superfluous.[10] To Lessing, this was half-baked religion as well as half-baked philosophy, inferior both to the older Lutheran orthodoxy and to the radical deism of Reimarus, both of which at least possessed the virtue of intellectual honesty. But as his friends Mendelssohn and Nicolai predicted, the effect of what soon became known as the 'Fragments' was not at all what Lessing had intended. The leading neologists and academic theologians kept well in the background, while the conservative wing of Lutheran orthodoxy, led by J. M. Goeze, reacted with a mixture of outrage and incomprehension to what they perceived as a mischievous assault on everything they stood for.

In retrospect, this result was hardly surprising. The neologists saw no compelling need to defend their theology of compromise against either

---

[9] See Allison, *Lessing and the Enlightenment*, pp. 83–95; also Karl Aner, *Theologie der Lessingzeit* (Halle/Saale, 1929), pp. 61–143.
[10] Allison, *Lessing and the Enlightenment*, p. 16.

of the extremes they sought to avoid, whereas the orthodox clergy felt directly threatened. In the first place, Lessing's rejection of the sole authority of Scripture, of what he himself described as 'bibliolatry' (LM XVI, 470–2), denied the central principle of Lutheranism, and not even his appeal to the spirit of Luther against Luther's ossified legacy (pp. 117–18) could disguise the gravity of this attack. Secondly, Lessing's style of writing – non-technical, accessible, often entertaining, and explicitly directed not just at theological specialists but at the educated public at large – seemed to Goeze and others like him to undercut their authority with their own parishioners. Furthermore, Lessing's 'counter-propositions' (pp. 62-82) did not substantially counter Reimarus's challenge to the resurrection as the ultimate confirmation of Christ's divinity. And finally, Lessing's failure to define his own position, his posture of neutrality (p. 95) while simultaneously sowing doubt and inciting others to combat, could only strike those whose immediate concern was the spiritual welfare of unsophisticated people as irresponsible. 'Take care', Lessing would warn those of more advanced insight, 'take care not to let your weaker classmates detect what you scent, or already begin to see!' (p. 233). But he did not heed his own warnings – and it would have been utterly out of character for him to do so. It was all very well to invoke, as the ultimate refuge from doubt, the 'inner truth' of religion as something which even the simplest believer could immediately feel (pp. 62–3 and 115–16). But how could this be reconciled with his claim that this same truth is still largely inaccessible to the most advanced efforts of reason (p. 234)? Such statements were profoundly unsettling, as Lessing surely meant them to be; but he could hardly protest if those whose main task was not to unsettle but to reassure took grave exception to them.

The result was the greatest controversy in German Protestantism in the eighteenth century, if not since the Reformation era. Apart from numerous reviews of the 'Fragments' and of Lessing's own responses, around fifty books and articles appeared, most of them highly critical of the 'Fragments', and many of Lessing for publishing them[11]. The first of these were from minor figures. Johann Daniel Schumann, headmaster and clergyman, to whom Lessing's first two replies are directed (pp. 83–94), attacked only the 'Fragments' and not Lessing himself –

---

[11] See Arno Schilson's editorial introduction to the controversy in B VIII, 960–3; on the chronology of the conflict and main publications by Lessing and his adversaries, see B IX, 760–7.

hence the relatively irenic tone of Lessing's responses; but Schumann's naive appeal to the miracles and fulfilled prophecies of Scripture did not begin to address Reimarus's basic objections. His second opponent wrote anonymously, but Lessing soon identified him as Johann Heinrich Ress, a senior clergyman and neighbour of his in Wolfenbüttel. On this occasion, Lessing's reply (*A Rejoinder*) is polemical – not because he was attacked himself, but because Ress dismissed the 'Fragments' by invective rather than by reasoned arguments, attributing wilful obtuseness and malevolence to the anonymous author, of whose intellectual stature Lessing was not in any doubt.

His third adversary, Johann Melchior Goeze, chief pastor of the Church of St Catharine in Hamburg and senior representative of the Hamburg clergy from 1760 to 1770, was a much more formidable figure. A prolific writer and seasoned controversialist, he was now the leading spokesman of Lutheran orthodoxy in Germany. Lessing had known and respected him in Hamburg for his scholarly interests (Goeze was an expert on German editions and translations of the Bible). But in his doom-laden sermons and implacable hostility to liberal theology, Goeze no longer had the public at large on his side, and it was partly for this reason that Lessing, in his usual spirit of contrariness, had defended him against the ridicule of enlightened opinion during his Hamburg period. Since then, Goeze had taken umbrage at Lessing's failure to reply to a bibliographical query, and although his initial response to the 'Fragments' was relatively restrained, he soon adopted the polemical tone for which he was renowned, accusing Lessing of 'direct and malicious attacks' on Christianity. This change of tone accounts for the parallel change of tone between Lessing's *Parable* (with its accompanying 'Request') and *Axioms* on the one hand (pp. 110–16 and 120–47), both of which were written before Goeze's full-scale denunciation began, and the 'Challenge' which Lessing added to the former work just as it went to press (pp. 116–19).

From this point onwards, the controversy became fiercely polemical and increasingly repetitive. Lessing's chief weapon in the eleven *Anti-Goeze* pamphlets which he now launched against his opponent – not included in this volume – is satire, and his main contribution to theology lies rather in the *Axioms* and *New Hypothesis* which preceded them (pp. 120–71). As the conflict intensified, his position grew increasingly precarious. From the start, Goeze made scarcely veiled attempts, as in most of his previous controversies, to incite the secular authorities (in the shape of the Corpus Evangelicorum, the body which represented Protestant interests in the Holy Roman Empire) to intervene against this latest threat to Lutheran orthodoxy. Lessing's response, as in his *Necessary Answer to a Very Unnecessary Question* (pp. 172–7), was to emphasise the importance of oral tradition, rather than the written word of the Bible, as the ultimate authority in matters of faith, in order to solicit support from the Corpus Catholicorum, which represented Catholic interests, if Goeze should succeed in mobilising the imperial authorities.

But the chief threat came from nearer home. Two local clergymen, J. H. Ress of Wolfenbüttel and J. B. Lüderwald, Lutheran Superintendant in Brunswick itself, had now become involved in the controversy, and Lessing, provoked to the limit by Goeze, now published the last and most virulent of his extracts from Reimarus's work, *On the Aims of Jesus and his Disciples*, in which the theory of the apostles' conspiracy and forgery of the resurrection was expounded in full (LM XIII, 215–327). This was the last straw. In July 1778, conservative elements at the Brunswick court prevailed upon the reigning duke to ban Lessing from publishing anything further in the dispute without the advance permission of the censor.

In the event, Lessing did publish several more items, including the *Necessary Answer to a Very Unnecessary Question*, outside Brunswick, despite the government's disapproval. In doing so, he may have reckoned on the more tolerant attitude of the duke's successor, Charles William Ferdinand, who was already effectively in charge and took over as ruler on his father's death less than two years later. And although the Corpus Evangelicorum did eventually call for punitive measures against Lessing, the new ruler at once reassured him that no such action would be taken. Lessing's postscript to the whole affair was not another polemic, but the drama *Nathan the Wise*, published by private subscription in 1779. With its moving appeal for universal tolerance, it shows remarkably little trace of the acrimonious dispute out of which it arose.

By this time, Lessing's health was failing, and there can be no doubt that the religious controversy, and the animosity which he encountered as a result of it, served to shorten his life. The damage it did was compounded by the death of his wife, after little more than a year of marital happiness, and her infant son shortly after the conflict erupted. As a result of these reverses and the problems he now faced with the censorship, he did not manage to respond publicly when some of the leading theologians he had hoped to involve, such as J. S. Semler and C. W. F. Walch, did eventually enter the debate in 1779; the replies which Lessing now began to draft were never completed (LM XVI, 450f. and 470–517).

The works in this volume associated with the so-called *Fragmentenstreit* (quarrel over the 'Fragments') vary in style and substance according to the exigencies of the debate and the attitudes of those at whom they are directed. *On the Proof of the Spirit and of Power*, with its image of the 'broad and ugly ditch' between the 'contingent truths of history' and the 'necessary truths of reason' – the latter equated with the central truths of Christianity – is an uncharacteristic work of Lessing. His self-stylisation as an agonised doubter who cannot make the leap of faith is unique in the writings of his maturity. It is out of keeping with that emotional certainty which, according to his commentary on the 'Fragments' and the later *Axioms* (pp. 62 and 115), even the simplest believer can feel, with the willing renunciation of certainty in *A Rejoinder* (p. 98), and with the rational optimism of *The Education of the Human Race*. It is a rhetorical posture, challenging his opponent to answer an argument which Lessing believes to be unanswerable. But the leap of faith which he claims he cannot make is not, strictly speaking, a leap of faith at all, for his professed aim is not the certainty of faith but the certainty of rational demonstration. Besides, the class of truths which he here describes as 'historical' is supposedly unreliable because it consists of second-hand reports, as distinct from direct experience; but he goes on to say that, even if the evidence for Christ's miracles or resurrection were wholly certain – as it would be if these events were directly experienced – this would still be insufficient to demonstrate his divinity. There seems, in short, to be a confusion of categories here.[12] Lessing's basic objection is not so much to the uncertainty of history as to the incapacity of any empirical evidence to demonstrate rational – and in this case counter-rational – propositions.

Be that as it may, the chief purpose of this little work is to drive a wedge between the historical authority of the Scriptures and the basic truths of religion, for which rational demonstration is allegedly indispensable. A secondary, pragmatic argument for the truth of Christianity is, however, advanced at the end of the work, reinforced by the lively dialogue entitled *The Testament of St John* which follows it: the truth of Christianity is sufficiently demonstrated by its fruits, by its auspicious consequences,

---

[12] As Søren Kierkegaard, whose theology of faith owes much to his reading of Lessing, noted: see Kierkegaard, *Concluding Scientific Postscript*, translated by David S. Swenson and edited by Walter Lowrie (Princeton, 1941), p. 88.

above all as a religion of love. This insistence on the primacy of ethics, so typical of the Enlightenment's attitude to religion, remains a constant feature of Lessing's subsequent writings.

These arguments against Schumann are more fully developed in *A Rejoinder*, written in reply to Ress. If the evangelists' accounts of the resurrection are full of contradictions, this ceases to matter if the Bible is treated like an ordinary historical document, for such contradictions are only to be expected in different accounts by different people of one and the same event. What Lessing omits to add is that, when the event in question is as extraordinary as a resurrection from the dead, far stronger evidence than normal is required to render it credible. But he is not himself greatly troubled by this lack, for he indicates on several occasions that he finds the divinity of Christ incomprehensible.[13] And on this occasion, in one of the most celebrated passages in all his writings, he makes a virtue out of necessity by declaring that the search for truth, even if accompanied by eternal error, is preferable to the possession of truth, which he associates with idleness and complacency (p. 98). Since he cannot, however, conclude on a note of total scepticism without appearing to share the position of Reimarus, he once more resorts to the pragmatic argument for the truth of Christianity: the fact that the building still stands is proof enough of its stability, and there is no need to dig up its foundations to see whether they are sound. 'How strange', he exclaims, 'that people are so rarely satisfied with what they have before them!' (p. 104). His rhetoric breathes confidence and reassurance; but it does not alter the fact that both he and Reimarus, far from satisfied with what stood before them, had excavated its foundations to the utmost of their ability.

This building metaphor is further elaborated in *A Parable*, Lessing's first reply to Goeze, which is supplemented by the discursive arguments of the simultaneously published *Axioms*. The latter work is Lessing's main statement of his theological position, a brilliant defence of those propositions or 'axioms' (Goeze's dismissive term for them) with which he had introduced his commentary on the 'Fragments' of Reimarus. After once more separating religious truth from the historical vehicle of the Bible (but not from that of oral tradition, to which he gives priority throughout), he again appeals to the simple faith of ordinary Christians as fully capable of discerning the 'inner truth' of religion by feeling alone, without any

---

[13] See Nisbet, 'The Rationalisation of the Holy Trinity', pp. 70–3.

need for rational demonstration. Stylistically, this work is varied, entertaining, and persuasive, from the tale of the shipwrecked islanders whose
religion survives without the Bible to the satirical 'pulpit dialogue' with
the uncomprehending preacher and the concluding quotation from J. D.
Michaelis, one of Germany's leading experts in Scriptural exegesis, in
support of Lessing's own position.

It is unfortunate that Lessing did not complete and publish his *New
Hypothesis on the Evangelists as Merely Human Historians*, which he rightly
saw as his most substantial contribution to the debate. Its aim is to reinforce
the conclusions of the *Axioms* by means of historical research, and it is
at this point that Lessing's formidable knowledge of the Church Fathers,
the main source of evidence on the origin of the New Testament canon,
comes into its own. For although he modestly described himself not as a
theologian but as an 'amateur of theology' (p. 122), his patristic learning
was equal to that of any of his contemporaries. By today's standards, his
main conclusions on gospel chronology are admittedly flawed. But along
with J. S. Semler's much more elaborate *Treatise on the Free Investigation of
the Canon* (1771–5), the *New Hypothesis* is a pioneering work in eighteenth-
century studies of this field.

The *Necessary Answer to a Very Unnecessary Question* is as interesting
for what it does not say as for what it does. For Goeze had demanded that
Lessing answer two fundamental questions, namely what he understood
by the Christian religion, and what religion, if any, he himself believed in.
As already noted, Lessing replied clearly – and astutely – to the first of
these questions, simultaneously inviting Catholic support by presenting
the early and orally transmitted creeds as definitive. But he conspicuously
fails to reply to the second question, on whose answer there is to this day
no general agreement among Lessing scholars.[14] Why he failed to respond
to it is probably best explained by the sceptical conclusion to the eight
short paragraphs, unpublished in his lifetime, entitled *The Religion of
Christ* (p. 179):

> The Christian religion [. . .] is so uncertain and ambiguous that there
> is scarcely a single passage which any two individuals, throughout
> the history of the world, have thought of in the same way.

---

[14] See Leonard P. Wessell, *Lessing's Theology: A Reinterpretation* (The Hague and Paris, 1977),
pp. 15–34, on some of the rival readings, to which Wessell himself adds yet another.

The positive corollary to the uncertainty and suspense of judgement which underlies this comment had already been formulated in *A Rejoinder*, in the famous passage on the search for truth: the uncertainty of our conclusions is more than made up for by the freedom which this affords for limitless speculation, and it is this activity, rather than any results it may yield, which exercises and develops our mental capacities. Enlarging on this conviction, Lessing speculates, in the curious fragment *That More than Five Senses Are Possible for Human Beings*, that our present psychophysical constitution is not necessarily unalterable: the human faculties may themselves evolve over time, so that human reason itself may be subject to further development. What he has in mind – in keeping with Charles Bonnet's theory of 'palingenesis', to which this fragment probably owes its inspiration – is not evolution in the usual biological sense, but a metaphysical process whereby the soul may migrate to progressively more complex bodies, perhaps in other parts of the universe. Such theories enjoyed considerable popularity in Germany around this time,[15] and Lessing puts forward other versions of them in his later years, most notably in the hypothesis of metempsychosis, of progressive reincarnations on earth, towards the end of *The Education of the Human Race*.

Other writings of Lessing's last years

Like the latter work, the Masonic dialogues *Ernst and Falk*, written around 1776–7 but not published in full until 1780, contain thoughts and speculations on the process of history. Apart from the immediate, practical objective of encouraging reforms within the Masonic movement – as evidenced by the work's dedication to that movement's senior representative in Germany, Duke Ferdinand of Brunswick – Lessing sees the role of institutional Freemasonry in history as analogous to that of institutional religion, of the Church with all its fixed doctrines and ceremonies. Both institutions represent the letter, rather than the spirit, of the beliefs they stand for. Like the Church, Masonic lodges can easily lose sight of their original purpose, as Lessing believed had happened to numerous lodges in Germany. (He had indeed dissociated himself from the movement after his own initiation in 1771, like that of Ernst in the dialogues, proved a

[15] See Lieselotte E. Kurth-Voigt, *Continued Existence, Reincarnation, and the Power of Sympathy in Classical Weimar* (Rochester, NY and Woodbridge, 1999), passim.

disillusioning experience.) But 'true' Freemasonry, like the true spirit of religion, ceaselessly strives to promote that human brotherhood which formal institutions and fixed doctrines – indispensable as they are to all organised societies – inevitably put at risk through the social, political, and religious divisions they reinforce and enshrine. (Lessing's liberal political opinions, which are akin to those of Kant, are plainly visible here.) The process described in the dialogues is one of endless approximation to a utopian ideal whose complete realisation is neither possible nor desirable. Like most of his later writings, this work is appropriately open ended.

In this respect as in many others, *Ernst and Falk* is closely parallel to *The Education of the Human Race*, at least the first half of which, if not the entire work, was also written in 1776–7. The subject-matter of the latter work is religion, and it arose out of Lessing's reflections on the fourth 'Fragment' of Reimarus (on the alleged inadequacy of the Old Testament as a religious revelation), in the context of which he published its first fifty-three paragraphs in 1777 (p. 79). The idea which underlies it, according to which revelation is to the human race what education is to the individual human being, was not a new one, but already expressed in early Christian times by the Church Fathers Clement of Alexandria and Origen. But Lessing develops it further. He withheld the second half of the work until 1780, and even then continued to deny his authorship of it – for good reason. For the second half makes it clear that what is here described is not just the history of Judaism and Christianity, but the wider process of enlightenment in which Christianity itself will eventually be superseded. Besides, it gradually becomes obvious that the parallel between education and revelation is not to be taken literally – that is, as directed by a transcendental pedagogue – but figuratively. Nevertheless, this work is no ordinary product of Enlightenment secularism: the chiliastic expectations of the concluding paragraphs, the invocation of the medieval mystics, and the prospect of continuous metempsychosis in the life to come restore at least something of the religious aura implicit in the original metaphor, reinforcing the suggestion in paragraphs 72–7 that there may yet be more to revelation than human reason has so far been able to penetrate.

This vision of permanent flux and spiritual evolution is a far cry from the kind of Wolffian rationalism to which many of Lessing's contemporaries remained attached. He duly became convinced that philosophy was ripe for change, declaring in 1777 that it had grown so superficial that it could scarcely retain any credibility for much longer.[16] He was right, of course. But he could not have foreseen the form that this change would take with the advent of Kant's critical philosophy. He had similar feelings about Christianity itself, and he eventually concluded that the controversies with orthodox Lutheranism into which he had latterly been drawn were a necessary prelude to fundamental change.[17] Here again, he was right, although he did not live to see the publication of, for example, Schleiermacher's *Addresses on Religion* (1794), in which emotional conviction – to which Lessing himself had appealed as the source of simple Christian faith – would replace both rational demonstration and literal interpretation of the Bible as the ultimate foundation of religious belief.

It should by now be obvious that, in his later years, Lessing repeatedly stressed the provisional nature of all philosophical and religious opinions. But he further underlined the provisionality of his own reflections, and by extension the elusive and unstable nature of truth itself, by the oblique modes of discourse to which he often resorted. He had always, as a poet and dramatist, been fond of metaphors, and in the religious controversies of the late 1770s, he regularly exploited the power of figurative language not only to add concrete vividness to abstract arguments, but also to reinforce the open epistemology to which he was now committed. It enabled him, for example in the images of architecture, construction, underpinning, undermining, demolition, and reconstruction which he often applies to religious criticism, to accentuate the activity of criticism itself – much to the annoyance of his adversary Goeze – without explicitly declaring which doctrines are to be rejected, modified, retained, or replaced. Similarly, his parable of the labyrinthine palace in flames – a false alarm, as it turns out – underlines the complexity and vulnerability, but also the enduring value, of the Christian religion, while the parable of the three rings in *Nathan the Wise*, with its rich and multiple meanings and avoidance of dogmatic closure, remains a classic example of its kind.

Figurative language such as this, and the use of fictional narratives to illustrate and amplify meaning, are of course the stuff of poetry – self-evidently so in the case of *Nathan the Wise*, which is itself a poetic text. This does not, however, mean that the philosophical texts of Lessing's last years, such as *The Education of the Human Race* and *Ernst and Falk*, are likewise

---

[16] Daunicht, *Lessing im Gespräch*, p. 432.
[17] See editor's note in B xii, 591.

poetic documents, for philosophers have always enriched their texts with figurative and narrative discourse, from Plato's parable of the cave to Leibniz's synchronised clocks and Nietzsche's reworkings of Greek myth. In Lessing's case, such devices are admittedly much more pervasive, and more consistently ambiguous, than in most of the great philosophers; but that is because ambiguity is a necessary part of his philosophical position, and the poetic means by which he sometimes expresses it are only one of the many strategies he employs for similar purposes. Another of these is dialogue, a favourite medium of philosophy since the time of Socrates and one in which Lessing, as a successful dramatist, is very much at home. Questioning, suggesting, encouraging, and qualifying, it serves in *Ernst and Falk* to explore rather than explain, as Lessing's interlocutors examine the divisive and cohesive forces in human society and possible ways of minimising the former and consolidating the latter, thereby advancing the cause of enlightenment. Numerous rhetorical devices are deployed in this and other works to reinforce the hypothetical and tentative nature of the enquiry, from the battery of rhetorical questions in the last quarter of *The Education of the Human Race* and the cluster of subjunctives in the passage on the search for truth in *A Rejoinder* to the riddles and paradoxes of Falk's definitions of 'true' Freemasonry and the repeated use of ellipsis and aposiopesis to deny the reader that definitive statement or affirmative conclusion to which a particular discussion appears to be leading. (The notorious contradiction – real or apparent – between paragraphs 4 and 77 of *The Education* is another instance of this kind.)

None of these devices is peculiar to poetic language, and it is worth pointing out that oblique modes of expression are not the only means which Lessing uses to enhance the openness and tentativeness of his reflections. Ordinary discursive language is at times used to the same end, as in the Latin quotation from Augustine on the title-page of *The Education of the Human Race*, which informs us that 'all these things are in certain respects true for the same reason that they are in certain respects false', or in the following exchange in *Ernst and Falk* on the definition of Freemasonry (p. 187):

Ernst. If I have a conception [*Begriff*] of something, I can also express it in words.
Falk. Not always; and at least often not in such a way that others derive exactly the same conception from the words as what I have in mind.

In itself, the language of both these quotations is literal and unambiguous. But its meaning is obscure, or at the very least perplexing. The first quotation presents a paradox which challenges straightforward definitions of truth. In the second, Falk's reply is perplexing because it questions the adequacy of conceptual language to do the job it is designed to do, namely to convey a clear idea of what it refers to. This doubt concerning the adequacy of language, particularly conceptual language, as a means of communication is a central theme of *Ernst and Falk*, and a fundamental feature of Lessing's thought in his final years. It is also one of the most modern features of his thought, and by no means typical of the Enlightenment. Nor is it simply a product of philosophical scepticism, for its underlying motive is practical and constructive: it is informed by a belief that concepts, especially those with an ideological loading, can all too readily harden into dogma and prejudice, and in questioning and subverting them, Lessing's aim is to encourage his readers to think for themselves. In short, he offers no system of philosophy; but he does offer guidance on how to philosophise. The real interest of his speculations accordingly lies not so much in the specific conclusions he reaches – many of which are not in any case original to him – as in the manner in which he presents them. His faith in a benevolent providence, in moral and intellectual progress, and in continued development in a life to come was shared by many of his contemporaries; but these articles of faith were to him of less importance in themselves than for the stimulus they might offer to further speculation and further enquiry. Far from regarding *The Education of the Human Race* as his definitive philosophical statement (as it is often portrayed), he never acknowledged it as his own work, even to his closest friends, and declared:

> *The Education of the Human Race* is by a good friend who likes to construct all sorts of hypotheses and systems to have the pleasure of pulling them down again [...] Let everyone say what he *thinks* is the truth, and let *truth itself* be entrusted to God.[18]

The conversations on Spinoza

All of these considerations must be borne in mind when we examine the last and most hotly debated aspect of Lessing's philosophical thinking,

---

[18] Lessing to J. A. H. Reimarus, 6 April 1778, in B XII, 143f.

namely his reported conversion to Spinozism in the last years of his life. He was certainly aware of Spinoza's importance (and notoriety) from his university years onwards, and his interest was fully aroused when his friend Moses Mendelssohn, while rejecting Spinoza's pantheism, discussed his work with respect in his *Dialogues* of 1755, a revised version of which was incorporated in his *Philosophical Writings* of 1761; as already noted, the two fragments which Lessing wrote in response to Mendelssohn's reflections are plainly sympathetic towards Spinoza's monism. But there are no further references to Spinoza in his writings and conversations until the last year of his life. It is therefore no wonder that his friends were astonished when, some years after Lessing's death, Friedrich Heinrich Jacobi reported that, in conversations with him in 1780, Lessing had declared himself a convinced Spinozist, saying: 'If I must call myself after anyone, I know of no one else [. . .] There is no other philosophy than that of Spinoza' (pp. 243–4).

There are indeed certain passages in Lessing's works which recall Spinoza's doctrines, such as those rationalisations of the Holy Trinity in *The Christianity of Reason* and in paragraph 73 of *The Education of the Human Race* which seem to indicate that the universe is a necessary creation of the divinity, or the suggestion in the latter work that God accommodated his revelations to the understanding of the early Jews and Christians.[19] But these are far from enough to confirm that he accepted Spinoza's philosophy as a whole. For even that determinism (or 'fatalism', as Jacobi called it) to which Lessing subscribed, telling Jacobi that he had no use for free will (p. 246), involves not a mechanical, causal necessity but a moral necessity of the kind in which Leibniz believed, as Lessing had made clear a few years earlier, echoing Leibniz's view that to understand the good is to be (morally) compelled to follow it (LM xII, 298):

> How much more welcome to me are the compulsion and necessity exercised by our perception [*Vorstellung*] of the best than the bare capacity to act, under the same circumstances, now in one way and now in another! I thank the creator that I *must*, that I must do what is *best*.

This is the language of Leibniz, not of Spinoza, and the same is true of Lessing's many affirmations of optimism, faith in progress, epistemological

---

[19] Cf. Benedict de Spinoza, *The Chief Works*, edited and translated by R. H. M. Elwes, 2 vols., revised edition (London, 1891–8), I, 37, 40, 70, and 162 (*Theological-Political Treatise*).

perspectivism, and belief in a dynamic universe of monads. Assuming that Jacobi's report of the conversations in 1780 is accurate – and none of Lessing's closest friends saw any reason to doubt its authenticity – why did Lessing assure his young visitor that he found Spinoza's philosophy the only tenable one?

In order to answer this question, one must first examine Jacobi's motives for introducing himself to Lessing and seeking his company. His interest had first been aroused, he tells us, by Lessing's writings on religion, and he visited him in the hope that he might 'conjure up through him the spirits of several wise men whose views on certain things I was unable to determine' (p. 241). The chief of these 'wise men' was, of course, Spinoza, and on the day of their first meeting, their conversation, as Jacobi reports, dealt largely with 'atheists, deists, and Christians'. Lessing must therefore have discovered almost at once what Jacobi's attitude to religion was, and certainly before the topic of Spinoza was explicitly raised: Jacobi was a Christian fideist who believed, unlike Lessing, that reason and rationality must inevitably lead to determinism and atheism, of which he saw Spinoza as the prime example, and that only free will and religious faith, as facts of experience which require no further demonstration, can lead the way to truth and salvation.

Lessing had been down this road before. He was familiar with the time-honoured debate on freedom and necessity at least since his first years in Berlin, when he studied and rejected the materialism of La Mettrie, and probably already as a student in Leipzig. But he had also encountered it in a similar context to that in which Jacobi reopened it, in the person of another earnest and devout young man, the playwright Joachim Wilhelm von Brawe, whose dramatic endeavours he had encouraged during his second period in Leipzig in 1757. Brawe, who was still at university, had been much impressed by the philosophy lectures of Christian August Crusius, who defended the freedom of the will and his own supra-rational Christian faith against the rationalism of Leibniz and Wolff, which he considered presumptuous and ultimately deterministic. As one who was present recalled, Lessing much enjoyed debating these issues with the hapless Brawe, regularly outmanoeuvring him with his dialectical skills and obliging other members of the company to turn the conversation to less contentious subjects.[20] Lessing's reaction

---

[20] Daunicht, *Lessing im Gespräch*, pp. 110–12.

to Jacobi was no different. No sooner had he discovered that Spinoza embodied everything that Jacobi found theologically and philosophically unacceptable than he pronounced himself a convinced Spinozist. When Jacobi published his account of these conversations after Lessing's death, Mendelssohn and others who had known Lessing well immediately recognised his ironic and provocative stance in the debate, even as reported by the stolidly literalistic Jacobi.[21] To anyone familiar with Lessing's opposition in principle to systems, especially in his later years, it is in any case inconceivable that he should suddenly have identified himself with the most rigorous systematist of the seventeenth century; his reluctance to do so can be detected in his initial reply to Jacobi's question whether he agreed with Spinoza: 'If I must call myself after anyone, I know of no one else' (p. 243). As in so many other cases, his affirmative statements were not designed to express a dogmatic position of his own; their character is essentially reactive, with the aim of questioning a received opinion and obliging its advocates either to abandon it or to find new and better ways of defending it.

Conclusion

As Jacobi's report shows, Lessing's interest in philosophy continued undiminished to the end of his life. In 1780, he read and recommended to Jacobi David Hume's recently published *Dialogues concerning Natural Religion*;[22] their dialogic mobility and analytical acuteness must have greatly appealed to him, although Hume's sceptical aversion to metaphysical speculation must have struck him as unduly restrictive. But only a few weeks after his death in February 1781, Kant's *Critique of Pure Reason* was published, transforming the landscape of German philosophy. This did not prevent Jacobi's report concerning Lessing's supposed Spinozism from causing another major controversy when it appeared in 1785: it led, in fact, to a Spinoza renaissance in Germany, as Herder, Goethe, and several of the German Romantics went on to construct monistic philosophies of nature on the model of Spinoza's pantheism and in reaction to Kant's

---

[21] See Altmann, *Moses Mendelssohn*, pp. 621 and 711.

[22] Heinrich Scholz (ed.), *Die Hauptschriften zum Pantheismusstreit zwischen Jacobi und Mendelssohn* (Berlin, 1916), p. 240.

dualistic metaphysics.[23] But despite their obvious differences – especially on metaphysical questions – Lessing and Kant had a good deal in common. Both defend the free exercise of reason and reject any attempt to declare religious dogmas unalterable for all time; both uphold liberal political principles and regard the state as a necessary evil; and both envisage history as a rational process leading to progressive moral improvement. Lessing's philosophical writings were also of interest to the Romantics and post-Kantian Idealists. Friedrich Schlegel and Hegel in particular found the openness, irony, and subversiveness of his later works congenial and akin to their own critical aspirations. Schelling and Hegel were attracted to his writings on religion and allude to them in their early works, and in Hegel's case, in his lectures on the philosophy of religion.[24] Hegel's search for a rational, speculative content in Christian revelation develops Lessing's parallel quest in a more systematic manner; and his philosophy of history as the product of an immanent rationality, as a natural theodicy, can be described as an expansion of Lessing's much simpler scheme, further enriched by Herder's insight into the distinctiveness and individuality of successive historical cultures.

But although Lessing's legacy to Idealism is historically important and consistently underestimated, it is not this aspect of his thought which resonates most strongly today. Those who incorporated his reflections into new philosophical systems were negating the fundamental tendency of his thought, which stands out more clearly today than it did to any of his contemporaries: his conviction that all philosophical doctrines and religious confessions embody a relative degree of truth, and his hope that, by subjecting them all to continuing scrutiny, we may at least keep moving in the direction of an ever-receding certainty.

---

[23] For the main contributions by Jacobi and Mendelssohn, see ibid., passim. On the conflict as a whole, see David Bell, *Spinoza in Germany from 1670 to the Age of Goethe* (London, 1984), pp. 71–96; also Frederick C. Beiser, *The Fate of Reason: German Philosophy from Kant to Fichte* (Cambridge, MA and London, 1987), pp. 44–108.

[24] See H. S. Harris, *Hegel's Development: Toward the Sunlight 1770–1801* (Oxford, 1972), pp. 43, 99, 101–3, 140f., 174n, and 189; also Nisbet, 'The Rationalisation of the Holy Trinity', pp. 77–84.

Philosophical and theological writings

The Christianity of reason

§1

The one most perfect being cannot have been occupied from eternity with anything other than the contemplation of that which is most perfect.

§2

That which is most perfect is himself; thus God can have thought from eternity only of himself.

§3

To represent, to will, and to create are one and the same for God. One can therefore say that everything which God represents to himself, he also creates.

§4

God can think of himself in only two ways: either he thinks of all of his perfections at once, and himself as the embodiment of them all; or he thinks of his perfections discretely, one separated from the other, and each divided by different degrees within itself.

§5

God thought of himself from eternity in all his perfection; that is, God created from eternity a being which lacked no perfection that he himself possessed.

§6

This being is called by Scripture the *Son of God*; or what would be better still, the *Son God*. A *God*, because it lacks none of the qualities pertaining to God. A *Son*, because that which represents something to itself seems, to our way of thinking, to have a certain priority to the representation.

§7

This being is God himself and cannot be distinguished from God, because we think of it as soon as we think of God and we cannot think of it without God; that is, because we cannot think of God without God, or because anything which we were to deprive of its representation of itself would not be a God.

§8

This being may be called an image of God, but an identical image.

§9

The more two things have in common with one another, the greater is the harmony between them. Thus the greatest harmony must be between two things which have everything in common, that is, between two things which together are only one.

§10

Two such things are God and the Son God, or the identical image of God; and the harmony which is between them is called by Scripture *the spirit which proceeds from the Father and Son*.

§11

In this harmony is everything which is in the Father, and thus also everything which is in the Son; this harmony is therefore God.

§12

But this harmony is God in such a manner that it would not be God if the Father were not God and the Son were not God, and that both could not be God if this harmony did not exist; that is, *all three are one*.

§13

God thought of his perfections discretely, that is, he created beings each of which has something of his perfections; for – to repeat it once more – every thought is for God a creation.

§14

All these beings together are called the world.

§15

God could think of his perfections divided in an infinite number of ways; thus an infinite number of worlds would be possible if God did not always think of the most perfect one, and if he had not consequently thought of the most perfect among all these possible varieties and thereby made it real.

§16

The most perfect way of thinking of his perfections discretely is that of thinking of them as divided by infinite degrees of more and less which follow each other in such a way that there is nowhere a jump or gap between them.

§17

The beings in this world must therefore be ordered by such degrees. They must form a series in which each member contains everything which the lower members contain, plus something more; but this additional something never reaches the final limit.

§18

Such a series must be an infinite series, and in this sense, the infinity of the world is incontrovertible.

§19

God creates nothing but simple beings, and the complex is merely a [secondary] consequence of his creation.

§20

Since each of these simple beings has something which the others have, and none can have anything which the others do not have, there must be a harmony among these simple beings; everything that happens among them – that is, in the world – can be explained by means of this harmony.

§21

Some fortunate Christian will one day enlarge the realm of natural science to this point, but only after long centuries, when all natural phenomena have been fathomed to the point where all that remains to be done is to trace them back to their true source.

§22

Since these simple beings are, so to speak, limited Gods, their perfections must also be similar to God's perfections, as parts are to the whole.

§23

It is also inherent in God's perfections that he is conscious of his perfection, and secondly, that he can act in accordance with his perfections; both are, so to speak, the seal of his perfections.

§24

The different degrees of his perfections must therefore also be associated with different degrees of consciousness of these perfections and of the capacity to act in accordance with them.

§25

Beings which have perfections, which are conscious of their perfections, and which have the capacity to act in accordance with them, are called *moral beings* – that is, beings which can follow a law.

§26

This law is derived from their own nature, and can be none other than: *act in accordance with your individual perfections.*

§27

Since there cannot possibly be a jump in the series of beings, beings must also exist which are not conscious of their perfections with sufficient clarity, -

On the reality of things outside God

However I try to explain the reality of things outside God, I have to confess that I can form no conception of it.

If it is called 'the complement of possibility',[1] I ask: Is there a concept of this complement of possibility in God or not? Who will venture to assert that there is not? But if there is a concept of it in him, then the thing itself is in him too:[2] all things in him are themselves real.

But, it will be said, the concept which God has of the reality of a thing does not preclude the reality of this thing outside him. Does it not? Then the reality outside him must have something which distinguishes it from the reality in his concept of it. That is, there must be something in the reality outside him of which God has no conception. An absurdity! But if there is nothing of this kind, if, in the concept which God has of the reality of a thing, everything is present that is to be found in its reality outside him, then the two realities are one, and everything which is supposed to exist outside God exists in God.

Or it may be said that *the reality of a thing is the sum of all possible attributes that may pertain to it.* Must not this sum also be present in the idea that God has of it? What attribute does the reality outside him have if its original image is not also to be found in God? Consequently this original image is the thing itself, and to say that the thing also exists outside this original image means duplicating the latter in a way that is as unnecessary as it is absurd.

---

[1] 'The complement of possibility' is Christian Wolff's definition of 'existence' (as in his *Philosophia prima sive ontologia*, Pt I, Section II, Ch. 3, §23)

[2] Cf. Spinoza, *Ethics*, Pt I, Prop. 15.

The philosophers do maintain, I believe, that to affirm the reality of a thing outside God is simply to distinguish this thing from God and to declare that its reality is of a different kind from the necessary reality of God.

But if that is all that they mean, why should the concepts which God has of real things not be these real things themselves? They are already sufficiently distinct from God, and their reality does not become in any way necessary because they are real in him. For must not the contingency which this reality would possess outside God also have a corresponding image in his idea of it? And this image is merely its contingency itself. What is contingent outside God will also be contingent in God, otherwise God could have no concept of the contingent outside him. – I use this term 'outside him' in the way in which it is commonly used, in order to show by its application that it should not be used at all.

But, people will cry, you are assuming contingencies in the immutable being of God! – And so? Am I the only one who does this? You yourselves, who must ascribe concepts of contingent things to God – has it never occurred to you that concepts of contingent things are contingent concepts?

Spinoza only put Leibniz on the track of [his theory of] pre-established harmony (To Moses Mendelssohn)

I begin with the first dialogue.[1] I still share the opinion you express in it that it was Spinoza who led Leibniz to [his theory of] pre-established harmony. For Spinoza was the first whose system confronted him with the possibility that all changes to the body might result purely and simply from its own mechanical forces. It was this possibility which put Leibniz on the track of his hypothesis. But it only put him on the track: its further elaboration was the work of his own sagacity.

For all that I think I have recently grasped of Spinoza's system leads me to doubt whether he can have believed in, or even had a remote inkling of, pre-established harmony itself, if only as it exists in the divine intellect prior to the divine decree [*antecedenter ad decretum*].

Just tell me this: if Spinoza expressly declares that body and soul are one and the same particular thing, which we merely conceive of at times under the attribute of thought and at times under the attribute of extension (*Ethics*, Pt II, Prop. 21, note),[2] what kind of harmony can he have had in mind? The greatest, it could be said, that can possibly exist, namely the harmony which a thing has with itself. But is this not just playing with words? The harmony which a thing has with itself! Leibniz seeks, by means of his harmony, to solve the problem of how two such different

---

[1] The reference is to the first of Mendelssohn's *Dialogues* (1755; revised edition, 1761): see Moses Mendelssohn, *Philosophical Writings*, translated and edited by Daniel O. Dahlstrom (Cambridge, 1997), pp. 96–104.

[2] Lessing's own references to Spinoza's *Ethics* follow the numbering of a now obsolete German translation he was using. The numbering used here is that of the original Latin edition and most modern editions.

things as body and soul can be united. Spinoza, on the other hand, sees no difference between them; he therefore sees no union and no problem requiring resolution.

The soul, Spinoza says in another passage (Pt II, Prop. 21), is united with the body in the same way as the soul's concept of itself is united with the soul. Now the concept which the soul has of itself belongs to the soul's essential being, and neither can be thought of without the other. Thus the body cannot be thought of without the soul, and it is only because neither can be thought of without the other, and because both are one and the same particular thing, that Spinoza considers them united with one another.

It is true that Spinoza teaches that 'the order and connection of concepts is the same as the order and connection of things'. And what he asserts in these terms merely with reference to the one self-sufficient being, he affirms elsewhere, and more explicitly, of the soul in particular (Pt V, Prop. 1): 'Just as thoughts and the concepts of things are ordered and connected in the soul, so are the conditions of the body or the images of things ordered and connected in exactly the same way in the body.' It is true that Spinoza expresses himself thus, and that Leibniz can express himself in precisely the same way. But if both of them use the same kind of words, will they both associate the same kind of concepts with them? Impossible! All that Spinoza has in mind in this connection is that everything which follows formally [*formaliter*] from the nature of God, and consequently from the nature of a particular thing, must likewise follow objectively [*objective*] in it, and in the same order and association. In his view, the sequence and association of concepts in the soul match the sequence and association of changes in the body simply because the body is the object of the soul; for the soul is nothing but the body as it thinks itself, and the body is nothing but the soul in extension. But Leibniz[3] – will you permit me to use a simile? There are two savages, both of whom see their reflection in a mirror for the first time. They have got over their astonishment, and they now begin to philosophise on this phenomenon. The image in the mirror, they both say, makes exactly the same movements as a body makes, and it makes them in the same order. Consequently, they conclude, the

---

[3] In Lessing's letter of 17 April 1763 to Mendelssohn, of which the present fragment is a draft, the discussion breaks off at this point and lacks the extended simile which follows.

sequence of movements of the image, and the sequence of movements of the body, must be explicable by one and the same cause.[4]

---

[4] The simile is clearly incomplete, but its implication is clear enough: the first savage will conclude that the two images are synchronised by an unseen cause (as in Leibniz's pre-established harmony), whereas the second will argue that the two images relate to one and the same body viewed from two different angles (as in Spinoza's monism). This in turn implies that Lessing finds Spinoza's account more convincing than that of Leibniz.

On the origin of revealed religion

1. To recognise one God, to try to form the worthiest ideas of him, to take account of these worthiest ideas in all our actions and thoughts, is the most comprehensive definition of all natural religion.

2. Every human being, in proportion to his powers, is disposed and committed to this natural religion.

3. But since this proportion differs in each individual, so that each individual's natural religion will also differ, it has been thought necessary to counteract the disadvantage to which this difference can give rise – not in man's state of natural freedom, but in his state of civil union with others.

4. That is: as soon as it was recognised as desirable to make religion a communal concern, it was necessary to agree on certain things and concepts, and to *attribute* to these conventional things and concepts the same importance and necessity which religious truths recognised by natural means *possessed in their own right*.

5. That is: out of the religion of nature, which was not capable of universal and uniform practice, it was necessary to construct a positive religion, just as a positive law had been constructed, for the same reason, out of the law of nature.

6. This positive religion received its sanction from the authority of its founder, who claimed that its conventional elements came just as certainly from God – albeit through the founder's mediation – as its essential elements did through the immediate evidence of each individual's reason.

7. The indispensability of a positive religion, whereby natural religion is modified in each state according to that state's natural and fortuitous condition, I call its inner truth; and this inner truth is as great in one as in the other.

8. All positive and revealed religions are consequently equally true and equally false.

9. Equally true: in so far as it has everywhere been equally necessary to reach agreement on various things in order to produce unanimity and accord in the public religion.

10. Equally false: inasmuch as that on which agreement has been reached does not simply coexist with the essential elements, but weakens and suppresses them.

11. The *best* revealed or positive religion is that which contains the fewest conventional additions to natural religion, and imposes the fewest limitations on the good effects of natural religion. - - -

Leibniz on eternal punishment

I see that the controversy on the eternal punishments of hell is about to flare up again among our theologians. Let us hope that it can finally be settled and put aside! For the most depressing thing about such disputes is without doubt the fact that they generally achieve nothing, so that twenty or fifty years later, the first zealot or quibbler who comes along thinks he is entitled to reopen the whole issue.

To avoid becoming like one of those scribblers, it is essential first of all to study the history of the disputed doctrine in all its ramifications. Only when we know exactly where each of our predecessors dropped his thread can we hope to pick them all up again and, by comparing their different directions, set off on that path to truth which has been lost or never discovered in the first place. And if these predecessors include men like *Leibniz*, what can possibly be more instructive than to follow every trace of their footsteps and take our bearings from there?

Nothing more is necessary, I think, to introduce the following few lines, hitherto unpublished, of that great man who, if I had my way, would not have written a single line in vain. The facts of the matter can perhaps best be described in the words of Mosheim – especially since this affords an opportunity to confirm the accuracy of these words and to furnish them with a literary commentary.

When Mosheim published his own relevant work in 1725, at the end of the first part of his *Sacred Addresses*,[1] he prefaced it with the following explanation:

---

[1] Johann Lorenz Mosheim, *Heilige Reden über wichtige Wahrheiten der christlichen Religion* [*Sacred Addresses on Important Truths of Christianity*] (1725); Lessing refers to the second edition, which

I have been asked to set down the appended thoughts on the doctrine of those who regard the punishments of hell as finite. Others have written more extensively and with greater learning on this matter, and I can well understand if my work is regarded as superfluous. The innocent haste of some of my friends to have it printed without my knowledge – and not entirely accurately – led me to promise them, when I heard of their plan, to supervise the publication myself. I now fulfil this agreement. And what is culpable about that? Would I not be just as blameworthy if I failed to keep my word as I am in keeping it? It is ultimately better to give the world too much rather than too little printed matter on such questions. And the more influence this doctrine has on certain truths of faith concerning the basis of salvation, the more one has cause to marshal the evidence in its support. On such occasions, it is always customary to appeal to reason. And many of the most famous men take the view that the cause of those who defend eternal punishment would be all but lost if one relied on reason alone. I take the opposite view, without therefore despising those who think otherwise. It seems to me that reason gives at least as much support, if not more, to those who defend the eternity of divine retribution as to those who regard it as finite. Certain human opinions of which the majority approves often pass for clear and indisputable laws of reason. And the justice of the divine court of judgement is often measured against the usual practice of human tribunals. The most acute arguments in favour of the finite punishment of the damned are those of a man who, though otherwise learned, is accused of having fallen in his latter years into the pernicious errors of the Socinians.[2] I have studied his comments closely and can testify that their author is a man of no mean intelligence. But if one removes certain ambiguities and denies that conclusions derived from human affairs are applicable to those of the divinity, the so-called proof becomes a phantom in which one looks in vain for any coherence. I have long intended to expound the history of the doctrine in question in a Latin treatise, and not only to discover its sources, but also to explore the various ways in which it has been given colour and

contains the passage which he proceeds to quote here, from Mosheim's introduction to his own appended 'Thoughts on the Doctrine that the Pains of Hell are Finite'.
[2] Followers of Lelio Sozzini (1525–62) and Fausto Sozzini (1539–1604), Unitarians who denied the Trinity, and consequently the divinity of Christ.

substance. A large number of other works, some of which will not be unfamiliar, have hitherto prevented me from completing this project. Perhaps I shall soon find a few hours in which to put the accumulated stock of ideas and testimonies in order and present them to the public.

The identity of the learned man who furnished the most acute arguments to date for the negative view is indicated by Mosheim himself in the appended title of the work in question, namely Ernst Soner's *Demonstratio Theologica et Philosophica, quod aeterna impiorum supplicia, non arguant Dei justitiam, sed injustitiam.*[3] He adds:

> The illustrious Leibniz planned to publish this little work, which is very rare. I have before me a copy which already has the preface which he intended to print along with it. I shall have occasion to say more about this in another context, and at the same time to acknowledge the kindness of the person to whom I am indebted for this and other related materials.

Unfortunately, Mosheim never found the opportunity he promised to his readers, and which he doubtless hoped would arise in that Latin treatise in which he intended to review the history of the contentious doctrine. But just as that work was never completed, so also did Leibniz's aforementioned preface to Soner's *Demonstration* remain hidden and almost entirely forgotten. For since 1737, when Ludovici, in his *History of the Leibnizian Philosophy* (Pt II, p. 27),[4] reminded Mosheim of his promise, I am not aware that it has been mentioned by anyone other than those dry bibliographers (for example Vogt, *Cat. libr. rar.*, p. 635)[5] who refer to it in connection with Soner's work on account of the latter's rarity. Not even Brucker mentions it, although he had an excellent opportunity

---

[3] [*A Theological and Philosophical Demonstration that the Eternal Punishments of the Godless Indicate not Justice, but Injustice on the Part of God*]. Ernst Soner or Sonner (1572–1612), Professor of Medicine at Altdorf, held Socinian views.

[4] Lessing's reference is to Karl Günther Ludovici, *Ausführlicher Entwurf einer vollständigen Historie der leibnizischen Philosophie* [*Circumstantial Draft of a Comprehensive History of the Leibnizian Philosophy*] (1737).

[5] Johann Vogt, *Catalogus historico-criticus librorum rariorum* [*Historico-Critical Catalogue of Rare Books*] (1747; earlier edition, 1732).

to do so in recounting Soner's services to Aristotelian philosophy (*Hist. cr. Phil.*, Vol. IV, Pt I, p. 312).[6] We should therefore not be in the least surprised that it has not been included in the new edition of Leibniz's collected works which we owe to M. Dutens,[7] given that Germany at large has been so very remiss in supporting the efforts of this worthy foreigner. Instead of competing to provide him with as many unpublished additions as could possibly be found, his informants did not even draw his attention to all of Leibniz's previously published essays. For as a foreigner, Dutens naturally could not be aware of them all himself, and the honest Brucker could not single-handedly supply him with an exhaustive list. But since the reason for this failure may simply have been that each German scholar feared that another scholar might have forestalled him, it is much less disturbing than the dead silence of our reviewers on the subject. Did they really know of no omissions in this collected edition? Nothing which might at least have deserved a brief mention?

But more of this on another occasion, for I do not wish now to stray too far from the subject which prompted the above censure. – In short, that preface which Leibniz wrote to Soner's work, which Mosheim had and which he intended to publish but then failed to do so, is what I here propose to make known from our library's resources.

So as not to overlook the manner in which it came into our library, I should mention that Mosheim himself appears to have received it from that source. At any rate, the person whose kindness he intended to acknowledge on another occasion was the then librarian Hertel.[8] But since Hertel had regularly associated with Leibniz and was himself keenly interested in rare and heterodox items, it is equally possible that he lent the preface to Mosheim, together with Soner's work, from his own literary collection, with which it subsequently passed into the library's holdings after his death. This seems to me all the more likely because a copy of Mosheim's reflections as well as a letter in his hand to Hertel is attached to it. The copy corresponds exactly to the later printed version, and I

---

[6] Johann Jakob Brucker, *Historia critica philosophiae* [*Critical History of Philosophy*] (1742–4).

[7] G. W. Leibniz, *Opera omnia* [*Complete Works*], edited by Louis Dutens, 6 vols. (1768).

[8] Lorenz Hertel, a predecessor of Lessing as Wolfenbüttel Librarian, who held office from 1705 to 1737.

shall quote the letter in full in a footnote.[a] Without further preamble, let me now introduce the reader to the main item.

Leibniz's preface

That work of Ernst Soner, once a highly respected philosopher in Altdorf, which he described as a theological etc. demonstration of the injustice of eternal punishment, is praised by some as supposedly irrefutable. It is all the more harmful because few have actually seen it, for people tend to place a high value on whatever they do not know. I therefore think that it is often useful to publish works of this kind, which need only be read in order to refute or dispose of this received opinion which has been handed down for so long a time. It certainly cannot be denied that Soner wrote in a subtle and ingenious manner; but his demonstration suffers from a major omission, which I shall briefly describe lest any incautious reader should be deceived by his specious argument, which can be summarised as follows. Sins are finite, and the finite and the infinite are incommensurable. Therefore punishments must also be finite. He further attempts to show that sins are finite by rejecting the senses in which they can be understood as infinite, and he lists these senses as follows. 'If the misdemeanours of the godless are supposed to be infinite or to be considered as such, then they acquire this infinite character either from within themselves or from the perpetrator, or

---

[a] 'With renewed and respectful thanks for the trouble you have recently taken on my account, I enclose my own reflections, together with Soner's objections concerning eternal punishment. Although the latter are sophistically enough contrived, one can quite easily settle the issue with this honest man by following his own principles. His basic assumption is that God's only form of justice is that he has to keep his own promises; in all other respects, his power is limitless. Very well! It then clearly follows that God's justice does not prevent him from imposing eternal punishment on the godless, for his power permits him to do so. The whole argument will therefore depend on whether, in the Scriptures, God really did threaten the godless with eternal punishment. But if this is so, the honest Socinian must lose, and the odds are ten to one against him. I would write more if time permitted. But I have to attend a disputation in two days' time, and I must complete my other lecture courses before Easter. I therefore have hardly a free moment, and I must devote those which I do have to [my translation of] Hales.[9] My reflections on the conduct of the fathers of Dordrecht [the Synod of Dort] will hardly please those who subscribe to that Synod's doctrines. I nevertheless base them on clear facts and rational propositions. I am, as ever, etc. Mosheim.'

[9] John Hales (1584–1656), English theologian; Mosheim refers to his own translation of Hales's *De auctoritate concilii Dordraceni paci sacrali noxia* [*On the Resolutions of the Synod of Dort as Prejudicial to Ecclesiastical Peace*], which criticised the Synod of Dort (1618–19) as excessively biassed in favour of radical Calvinism.

from those on and against whom the offence is perpetrated, and either from some of those persons or from all of them simultaneously. But they cannot be infinite, or be considered as such, in any of these senses. Yet apart from these, there is no other possible sense in which they can be infinite, or be described as such. Therefore they are not infinite at all.'

What the theologians usually reply to this argument, which is based on the relation between crimes and punishments, can best be read in their own works. In the present context, I would prefer to indicate another flaw in Soner's argument, namely his incomplete list of the senses in which something can be described as infinite. For sins can be described as infinite not just in relation to the object which is sinned against, i.e. God, or in relation to the type of sin or its degree of intensity or the other senses to which the author refers, but also in relation to their number. Thus, even if we should ourselves concede that no sin is infinite in itself, it can certainly be argued that the sins of the damned are infinite in number, because they persist in sin throughout all eternity. It is therefore just that, if the sins are eternal, the punishments should also be eternal. For evil men condemn themselves, as wise men rightly say, because they remain forever impenitent and turn away from God. God cannot therefore be held responsible, or accused of disproportionate severity in relation to the sin in question.

That is all there is to this so-called preface. I hope I shall not be expected to include Soner's work as well. Admittedly, it is still just as scarce, as a printed book, as it was in Leibniz's time, for I am not aware that it has ever been reprinted. But its content no longer has the merit which it may once have possessed for those who favoured free enquiry in matters of faith, for since then, it has been reproduced in a hundred books to which everyone has access. And since it has become easier, in recent times, for supporters of apocatastasis[10] in particular to state their views as openly as they please, they and those who respond to them have no less frequently defended or opposed the doctrine of finite punishment of the damned (which is clearly implicit in the doctrine of apocatastasis) with all kinds of argument – and, indeed, with all kinds of zeal and fanaticism. In short, Soner's demonstration, apart perhaps from one or two niceties, is now a spent force.

[10] The extension of God's kingdom (i.e. the Christian faith) throughout the earth, and (according to Origen) the restoration of all souls to their original purity; see Matthew 19.28; also Acts 3.21 and 2 Peter 3.7–13.

But could and should I not, it may be thought, for this very reason have left Leibniz's preface in similar obscurity? For what he says there in reply to Soner is equally familiar nowadays, because he himself has said the same thing in other contexts. – I am well aware of this. But my intention in publishing it has less to do with the defence of truth than with its defender, with the attitudes and reasons which underlay his defence; for both of these have been misinterpreted and misrepresented.

Mosheim himself, who was certainly in a good position to know the real content of Leibniz's preface, still gives readers a completely false impression of it. When he first mentioned it,[b] he did so in such general terms that the good Pagenkopen[11] imagined that, since Leibniz had intended to publish Soner's demonstration, he must have approved of it. In order to enlighten him on this matter, Mosheim wrote in reply:[c]

> Herr von Leibniz did not propose to publish this material because he regarded it as important and accepted Soner's opinion. He wished rather to furnish it with a preface, now in my hands, in which he refutes Soner himself with the help of Aristotle's principles, and exposes the weakness of his proofs. His plan was to show the world the inadequacy of a work which was regarded as irrefutable merely because it was rare and known to few people.

But if Mosheim initially said too little, he now obviously says too much, and his opponents had reason to suspect that he was deliberately seeking to misuse Leibniz's authority. For we now have Leibniz's preface before us, and one must be able to read a great deal out of very little in order to find everything that Mosheim claims to have found in it. So Leibniz refuted Soner with the help of Aristotle's principles? He exposed the weakness of his proofs? His proofs? Are then his proofs the sole dilemma? And what exactly were those Aristotelian principles? I can as little discover them in Leibniz's preface as I can in Soner's work itself, which Mosheim likewise says is related to Aristotle's principles. The only Aristotelian element in Soner's work is that it is expressed throughout in

---

[b] In the preface to Part I of his *Sacred Addresses*, as already noted [see note 1 above].

[c] In the epistle on various matters at the end of Part II of his *Sacred Addresses* [see note 1 above].

[11] Pagenkopen (biographical details unknown), author of *Gründliche Erklärung der ewigen Liebe Gottes in Christo, gegen alle gefallene Creaturen, oder ausführlicher Beweis, daß die Lehre von der Wiederbringung aller Dinge in der Natur und Schrift unumstößlich gegründet* [*Thorough Explanation of God's Eternal Love in Christ towards All Fallen Creatures, or Circumstantial Proof that the Doctrine of Apocatastasis is Incontrovertibly Grounded in Nature and Scripture*] (1726).

terms of scholastic deductions. But the premises of these deductions are merely commonsense propositions, and certainly not doctrines peculiar to Aristotle. So even if Soner's dilemma does lose its force as a result of Leibniz's comment, this is surely accomplished without any assistance from Aristotle. But with or without this assistance, is it really true in the first place that this one comment by Leibniz is so powerful and decisive? To be frank, I am totally unconvinced. For even if it were undeniable that human sins can, or indeed must, become infinite in number, what did this one further possible kind of infinity matter to Soner? What need did he have to concern himself with it? And against whom did he have to do so? Even if some of his adversaries did recognise this infinity, did they therefore recognise it as the most important, or even the sole, basis of their doctrine? Would they therefore cease to maintain what Soner actually denies – namely that, even if there were no infinity of sins such as that described above, the purely finite sins of this life are nevertheless subject to eternal punishment? And that even one of these sins merits this eternal punishment? Leibniz's objection in fact alters the whole point at issue. For Soner was concerned only with the sins of this life, which can only be finite in number. But Leibniz wants him to take account of the sins of our future life as well, which would in themselves merit perpetual punishment if their own duration were necessarily perpetual.

It may well be that, on further reflection, Leibniz himself could not deny this fact, and for that reason withheld the entire preface. For once it was written, why else would he not have published it? One cannot at any rate argue that he nevertheless made essentially the same point many years later in another context, namely in his *Theodicy*,[12] for in another context, the same idea can have a completely different significance. What Leibniz had recognised on the first occasion as an invalid rebuttal he could now quite properly use as an additional means of elucidating another question. Its original aim had been to refute all of Soner's objections and to provide a basis for the disputed doctrine, and it was quite inadequate for this purpose. But now, in the *Theodicy*, where he could assume as already demonstrated what he could not prove by this means alone, it was merely designed to establish a more direct connection between the greatest physical evil whose existence he was obliged to admit in his best

---

[12] *Essais de Théodicée sur la bonté de Dieu, la liberté de l'homme et l'origine du mal* [*Essays on Theodicy, on the Goodness of God, the Freedom of Man, and the Origin of Evil*] (1710), Leibniz's main exposition of his philosophical optimism.

of possible worlds, and the evil of human guilt – but without any reference to the infinity of the object of this guilt, because this infinity could not be treated as part of the [finite] universe.

And that would be all I needed to add, had I not discovered one of our most recent writers working along the same lines. Herr Eberhard, in his *Apology for Socrates*[13] – an in many ways excellent book, in which he examines the doctrine of the salvation of the heathens – has also thought it necessary to include the doctrine of eternal punishment in his investigation. Now I have a very specific reason for wishing that he had not opposed the latter doctrine – not, at least, in an apology for Socrates. This alone, however, would scarcely have led me to permit myself the least criticism of his work, had he not at the same time – since his topic also drew his attention to Leibniz's comments on the subject – raised various objections to that philosopher and to the comments in question, objections which I have such good reason to consider in the present context. I shall say what I have to say as briefly as possible, and if I do not put my thoughts into proper order, I shall at least number them.

I. I shall begin with the general judgement which Herr Eberhard passes on Leibniz with regard to his attitude towards accepted articles of religion. For after touching on that proof of eternal punishment referred to above, he shows very well that it cannot take us beyond the limits of mere possibility, and continues:

> The most perceptive advocates of this view, such as Leibniz, were well aware that a proof of this kind does not extend any further. Thus Leibniz was arguing only in support of those who had already been convinced by Scripture of the real eternity of the pains of hell. Since he was so anxious to make his philosophy universally acceptable, he tried to adapt it to the dominant principles of all parties and to show that it was agreeable and advantageous to the opinions of them all, in order to secure their approval. He took their doctrines as given and attributed a tolerable sense to them, thereby reconciling them with his system, but without subscribing to them himself.

Does this judgement not make our philosopher seem a little too vain? Does it not render his attitudes towards religion in general more suspect

---

[13] Johann August Eberhard, Berlin clergyman and author of *Neue Apologie des Sokrates oder Untersuchung der Lehre von der Seligkeit der Heiden* [*New Apology for Socrates, or An Examination of the Doctrine of the Salvation of the Heathen*], the first volume of which had recently appeared (1772).

than is good for religion itself? It is quite certain that neither of these conclusions was intended by Herr Eberhard. But it cannot be denied that, on this occasion, he did not express himself throughout as felicitously and precisely as he usually does. For however biassed in favour of his own philosophy we may think, or wish to think, Leibniz was, we really cannot say that he tried to adapt it to the dominant principles of all parties. How could he possibly have done so? How could it have entered his mind, to quote an old proverb, to make a dress for the moon? Everything that he did from time to time in the interest of his system was quite the opposite: he tried to adapt the dominant principles of all parties to that system. Unless I am much mistaken, the two are very far from identical. In his quest for truth, Leibniz never took any notice of accepted opinions; but in the firm belief that no opinion can be accepted unless it is in a certain respect, or in a certain sense true, he was often so accommodating as to turn the opinion over and over until he was able to bring that certain respect to light, and to make that certain sense comprehensible. He struck fire from stones, but he did not conceal his own fire in them. But that is basically all that Herr Eberhard intended to say, and part of his statement actually does say it: 'He took their doctrines as given, and attributed a tolerable sense to them, thereby reconciling them with his system.' Very good; but Herr Eberhard ought not to have added: 'but without subscribing to them himself'. For Leibniz did indeed subscribe to them, namely in that tolerable sense which he did not so much attibute to them as discover in them. That tolerable sense was truth, and how could he not subscribe to truth? Besides, he should not be accused either of falsehood or of vanity for so doing. He did no more and no less than what all the ancient philosophers used to do in their *exoteric* pronouncements. He displayed a sagacity which our most recent philosophers have, of course, become far too wise to employ. He willingly set his own system aside, and tried to lead each individual along the path to truth on which he found him.

II. Herr Eberhard continues:

> This is obviously the case with the present proof. In order to make his best of possible worlds acceptable to those who believe in the eternal torments of hell, he sought to demonstrate that these, too, can be reconciled with his propositions on the best of possible worlds and with his notions of divine justice.

Let us not forget what kind of a proof this is. It is that which deduces the endless duration of punishments from the perpetual continuation of sin. But what connection does this proof have with the doctrine of the best of possible worlds? How can it make this doctrine acceptable to those who believe in the eternity of the torments of hell even without this proof? Do these eternal torments cease to constitute an objection to the best of possible worlds because they are just? Whether just or unjust, they in both cases attribute infinite consequences to evil, and it was against these consequences, not against their injustice, that Leibniz ought to have defended his best of possible worlds. And he did so defend it – not, however, by means of the proof in question, but by an entirely different expedient. For if this same objection to his best of possible worlds on the grounds of eternal torment gained additional strength from the fact that the actual number of those condemned for ever must become immeasurably greater than the number of those saved, what did he say in reply? Merely, perhaps, that the vastly greater numbers of damned individuals were rightfully damned? What benefit would he have gained for his best of possible worlds from this conclusion, which is in any case self-evident if the theory is otherwise correct? Instead, he took both propositions – the eternal damnation of the majority of mankind, and the justice of their damnation – as fully established, and simply denied the corollary by showing what an infinitely small part of the world the whole of mankind is, and how, in the universal city of God, evil nevertheless counts as virtually nothing in comparison with the good (*Theodicy*, Pt I, §19). And that, I suggest, does mean making the doctrine of the best of possible worlds acceptable even to those who believe in the eternal torments of hell. But the thought from which this eternity is deduced was merely intended to cast more light on the working of God's justice. This alone is true in Herr Eberhard's statement. But I confess that I cannot see why he says that this involved only Leibniz's *own* notions of divine justice. It is bad enough that the doctrine of the best of possible worlds continues to be called *his* doctrine; but why should the only true notions of divine justice also be described as *his* notions?

III. Herr Eberhard further adds: 'He [Leibniz] accepts eternal torments only conditionally, and shows that they contain no injustice if we assume that the transgressions are also eternal.' I know the passage in the *Theodicy* where Leibniz says precisely that (*Theodicy*, Pt II, §133). But he would scarcely have acquiesced if this had been taken to imply that he therefore completely rejected everything else that theologians usually adduce in support of eternal punishment. He is so far from doing so that he is in fact more than at one with them on the most important point at issue. What I mean is that he does not merely allow this point to stand on its merits or demerits, but actually defends it with great perspicacity. Herr Eberhard declares that the one and only end which God can and must pursue in his punishments is the correction of those whom he punishes. Leibniz, on the other hand, not only extends this correction to those who merely witness the punishment, even if it has no effect on those who are themselves punished; he also speaks very seriously in support of a purely retributive divine justice, whose intention is neither to correct, to set an example, 'nor even to make restitution for evil'. And he bases this justice not just on the divine threat identified by the theologians, but on a genuine appropriateness, a certain indemnification of the understanding.[d] Nor does he anywhere reject, or even disapprove of, the proposition that sin receives infinite punishment because it offends an infinite being. He does indeed say on one occasion that there was once a time 'when he had not yet examined this proposition sufficiently to pass judgement on it' (*Theodicy*, Pt III, §266). But I find no evidence that he passed judgement on it later, no doubt because he realised, once he had examined it sufficiently, that it is not possible to reach any conclusion on it. For if that retributive justice really does pertain to God, what finite intellect can define its limits? Who can presume to decide what criterion it has to adopt in imposing these punishments, and what it cannot adopt? The criterion of its own infinity is at least as probable as any other.

IV. But what is the point of all this? Do I wish to increase the suspicion that Leibniz merely pretended to be orthodox? Or do I wish in all seriousness, to the annoyance of our philosophers, to make him orthodox? I wish neither of these things. I admit that Leibniz treated the doctrine of eternal damnation very *exoterically*, and that he would have expressed himself quite differently *esoterically*. But I would certainly not wish anyone to see in this anything more than a difference in teaching methods. I would

[d] 'The end of this kind of justice is neither to correct, to set an example, nor even to make restitution for evil...Hobbes and some others do not recognise this punitive justice, which is actually retributive...But it is always based on a relation of appropriateness, which satisfies not only the offended party but also discerning observers, just as fine music or good architecture satisfies cultivated minds' (*Theodicy*, Pt I, §73).

certainly not wish anyone to accuse him outright of internal ambivalence with regard to this doctrine – that is, by publicly paying it lip-service while secretly and fundamentally denying it. For that would be going too far, and it could not possibly be excused by any didactic strategy or by a desire to become all things to all men. On the contrary, I am convinced – and I believe that I can prove it – that Leibniz did not object to the ordinary doctrine of damnation, with all its exoteric reasons, and would even have preferred to reinforce it with new reasons, simply because he realised that it was in closer agreement than the opposite doctrine with a major truth of his esoteric philosophy. Of course he did not interpret it in the crude and dismal sense which some theologians attach to it. But he found that there was more truth even in this crude and dismal sense than in the equally crude and dismal notions of the fanatical adherents of apocatastasis; and this alone impelled him rather to go a little too far with the orthodox than not far enough with the latter.

V. Herr Eberhard certainly does not share this view of Leibniz and his esoteric philosophy. He believes that its main principle, that of the best possible world, becomes fully convincing only if one assumes that all rational beings will eventually attain happiness. In his own words:

> Leibniz was undoubtedly conscious of this, and despite the fact that, as I have already noted, he even tried to accommodate his philosophy to the opposite view, he still gave clear indications that he disapproved of it. One of his most able pupils and defenders (Vattel)[14] does not hesitate to acknowledge this. Besides, a more merciful fate for sinners is too deeply ingrained in his principles (provided one understands their full force and extent, and has explored their innermost secrets) for these to be accepted and the former rejected. He recognises no immobility or rest in the universe; everything, down to the smallest particle, is in constant movement, with a tendency to greater expansion. He obviously prefers this growth to uniform perfection, whether this growth is explained by the ordinates of the *hyperbola* or of the *triangle* (letter to M. Bourguet, *Opera omnia*, Pt II, p. 332).[15]

[14] Emmerich de Vattel, *Défense du système Leibnitien contre les objections de Mr. Crousaz* [*Defence of the Leibnizian System against the Objections of Mr Crousaz*] (1741).

[15] The geometrical terms here and in the following paragraph are those used by Leibniz to illustrate different hypotheses concerning the perfection of the universe. The hyperbola, a curve whose branches both tend towards infinity, denotes infinite progress towards perfection without a beginning; the triangle denotes infinite progress with a beginning; and the rectangle denotes equal perfection with neither a beginning nor an end.

With due respect to Herr Eberhard, I must point out that, although he is not entirely wrong with regard to this last reason drawn from Leibniz's philosophy, he is certainly quite mistaken with regard to the passage cited in his note. What Leibniz actually says is 'I do not yet see any means of showing by demonstration which of them one should choose in accordance with pure reason.' Herr Eberhard apparently takes this to refer to the two hypotheses for explaining the ever-increasing perfection of the whole, by the ordinates of either the hyperbola or the triangle. But it plainly refers to the two general hypotheses which postulate either an ever-increasing perfection or an ever equal perfection of the whole.[e] Now if Leibniz himself, in the year 1715, did not yet see any means of demonstrating either the one or the other from irrefutable principles, how can one say that he nevertheless obviously preferred the former? His system did not in the least oblige him to declare his preference for one or the other; it remains exactly the same on either assumption, and he said of both until the end of his life[16] that he did not yet see which of the two he definitely had to accept. For just as he elucidates the theory of ever-increasing perfection – whether or not one assumes a first beginning – either by the hypothesis of the hyperbola or by that of the triangle, he elucidates the theory of ever equal perfection by means of the rectangle. Of all these three hypotheses taken together, he says expressly in a different letter from that cited by Herr Eberhard: 'Thus it is not so easy to decide between the three hypotheses, and much further reflection is needed to reach a conclusion.' He also says in yet another letter:

> As for the grand question of whether it is possible to demonstrate by reason which hypothesis – viz. of the rectangle, the triangle, or the hyperbola – is preferable in explaining the constitution of the universe, I believe that one must adhere to a rigorous form of logical reasoning. For since, in metaphysics, one does not have the advantage

---

[e] Here is the passage in its full context: 'One can form two hypotheses – the first that nature is always equally perfect, and the second that it is always growing in perfection. If it is always equally perfect, though subject to variation, it is more probable that there is no beginning. But if it is always growing in perfection (assuming that it was not possible to give it the whole of perfection simultaneously), the matter might again be explained in two ways, namely by the ordinates either of the hyperbola or of the triangle. On the hypothesis of the hyperbola, there would be no beginning, and the moments or conditions of the universe would have grown in perfection from all eternity; but on the hypothesis of the triangle, there would have been a beginning. The hypothesis of equal perfection would be that of the rectangle. I do not yet see any means of showing by demonstration which of them one should choose in accordance with pure reason.'

[16] Leibniz died on 14 November 1716.

of the mathematicians who can define ideas by means of figures, one must make up for it by rigorous reasoning, which can scarcely be attained in such matters except by observing the form of logic. – I would therefore ask you, Sir, to consider how you might reduce your reasonings on this subject to an appropriate form, because I do not yet see a way of doing so myself.

As already noted, he wrote all this in 1715 – that is, at the end of his career – in letters which contain his final commentary on his system. That is why these letters to M. Bourguet, which first appeared in Dutens's edition of the complete works, are one of this edition's most valuable assets.

VI. But if Herr Eberhard did not mean his words to be taken so literally, and only wished to say that, although Leibniz could not properly demonstrate any of the relevant hypotheses, he nevertheless had a marked preference for that of constant progress towards greater perfection, I must admit that I cannot concur with him here either. Leibniz seems to me rather to have been much more favourably disposed towards ever equal perfection, and indeed almost to have persuaded his friend to supply a formal demonstration of it, which he perhaps had reasons for eliciting from him rather than simply putting it into his mouth. I base this comment particularly on that passage where he writes:

> You are right, Sir, in saying that it does not follow from the fact that finite beings are infinite in number that their system must acquire from the start all the perfection of which it is capable. For if this conclusion were correct, the hypothesis of the rectangle would be demonstrated.

It in fact seems to me that, even if this conclusion is not necessary but only possible, the hypothesis of the rectangle has already gained a great advantage, because the whole could then at every moment have that perfection which, according to the other hypothesis, it merely approaches constantly without ever reaching it; and I do not see why it should not for that very reason have struck the eternal wisdom as the more attractive choice. Leibniz, however, not only admits the possibility that the infinite number of finite beings could have been placed from the very beginning in the most perfect combination of which they are capable, but actually defends it against the accusation of eternal sameness; he does so by showing that, even if the degree of total perfection remained the same, the individual perfections would constantly change.

VII. But even supposing that all this were not as I say, and that Herr
Eberhard's assertion that Leibniz obviously preferred incessant growth to
uniform perfection were undeniably true, would he not at least be stretch-
ing quite excessively the meaning which Leibniz attached to this growth?
For Leibniz would surely have understood this growth as applying only
to the general conditions of the whole, yet Herr Eberhard extends it to all
individual beings. But even if the latter were also in constant movement
towards greater expansion, I should like to know how sin could ever occur
at all among moral beings, unless sin itself were nothing but a movement
towards greater expansion. No, that is certainly not how Leibniz thought.
For when, in accordance with the hypothesis of uniform perfection, he
says of a particular state of the whole 'this collection can have perfection as
a whole, *although the individual things of which it is composed may increase or
diminish in perfection*', this certainly also applies to every state of the whole
under the hypothesis of perpetual growth. The whole may continue in the
same degree of perfection, or grow in perfection at every moment, but in
neither case are individual beings prevented from increasing or decreas-
ing in perfection. Without this possible decrease in perfection, sin among
moral beings is inexplicable; and no more than this possible decrease is
required, even in the system of ever-growing perfection, to explain the
punishment, indeed the eternal punishment, of sin.

VIII. But I must first of all draw attention to that great esoteric truth
itself in whose interest Leibniz found it helpful to speak on behalf of the
common doctrine of eternal damnation. And what else can that truth be
but the fruitful proposition that nothing in the world is isolated, nothing
is without consequences, and nothing is without eternal consequences?
Thus if no sin is without consequences either, and these consequences
are the punishments of sin, how can these punishments be anything but
eternal in duration? How can these consequences ever cease to have consequences? Herr Eberhard himself acknowledges their eternity in this
respect, and comments on it with all possible forcefulness and dignity:

> If eternal hell is nothing but this eternal harm which is said to attach
> to us from every act of sin, no one will be more willing than I to
> grasp this opinion with both hands. For the sake of the end itself, I
> shall gladly overlook all the misconceptions to which this expression
> might be subject. I shall endeavour with all the zeal and all the
> eloquence that God has given me to impress on people's minds that

all immorality has infinite evil consequences, and that each backward step we take on the road to perfection will be subtracted, throughout our entire eternal existence, from the sum of that perfection and from the distance we have already covered.

All well and good! But how did he come to think that Baumgarten[17] alone had hinted at this eternity of punishment? How did he come to award to Baumgarten alone the distinction of having coupled it with so true and great a significance? Does it not also follow from Leibnizian principles? And even in Baumgarten's case, does it rest on any other principles than those of Leibniz? As for the proposition from which Baumgarten directly deduces it – namely that no negative thing can be a ground for reality in a real thing – what else is this but a more useful formulation, in certain instances, of the principle of sufficient reason? – Not to mention the fact that not only the eternal duration of damnation follows from this proposition, but also the impossibility of passing from damnation through damnation to salvation.

IX. But if the eternity of punishments is so obviously based on un-doubted Leibnizian doctrines, it must also be compatible with both hypotheses of universal perfection, whether equal or growing, if Leibniz's whole system is, as I have said, indifferent to these hypotheses. And it really is indifferent to them, provided that neither kind of perfection is attributed to each individual being, but only to the total states of all beings collectively. Irrespective of which hypothesis is adopted, a moral being can not only stop short or take several backward steps in its progress towards perfection: on the contrary, I do not see why it *might* not even persist eternally in this retrogression, and move further and further away from its perfection. On this possibility rests the exoteric reason which Leibniz employs in deriving the eternal duration of damnation from the endless continuation of sin – except that, if he were to be completely orthodox, he ought to have deduced from it not just eternal damnation, but also an eternal damnation which grows throughout eternity.

X. Humanity certainly shudders at this thought, even if it refers to no more than a possibility. But I do not therefore wish to raise the question of why one should frighten people with a mere possibility, because I fear

---

[17] Eberhard's reference (*Neue Apologie*, p. 427) is to Alexander Gottlieb Baumgarten, *Metaphysica* (1739; fourth edition, Halle, 1757), §791.

I might be asked in reply 'Why not frighten them with it if it can really only be frightening to someone who was never serious about mending his ways?' But supposing that not even this possibility existed, and that, although it might be compatible with the perfection of the whole, the eternal regression of a moral being were internally contradictory, the eternity of punishments nevertheless remains wholly consistent with the strictest Leibnizian principles. It is enough that no delay along the road to perfection can ever be made up in all eternity, and it therefore punishes itself throughout all eternity by its own agency. For even assuming that the supreme being cannot possibly administer punishment other than to correct the punished individual, and even assuming that this correction is sooner or later a necessary consequence of the punishment, is it therefore certain that any punishment can ever act as a corrective unless it last eternally? It may be replied 'Of course – through the vivid memory which it leaves behind.' But is this vivid memory not also a punishment?

XI. But why dwell on things which no one denies? It is not the eternity of natural punishments which is denied, but – what then? – the eternity of hell. But are the two not identical? Or is hell something different from, or at any rate more than, the quintessence of those punishments? – I am fully aware that there are theologians who take this view. But I find that Herr Eberhard at least is not among them, and that he is not for that reason any less orthodox than they. For there is nothing in all religion which compels us to believe such a thing. On the contrary, one can and may assume with every confidence that the punishments of which Scripture warns us are none other than the natural ones which would follow from sin, even without this threat. But if the higher wisdom considered that such extraordinary threats were necessary in addition, it recognised that it was also salutary to express them purely in terms of our present sensibilities. And here, I think, we come to the source of all the difficulties which have impelled people to deny eternal damnation. For since Scripture, in order to convey the liveliest impression of the misery which awaits the depraved, has taken nearly all its images from physical pain – with which all human beings, without exception, are most familiar –, people have interpreted if not physical pain itself, then at least its character and relation to our nature, not as an image, but as the thing itself; and on the basis of this misconception, they have denied something which is in every respect better founded. Thus punishments have become torments,

54

torments have become a condition of torment, and our awareness of this condition has become an exclusive sensation permeating our entire being. In short, that *intensive* infinity which – tacitly or implicitly, and to a greater or lesser degree – people have unthinkingly attributed, or even felt obliged to attribute, to the punishments of hell has no basis in either reason or Scripture; and it is this intensive infinity which makes, has always made, and must necessarily make the infinite duration of these punishments so incomprehensible, so incompatible with the goodness and justice of God, and so repellent to our understanding and sensibility.

XII. And it *must* make this impression, especially on those who cannot conceive of any divine punishments which do not aim at correction. Their feeling is fully justified, but their understanding draws a false conclusion. It is not the infinite duration of punishments which rules out correction, but their intensive infinity. For the main feature of this intensive infinity is its unremitting quality, and it is this unremitting quality which makes all correction impossible. What I mean to say – and have said in part already – is that if the punishments are to be corrective, the perpetual duration of the physical evil they inflict is so far from impeding the correction that the correction is actually a product of this duration. But the sensation of this enduring evil must not be unremitting – or at least, its unremitting quality must not always be dominant – because it is inconceivable how the initial resolve to improve could ever arise under such circumstances. Herr Eberhard himself affirms the former possibility explicitly and no less emphatically: 'The physical aspect of punishment may last indefinitely, but the better informed sinner will no longer call it an evil; he will no longer consider himself unfortunate, however painful it may be to his sensuous nature.' What else does this mean but that the sinner can better himself, even if his punishment never ceases? But when could he even begin to think that the enduring physical evil might be a salutary evil for him, and when could he begin to be better informed, if the sensation of this evil were as intensive and unremitting as people believe is implied by some figurative expressions of Scripture?

XIII. I deliberately say 'by *some* figurative expressions'. For other such expressions, especially if we may include the parables among them, yield far more accurate notions which are compatible both with the endlessness of punishments and with the correction of the punished individual. That the two are not mutually exclusive is evident not just on the assumption that the correction can only be sustained if the punishments continue to operate: that it is more than probable can also be demonstrated by another means – namely if we bear in mind that, although punishment and reward will and must be positive factors, a condition of punishments and a condition of rewards are also relative concepts which remain the same so long as they decrease or grow in equal proportion. The rich man in hell may better himself; he may even, from the first moment when he felt his punishment, have turned once more towards his perfection and drawn ever closer to it with every succeeding moment. Does he therefore cease to remain in hell in comparison with Lazarus,[18] who, from the first moment when he felt his salvation, has meanwhile hastened on by an equal number of steps towards ever higher perfection? – Anyone who can seriously object that, in this way, heaven and hell flow into one so that every sinner can console himself with the thought that he will sooner or later reach heaven is precisely the kind of person with whom one should not begin to discuss such matters. Let him continue to cling to the letter alone, for it was for him and his kind that the letter was intended.

XIV. I may, however, ask a man like Herr Eberhard whether that unbroken progression which links the two conditions, heaven and hell, through infinite stages, without either of them ever losing its relative designation, does not already follow from the system of corrective punishments. And similarly, whether the complete distinction which the ordinary understanding makes between heaven and hell, with their boundaries which form no boundary and their abruptly demarcated limits which are supposedly separated by I know not what gulf of emptiness, on one side of which there is absolutely nothing but one kind of sentiments and on the other absolutely nothing but sentiments of a different kind – whether all such things are not far more unphilosophical than the very crudest notion of everlasting punishments can ever be. The latter, at least, is based on a great and undisputed truth, and it only becomes so nonsensically crude because it is made to include those absurdities which conflict both with the nature of the soul and with the justice of God.

XV. That they conflict with the nature of the soul is clear, because the soul is not capable of any pure sentiment – that is, of any sentiment which is capable of being, even in its smallest elements, exclusively pleasant or

---

[18] See Luke 16.22–31.

exclusively unpleasant – let alone of a state in which it experiences nothing but such pure sentiments of the one kind or the other. But that they also conflict with the justice of God is, I fear, something which may have received less consideration than it deserves. Yet what does such a conflict more obviously signify than the assumption or assertion that even the justice of God cannot, in its punishments, escape an imperfection which, in certain cases, is inevitable in human justice? This imperfection consists in the fact that human justice, when punishments and rewards overlap, can only reward by a reduced punishment and punish by a reduced reward – in other words, it must, in such cases, punish and reward, as the expression goes, in a single package. But does this also apply to God? Never! On the contrary, if it is true that the best human being still has much evil and the worst is not devoid of all good, the consequences of evil must follow the former into heaven, and the consequences of good must also accompany the latter into hell: each must find his hell even in heaven, and his heaven even in hell. The consequences of evil must not simply be subtracted from the more numerous consequences of good, or the consequences of good from the more numerous consequences of evil; instead, each of them must, in its whole positive nature, express itself independently. Nothing else is meant by Scripture itself when it refers to the stages of heaven and hell. But do the more unthinking of its readers also imagine these stages in this way? Or do they not rather give each one of these stages, however low it may be, so to speak its own intensive infinity? They of course recognise that the lowest stage of heaven is only the lowest one; but it is nevertheless heaven, nothing but joy and bliss, nothing but blessedness.

XVI. And so, why should we not rather turn our weapons against these erroneous notions, which are also far easier to eliminate from Scripture by means of reinterpretation than the eternal duration of punishments? It seems to me at least that even the most acute interpreter, if he tries to oppose the latter, must take as established certain things which remain open to many objections. For example, when Herr Eberhard insists that the word 'eternal', in the Hebrew and Greek languages, denotes merely an indefinite but by no means infinite duration, he says, among other things:

> One must take particular note of the chronological progression in the gradual elevation of so abstract a concept as that of eternity. This concept was not always so transcendental as the staunchest efforts of the most sublime philosophy have finally made it.

The reminder which this passage contains may apply very appropriately to many metaphysical concepts, but hardly to that of eternity. Since it is purely negative, I fail to see what kind of gradation is possible within it. Either it was not present at all, or it was present all along as completely as it ever can be. The fact that it was customary to describe a long and indefinite time as an eternity does not remotely prove that eternity was also at first envisaged only as a long and indefinite time. For the word is still used every day in the former sense by people who know very well what the word 'eternity' really means. And it is even less true that, although the poverty of early language could only express the abstract concept of eternity by piling one age on top of another, the concept itself ever lacked its essential character. The history of philosophy suggests the very opposite. For even if this concept of eternity does represent a special effort of the most sublime philosophy, philosophy was certainly capable of such an effort at a very early stage, and this most sublime philosophy is none other than the oldest philosophy of all. Even the most transcendent level which this concept of eternity is capable of reaching (I refer to the exclusion of all temporality), and to which so few are able to raise themselves even now – even this was already very familiar to the ancient philosophers, and as already noted, almost more familiar to them than to our philosophers of today.

XVII. I am equally reluctant to associate myself with various other pronouncements of Herr Eberhard on this matter, for without addressing the essential point at issue, they nevertheless present it in a false light. This is true of his suggestion, which is clearly implied even if it is not directly asserted, that the doctrine of eternal punishment originated with the Christians. He says:

> I am admittedly not in a position to specify the precise moment when it arose and spread among the Christians. But whenever it was, it must have been at a time when barbarism had already gained sufficient ground for the sophistry of the schoolmen to find ready access to the minds of men. For I hope to prove so conclusively that reason rejects this terrible doctrine that they will have no option but to put it down to misunderstandings of Scriptural passages.

As already noted, even if he does not deny, in these words, that other religions besides Christianity teach, and have taught, the eternal punishment of sinners, his formulation is not entirely blameless if those unfamiliar with the question gain the impression that it is not, and never has been, taught by any other. This is nevertheless so mistaken that he would find it difficult to name even one religion which clearly teaches that punishments are finite, and does not in fact teach the opposite in terms no less severe than those which, as he must admit, seem at least to be used in the Scriptures. Thus, each Christian convert brought the offending doctrine with him from his former religion into Christianity, and did not need to be introduced to it by the misunderstood passages of Scripture, which could at most reinforce his existing belief. It would, on the other hand, be much easier to specify the moment when, in Christianity, a doctrine so common to all religions first began to be contested, partly on supposedly philosophical grounds and partly on the basis of prior misunderstandings on the part of those involved. And this consensus of all religions would alone prevent me from agreeing with Herr Eberhard 'that reason rejects this terrible doctrine', or, as he says even more emphatically on another occasion, 'that reason cannot be blamed for this doctrine, that there is not one among the whole range of rational truths from which it can properly be deduced'. What all religions have in common can surely not lack a basis in reason; and the truth of the eternal consequences of sin, albeit obscurely felt rather than clearly recognised since time immemorial, was undoubtedly enough to generate the doctrine in question. Or rather, this truth and the doctrine of eternal punishment are basically one, although they are more or less distorted in the various religions by the attempt to represent these punishments in sensuous terms.

XVIII. I shall conclude by indicating more precisely the reason, mentioned near the beginning of this work, why I could wish that Herr Eberhard had not opposed the doctrine of the eternal punishment of sinners – not, at least, in an apology for Socrates. It is because Socrates himself believed in all seriousness in such eternal punishment, at least to the extent of considering it helpful to teach it in the most unexceptionable and explicit terms. He does so in his speech at the end of Plato's *Gorgias*, in which the following passage leaves absolutely no room for doubt:[19]

> And it is fitting that every one under punishment rightly inflicted
> on him by another should either be made better and profit thereby,
> or serve as an example to the rest, that others seeing the sufferings

---

[19] Plato, *Lysis, Symposium, Gorgias*, with an English translation by W. R. M. Lamb, Loeb Classical Library (Cambridge, MA and London, 1925), p. 525.

he endures may in fear amend themselves. Those who are benefited by the punishment they get from gods and men are they who have committed remediable offences; but still it is through bitter throes of pain that they receive their benefit both here and in the nether world; for in no other way can there be a riddance of iniquity. But of those who have done extreme wrong and, as a result of such crimes, have become incurable, of those are the examples made; no longer are they profited at all themselves, since they are incurable, but others are profited who behold them undergoing for their transgressions the greatest, sharpest, and most fearful sufferings evermore, actually hung up as examples there in the infernal dungeon, a spectacle and a lesson to such of the wrongdoers as arrive from time to time.

No evasions are possible here. The 'evermore' (τὸν ἀεὶ χρόνον) is not as ambiguous as αἰὼν or αἰώνιος.[20] And what would it matter if there were an ambiguity, given the explicit contrast between the damned who suffer punishments and torments for the purpose of correction, and the damned who cannot better themselves but are tortured and tormented eternally simply as an example to others, suffering 'the greatest, sharpest, and most fearful sufferings evermore'? It is true, of course – at least on this evidence – that Socrates did not treat the punishments of hell, in general and without distinction, as eternal. But if this alone makes his doctrine more tolerable, what is there in our religion to prevent us from making the same distinction? To prevent us? As if the greater part of our fellow-Christians had not already adopted it! That intermediate state [of purgatory] which the older Church believes in and teaches, and which our reformers, despite the grievous abuse it had occasioned, ought not perhaps to have rejected so completely – what else is it but the corrective hell of Socrates? And even if it were merely possible, and indeed remained merely possible for all eternity, that there might be utterly incorrigible sinners who could never desist from sinning, why should we not assume or accept merely possible punishments for these merely possible monsters alone? –

– O my friends, why should we try to appear more sharp-witted than Leibniz, and more philanthropic than Socrates?

[20] These terms can mean either 'eternity' and 'eternal' or 'a long time' and 'long lasting'.

[Editorial commentary on the 'Fragments' of Reimarus, 1777]

[Introduction]

The anonymous fragment 'On the Toleration of Deists', published in the last issue,[1] made a particular impression on one or two of my readers, to whose approval I am by no means indifferent. The less I expected it here, the more agreeable it was, 'like a green oasis unexpectedly encountered in a desert'. The image is not my own, as can well be imagined: it was used by one of the readers in question,[2] who wrote to reward and encourage my efforts. For he adds that he would regard it as true pedantry if I, as a librarian, were now to put aside completely a set of thirty-year-old papers merely because they were perhaps not yet sufficiently decayed and illegible. He even begs me to provide the public with further extracts in the next issue, including, if possible, the boldest and strongest sections, so as not to lead those of weak faith to suspect that all sorts of unanswerable objections were being kept secret.

Now I fear the charge of pedantry too much, and am too convinced that the good cause can stand up to the above suspicion, to hesitate for one moment in fulfilling this request, which I know is supported by other like-minded readers. But I can hardly come up at once with the boldest

---

[1] The first issue of Lessing's periodical *Zur Geschichte und Literatur. Aus den Schätzen der Herzoglichen Bibliothek zu Wolfenbüttel* [*On History and Literature: From the Treasures of the Ducal Library in Wolfenbüttel*], in which he was authorised to publish new discoveries from the library without referring them to the Brunswick censors. Although he claimed to have discovered the anonymous 'Fragments' in the library, he had in fact obtained them from the late Reimarus's daughter in Hamburg.

[2] No evidence of such appeals by readers survives.

and strongest material, for the papers are still too disorganised, and the continuity is often lost where one least expects it. So until I have become more familiar with them, readers will have to make do with the following fragments, which I append without further preamble.

I merely ask permission to add, in conclusion, a few hints concerning the manner in which critics have sought, especially in recent times, to counter and negate all these arguments. I regard it as my duty to add such an appendix, however unequal I consider myself to the task.

[Five substantial extracts (or 'fragments') from the anonymous work of Reimarus, all sharply critical of the Bible, are inserted at this point; Lessing gives them the following self-explanatory titles:

1 On the denunciation of reason from the pulpits
2 On the impossibility of a revelation which can justifiably be believed by all of mankind
3 On the crossing of the Red Sea by the Israelites
4 That the books of the Old Testament were not written in order to reveal a religion
5 On the story of the resurrection].

Counter-propositions of the editor

And now enough of these fragments! – But any one of my readers who would rather I had kept them to myself is surely more *faint-hearted* than *well informed*. He may be a very *pious* Christian, but he is certainly not a very *enlightened* one. He may genuinely *mean* well by his religion, but he ought also to have more *faith* in it.

For how much remains to be said in reply to all these objections and difficulties! And even if nothing whatsoever could be said in reply – what then? The learned theologian might ultimately find them an embarrassment; but what of the Christian? He certainly would not! The former might at most be at a loss to see the supports with which he had hoped to underpin religion so badly shaken, and to find the buttresses with which, God willing, he had so well preserved it completely demolished. But what do this man's hypotheses, explanations, and proofs matter to the Christian? For him, Christianity is simply *there*, that same Christianity which he *feels* is so true and in which he *feels* himself so blessed. – When the paralysed patient *experiences* the salutary shock of the electric spark, what does he care whether Nollet, or Franklin,[3] or neither of the two is right? –

In short, the letter is not the spirit, and the Bible is not religion. Consequently, objections to the letter, and to the Bible, need not also be objections to the spirit and to religion.

For the Bible obviously contains more than what pertains to religion, and it is merely a hypothesis that it must be equally infallible in this additional respect. Religion also existed before there was a Bible. Christianity existed before the evangelists and apostles wrote about it. Some time elapsed before the first of them wrote, and a very considerable time elapsed before the whole canon was established. Thus, however much may depend on these writings, it is impossible for the whole truth of religion to be based on them. If there was a period in which this truth was already so widely disseminated, and in which it had already won over so many souls – but without a single letter of *that* material which has come down to us having yet been recorded – then it must also be possible for everything that the evangelists and apostles wrote to be lost once more and for the religion they taught to continue to exist. The religion is not true because the evangelists and apostles taught it; on the contrary, they taught it because it is true. The written records must be explained by its inner truth, and none of the written records can give it any inner truth if it does not already have it.

This, then, might be the general response to a large portion of these fragments – in the worst case, as already noted. This case would arise if a Christian who is also a theologian should find no satisfactory answer within the spirit of his own confessional system. But how can he discover whether he has the answer, and how can we be confident that he does have it, if it is not permissible to state, freely and plainly, every variety of objection? It is not true that all the objections have already been stated. It is even less true that they have all been answered. A great many of them, at least, have been answered as deplorably as they were stated. To the superficiality and ridicule of the one side, the other has not infrequently replied with pride and disdain. Great offence has been taken if one side equated religion with superstition; but the other side has not scrupled to denounce doubt as irreligion, and belief in the sufficiency of reason

---

[3] Jean Antoine Nollet (1700–70) and Benjamin Franklin (1706–90) were among the pioneers of electrical theory.

as infamy. The one party has disparaged every clergyman as a scheming priest, while the other has disparaged every philosopher as an atheist. Thus each side has turned its adversary into a monster so that, if it cannot defeat him, it can pronounce him beyond the law.

In truth, that man has yet to appear, he has yet to appear on either side, who can attack or defend religion in a manner befitting the importance and dignity of the subject – with all the knowledge, all the love of truth, and all the gravity it requires! – To launch or repel assaults on individual bastions is neither to mount a siege nor to raise it. Yet little more than this has so far been attempted. No enemy has yet surrounded the fortress completely; none has mounted a simultaneous assault on all its fortifications. The attacks have always been mounted only on an outwork, often of very little significance, which has been defended with more fervour than astuteness on the part of the besieged. For their usual maxim was to direct all their fire at the single point of attack, regardless of whether or not another enemy was meanwhile scaling the undefended walls. What I mean is that a single proof has often been overstretched, to the detriment of all the others as well as itself. A single nail was supposed to support everything, and it supported nothing. A *single* objection was often answered as if it were the *sole* objection, and often by means of arguments which were very open to objections of their own. Another even more ill-conceived procedure was to leave the attacked position undefended, abandoning it contemptuously to the enemy and moving to another instead. For in this way, the defenders gradually let themselves be not so much *expelled* as *frightened away* from all their defences, only to be obliged, before long, to throw themselves once more into the position which they originally abandoned. Anyone with the least knowledge of the latest works on the truth of Christianity will readily think of examples to fit every feature of this allegory.

How close our author came to the ideal of a true opponent of religion can certainly be deduced, to some extent, from these fragments, but not adequately appreciated. He seems to have occupied enough ground for his approach trenches, and he sets about his work in earnest. – May he soon call forth a man who comes at least as close to the ideal of a true defender of religion!

So as not to pre-empt this man but merely to let others judge how much he would have to say, and secondly, to counteract the initial panic which might seize the timorous reader, I hasten to add to each individual fragment some thoughts which have impressed themselves on me. But if I do more in the process than I initially asked permission to do,[4] this is because I abhor that tone of derision into which I could easily lapse if I tried to do *only* the latter. For there are certainly enough men now who defend religion as if they had been expressly suborned by its enemies to undermine it. But it would be an insult to religion if I were to suggest that these were the only men who still stand before the breach. And how do I know whether they too do not have the best intentions in the world? If *they* cannot defend their good intentions, what defence will *I* have if I miss the mark as widely as they do?

I

The first fragment takes issue with something which can do nothing to make Christianity acceptable. So if there have been theologians who insisted on it, they must have been very strongly convinced of its necessity. Would they otherwise have tried, in full view of everyone, to set mantraps beneath the very gate which they urged people to enter?

And there certainly were such theologians. But where are they today? Has the boot not long since been on the other foot? The pulpits no longer resound with the need to subordinate reason to faith; they now resound only with talk of the intimate bond between reason and faith.[5] Faith has become reason reinforced by miracles and portents, and reason has become faith reinforced by rational thought. The whole of revealed religion is nothing but an additional endorsement of the religion of reason. It either contains no mysteries at all, or if there are any, it is immaterial whether the Christian associates them with this or that concept or with no concept at all.

How easy it was to refute those incompetent theologians who had nothing to fall back on but a few misunderstood passages of Scripture, and who, by condemning reason, ensured that the reason they offended continued to fight back! They incensed everyone who had, or wished to have, reason.

---

[4] See p. 62 above.

[5] Lessing refers to the so-called 'neologists', including A. F. W. Sack, J. F. W. Jerusalem, J. G. Töllner, and J. A. Eberhard, who preached a rational form of Christianity, ignoring or playing down those elements (including the central mysteries) which could not readily be rationalised.

How delicate a matter it is, on the other hand, to start an argument with those who both glorify and neutralise reason by denouncing the opponents of revelation as opponents of common sense! They hoodwink all those who claim to have reason but do not have it.

Nevertheless, the truth must undoubtedly lie once more where it always lies – between the two extremes. Whether there can and must be a revelation, and which of so many self-proclaimed revelations is likely to be true, is something which only reason can decide. But if there can and must be a revelation, and once the true revelation has been identified, reason must regard it rather as an additional proof of its truth than as an objection to it if it finds in it things which are beyond its comprehension. Anyone who polishes such things out of his religion might as well have no religion at all. For what is a revelation which reveals nothing? Is it enough to retain only the name while rejecting the substance? And is it only the unbelievers who discard both?

Thus a *certain* subjugation of reason to the discipline of faith is based not on this or that passage of Scripture, but on the essential definition of revelation. It may well be that our author had a better grasp of the passages in question (and I could name more than one worthy interpreter who found nothing more in them than he did). It may well be that he is more accurate than those wretched preachers who resort to our earliest ancestors' lamentable fall from grace in order to prove something which has no need of this proof. He himself acknowledges that the Mosaic story is not to blame for this abuse. But while it is not true that it can be held responsible for a *subsequent* corruption of human reason, he does seem to me not to have realised its full implications either. For when he says 'that given this story, it was rather the duty of the preachers, as true pastors, to recommend sound reason and its employment to their congregations as an infallible criterion of divine knowledge and pious living, given that our earliest ancestors fell from grace precisely because they failed to make use of it', he addresses only half of the problem. For the story also indicates the cause which prevented their reason from functioning. In a word, it is the power of our sensuous desires, of our obscure representations [*Vorstellungen*] over even our clearest knowledge, which the story expresses so vividly. The Mosaic narrative either reports the first sad experience of this power, or furnishes the most telling example of it. Whether it is fact or allegory, it shows that the source of all our transgressions was this power alone, which was as firmly implanted in Adam, notwithstanding his creation in God's image, as it is innate in us. We have all sinned in Adam because all of us must sin; and we are image enough of God if we are not exclusively sinners, if we have it in us to reduce that power and can use it as readily for good as for evil actions. The so frequently ridiculed 'fairytale' of Moses is at least fully open to this edifying interpretation, provided we do not import into it those accommodations which a later system discerned in it, and leave accommodations to themselves.[6]

As already stated, a *certain* subjugation of reason to the discipline of faith is simply based on the essential definition of revelation. Or rather – for the word 'subjugation' seems to suggest violence on one side and resistance on the other – reason *surrenders* itself, and its surrender is merely an acknowledgement of its limits as soon as it is assured that the revelation is a genuine one. This, then, is the outpost in which we must firmly stand our ground; and it betrays either woeful vanity if we let mischievous mockers *ridicule* us out of it, or despair over the proofs for the reality of revelation if we *withdraw* from it in the belief that we need no longer take such proofs very seriously. What is meant to be rescued by such means is all the more irrevocably lost; and when the opponents of Christianity exaggerate the incomprehensible aspects of revelation, they are merely setting a trap for those of its defenders who are not entirely sure of their ground, and whose main concern is to salvage their reputation for shrewdness.

Another trap which is laid even for the better sort of theologians is to express dissatisfaction with existing versions of the catechism, and to make their defective presentation responsible for the fact that religion makes so little impact. Now I do not wish to deny that there is room for improvement in such textbooks; but caution is required before one proceeds, with well-intentioned haste, to correct those very things which some people are so anxious to correct, including our author himself when he accuses them of 'a lack of rational religion and of a rational progression from it to revelation'.

In my opinion, this lack is on the one hand no lack at all, and on the other, it would be extremely dangerous to remedy it. I mean *really* to remedy it, for there can be no question of anything else, because any minor adjustments would only make those dear old books more stark and stale than ever.

---

[6] Accommodations: here, theories that human reason is inherently flawed by original sin.

Revealed religion does not in the least presuppose a rational religion, but includes it within itself. If it did presuppose it – that is, if it were unintelligible without it – the deficiency of which the textbooks are accused would be a genuine deficiency. But since it actually includes it, since it contains all the truths which rational religion teaches and merely supports them with another kind of evidence, it is still very relevant to ask whether the unitary mode of demonstration employed in textbooks for children and ordinary people is not more convenient and more useful than a rigorous separation of rational and revealed doctrines, each demonstrated in accordance with its own distinct source.

It is at least certain that the transition from purely rational truths to revealed truths is extremely difficult to accomplish if one has first enjoyed the luxury of the precise and comprehensible proofs of the former. One then expects and demands the *same* clarity and comprehensibility from the proofs of the latter, and anything not proved *in the same way* will seem not to be proved *at all*. I recall here what happened to me in my youth. I wanted to study mathematics, and I was given the elder Sturm's *Tables*,[7] in which chiromancy was still included among the mathematical sciences. When I encountered this, I was completely nonplussed. My limited understanding suddenly ceased to function altogether; and although an art which promised to acquaint me with my future destiny held no small attraction for me, I felt as if I had exchanged a pleasant wine for insipid sugar-water when I transferred my attention to it from geometry. I did not know what to think of a man who had combined two such disparate things in a single book, so I took my leave of him and sought another teacher instead. But had I been obliged to regard this man as infallible, the question-begging proofs of chiromancy, whose arbitrariness was so apparent to me, would have filled me with fear and distrust towards those mathematical truths which were so congenial to my understanding, even if I had as yet grasped some of them only by memory. I could not possibly have regarded them both, geometry and chiromancy, as equally certain; but I might well have come to regard chiromancy and geometry as equally uncertain.

I hardly think it worth the effort to repudiate the suspicion that I am trying to insinuate that the proofs of revelation and the proofs of

---

[7] Johann Christoph Sturm, *Mathesis compendiaria . . . tabulis . . . comprehensa* [*A Brief Guide to Mathematics, in Tabular Form*] (1670).

chiromancy are of equal weight. Of course they are not of equal weight: their specific weights are absolutely incommensurable. But both kinds of proof nevertheless belong to a single class: both are based on evidence and on empirical propositions. And the contrast between the strongest proofs of this kind and proofs which flow from the nature of things is so striking that every artifice designed to reduce this striking divergence and to smooth it out by introducing all kinds of intermediate gradations is futile.

II

The second fragment says a great many perfectly correct and wholly unexceptionable things. Let us suppose that it contains only such things! Let us suppose that its proof that a revelation which could justifiably be believed by *all* of mankind is impossible is conducted with all due rigour – as indeed it is!

But does not this problem immediately suggest its own answer? If *such* a revelation is impossible – well, then, God could not make it possible either. If, however, a revelation is nevertheless useful and necessary, would God choose to provide *no revelation at all* just because he could not provide *such* a revelation? Would God deny this benefit to the whole human race just because he could not enable all human beings to partake of it at the *same* time, and to the *same* extent? Who has the heart to answer this question in the affirmative?

It is enough if the highest wisdom and goodness, in providing a revelation which it could not provide in a universal and absolutely clear form, adopted the only means whereby the *greatest* number of people could enjoy it in the *shortest* possible time. Or will anyone presume to demonstrate that this did not happen? That if this revelation had been imparted at another time, to another people, in another language, it would have equipped more people, in a shorter time, with those truths and motives for virtue on which Christians, as Christians, can now pride themselves?

Let anyone who presumes to do so first name to me a people in whose hands that initial capital of revelation would have been more likely to gain greater interest than in the hands of the Jews. That infinitely more despised than despicable people was nevertheless absolutely the first and only people in the whole of history to make a business out of communicating and disseminating its religion. The zeal with which the Jews conducted this business was already censured by Christ,[8] and ridiculed by Horace.[9] All other peoples were either too secretive and jealous with regard to their religions, or much too coldly disposed towards them to trouble themselves in the least with their dissemination. The Christian peoples, who subsequently followed the Jews' example in their zeal, inherited it only in so far as their religion was grafted on to Judaism.

But even if, our author might insist, a well-founded knowledge of revelation, such as *all* human beings cannot possibly possess, is indispensable to *all* human beings for salvation, how can the millions of people acquire it – ?

Let us not think such a cruel thought through to its conclusion! – Woe betide the human race if no reply can be given to this thought, other than perhaps to point out that the author has added up the total before the account was closed, and to inform him: 'Christianity is for all time; it gains new ground every year, although neither missions nor learned proofs of its truth help it to do so; even if the Christian nations have hardly increased in number over the last few centuries, more people have surely become Christians within these nations; the time must come when this imperceptible growth will reveal itself to the eyes of an astonished world, and a fair wind must arise which will combine the as yet scattered flames into one all-consuming fire, so that the number of lost souls will finally stand in the same ratio to the number of saved as the latter now does to the former.' –

Woe betide the human race if this alone, or some other petty distinction, is to be its consolation! – For example, that we must distinguish between revelation and the books of revelation; that the former is only a single, very comprehensible truth whose history is contained within the latter; or that salvation is not tied to laborious study of the books in question, but to the sincere acceptance of the revelation itself, which must lead to considerable reductions in the cumulative total [of lost souls].

For woe betide the human race if even a single soul is lost in this *economy of salvation*! The loss of this *one* must be of the most pressing concern to *all*, because any individual could well have been that one. And what everlasting bliss is so rapturous as not to be marred by this concern?

[8] Matthew 23.15.   [9] Horace, *Satires* I.4 and I.9.

But what need is there for this agonising? – So unmerited a defeat for mankind, a victory awarded to hell by God himself, is a miserable fantasy. Let us trace this false alarm to its source. One word will be enough to dispose of it.

It was neither a doctrine of Christ, nor has it ever been a generally accepted doctrine of the Church, that revelation is also necessary for the salvation of those who are ignorant of it, or who cannot attain reliable knowledge of it. Even those who, in all the various [Christian] denominations, have made the harshest pronouncements on this matter and taken the view that no exceptions can be made to that universal necessity have nevertheless circumvented its sad consequences, giving back with one hand what they had taken with the other. It is immaterial with how good or ill a grace they did so, how unphilosophical a view they adopted, or how faithful or unfaithful they were to their own doctrinal system; it is enough that they acted as they did, and that they did so willingly and joyfully. Their wish itself exonerates their hearts, and their acknowledgement that God can grant dispensation where the theologian cannot, and that God will know of alternative solutions with no need for any dispensation, reconciles us to their system.

And it is here that I must explicitly repeat that general criticism of our author to which I have already alluded, although it serves as much to excuse him as to censure him. He treats everything contained in a certain doctrinal system of Christianity expounded in certain symbolic books as the only true and authentic Christianity. Propositions without which Christianity cannot survive and which were explicitly taught by its founder and propositions which were merely inserted in order to provide better links between the former or were thought to follow necessarily from them are treated by him as identical. It is nevertheless right and proper that, when Christianity is attacked, all its sects should be treated as one, and no objection to Christianity should be accepted as valid unless none of these sects can answer it. But this does not really apply to that doctrine of the complete corruption of human reason in divine matters which our author found it so easy to refute in the first fragment, or to that doctrine of the indispensable necessity of a clear and distinct faith for salvation which is the object of the second fragment, or to the doctrine of the divine inspiration of Scripture as he expounds it here – and as indeed he had to expound it in order to lend all his objections, including the most trivial ones, an equally high degree of credibility. – This, at least, is the judgement I am bound to reach on the evidence before us.

III

The objection contained in the third fragment has often been raised and often answered. But *how* was it raised and answered? It has surely never been presented so thoroughly, so circumstantially, and taking such full account of all possible evasions as it is here. One need only ask how successful such authorities as Clericus, Calmet, Saurin, or Lilienthal[10] have been in answering it: their success, I fear, has been minimal. The orthodox believer will therefore have to think of a completely new solution if he is unable to defend his position, yet also unwilling to make any concessions.

He will, however, regard it as a major concession if he were to admit that so great a multitude could not possibly make such a crossing [of the Red Sea] in so short a time, and to try to overcome the difficulty by suggesting an error of transcription in the number of Israelites specified in the text, so that instead of 600,000 fighting men, only 60,000, or even 6,000, departed from Egypt. – Now I really cannot see what harm such an error could do, even if it were quite deliberately committed. In the earliest times, people had a very unclear conception of large numbers, and there will often be a perfectly innocent explanation for the fact that a very large number was sometimes expressed as one figure and sometimes as another. There would be ample scope for doubt regarding all those ancient battles where one writer gives one figure for the number of enemy casualties, another gives a different figure, and all of them give far higher figures than are compatible with the other circumstances they relate. Why should we be more exacting in the case of miracles, where the precise number of people rewarded or punished by them is much less important, and nothing whatsoever depends on it? For whether Moses divided the sea with his rod and led millions across over dry land, or Elisha did the

---

[10] Jean Le Clerc (Clericus) (1657–1736), Dutch Arminian theologian, author of a commentary on the Pentateuch; Augustin Calmet (1672–1757), Catholic theologian, author of a Bible commentary; Jacques Saurin (1677–1730), French Calvinist, author of a work on the principal events in the Old and New Testaments; Theodor Christoph Lilienthal (1717–82), Lutheran theologian, author of a work defending the literal accuracy of the Scriptures.

same to the Jordan with the cloak of his master and crossed it alone,[11] is not the one as much a miracle as the other?

That is certainly what I would think. But the orthodox believer cannot readily concede this much so long as any possibility of salvaging even the smallest details of the report remains unexplored. – As perhaps here. – For what if the miracle assumed the following form? – When the Israelites had reached an arm of the Arabian Sea which they necessarily had to cross if they were not to fall into their pursuers' hands, a strong wind – helped, if we wish, by the receding tide – drove the water out *seawards*, and held it back long enough for them to cross at their leisure. Meanwhile, the dammed-up water sought another way out, broke through behind the Israelites, rushed in *landwards* by another route, and it was in this new inlet that the Egyptians perished. What could be less contrived than this explanation? Is it not in the nature of water, if its usual course is blocked, to overflow or break through at the first weak or low point in the surrounding land and scour out a new course for itself? And what difficulty in our fragment is not removed by this explanation? The Israelites, however great their number, no longer need to hurry; they can move just as slowly as they need to with their children and cattle, bag and baggage; and if they had not crossed the whole of the broad, dried-up inlet by the beginning of the morning watch, the water of this inlet was already behind them, and their enemies drowned in the very water on whose bed the Israelites had escaped.

I am not aware that any interpreter has offered a similar explanation and treated the text accordingly, for many passages in it would certainly lend themselves very well to it – better all round, in fact, than to any other explanation. Even on the closest scrutiny, I can find only one word in Luther's version of the Mosaic account which appears to conflict with it, namely 'and at daybreak the sea returned to *its* course', or in Herr Michaelis's translation,[12] 'in the morning the water returned, and resumed its *usual* flow'. If it was to *its* course that the sea came back, or if it was its *usual* flow that it resumed, any new inlet or overflow certainly does seem a very contrived assumption. It does, however, appear that Luther was following here not so much the original [Hebrew] text as the Vulgate,

[11] 2 Kings 2.14.
[12] Johann David Michaelis, *Deutsche Übersetzung des Alten Testaments, mit Anmerkungen für Ungelehrte [The Old Testament in German Translation, with Notes for the Uneducated]* (1769–85).

which reads 'at daybreak the sea returned to its previous place'; and Herr Michaelis has perhaps read a little too much of his own hypothesis into the text, for the literal reading is simply 'and the sea returned with the morning in its strength', so that it is not even certain whether the sea returned in its strength, or whether it returned when the morning was in its strength.

But be that as it may, whether or not my interpretation is defensible, I am far from believing that the orthodox believer needs to take refuge in any idea of mine. As already stated, he need only hold fast to his position, and he can dispense with all the ingenious ideas with which others pretend to come to his assistance while in fact merely trying to lure him out of his defences.

But what I call his position is that small, impregnable area in which no attacks from without need trouble him, namely the one satisfactory answer which he can and should give to so many objections, as in the present instance. He need only say 'But what if the *entire* crossing was a miracle? What if the miracle consisted not only in the drying up of the inlet, and the speed with which such a multitude crossed over in so short a time was also part of the miracle? – I have no objection if, in the first part of this miraculous occurrence, it is also claimed that natural causes were also involved – not just the wind, which is mentioned in the Scripture itself, but also the ebb tide, which it does not mention; and if *one* ebb tide is not enough, I could even accept two successive tides, ebb upon ebb, of which neither Scripture nor the admiralty pilots at Cuxhaven have ever heard.[13] I readily concede that it is sufficient for a miracle if these natural causes are no longer active now, or no longer in this particular way, although their past operation, directly based on the will of God, was nevertheless predicted in advance. This much I readily concede. But no one must try to defeat me with my own *concessions*; no one must turn what I admit may accompany a miracle, without its ceasing to be a miracle, into an indispensable requirement of miracles in general; no one must flatly deny a miracle just because no natural forces can be specified which God might have used. The drying up of the inlet was caused by the wind

---

[13] Lessing adds a reference here to the explorer Carsten Niebuhr's *Reisebeschreibung nach Arabien und anderen umliegenden Ländern* [*Travels in Arabia and Neighbouring Countries*] (1774–8), on how Niebuhr received a negative answer on consulting the Hamburg pilots as to the soundness of Michaelis's theory that a double ebb-tide might be caused by a landwind.

and an ebb tide: good – but it was still a miracle. The speed with which the people crossed was achieved – I know not how; but is it therefore any less miraculous? It is for that very reason all the more miraculous. It certainly sounds very clever when your author refuses "to let anyone give wings to the Israelites and their oxen and carts". But God himself does in fact say that he carried the Israelites out of Egypt "on eagles' wings" (Exodus 19.4). And what if the language has no means of expressing the nature of this miraculous speed other than this metaphor? Permit me to discern even in a metaphor employed by God more reality than in all your symbolic demonstrations.'[14]

And if the orthodox believer answers thus, how can one refute him? We can shrug our shoulders at his answer as much as we like, but we must still let him stand where he stands. That is the advantage enjoyed by a man who remains true to his principles, and who would rather follow *less than fully demonstrated* principles than not follow them *consistently* in his words and actions. This consistency, which enables one to predict how a man will speak and act in a given instance, is what makes him a man and gives him character and constancy, those major assets of a thinking individual. Character and constancy can even correct one's principles over time; for it is impossible for a man to act for long in accordance with certain principles without noticing if they are false: anyone who regularly makes use of calculations will soon notice whether or not his multiplication tables are correct.

Not orthodoxy itself, therefore, but a certain squinting, lame, and inconsistent kind of orthodoxy is so obnoxious! So obnoxious, so repellent, so flatulent! – These, at least, are the appropriate words to describe *my* sentiments.

IV

The Old Testament makes no mention of the soul's immortality, or of any rewards and punishments in an afterlife. So be it! If we wish, we may go even a step further. We may assert that the Old Testament, or at least the Israelite people as we encounter them in the Old Testament writings before the time of the Babylonian captivity, did not even have

---

[14] Demonstrations based on the 'symbolic books' or doctrinal compendia.

the true concept of the oneness of God. If we consider the people at large and disregard those more enlightened souls such as the sacred writers themselves, we can even lend this assertion a high degree of probability. It is certain at least that the oneness which the Israelites attributed to their God was not at all that transcendental, metaphysical oneness which is now the basis of all natural theology.[15] The ordinary human understanding had not yet risen to *that* level in such early times, least of all among a people who were so indifferent to the arts and sciences, and who so stubbornly refrained from all dealings with peoples more knowledgeable than themselves. Had they possessed the true and genuine concept of a single God, they could never have abandoned it so often in favour of other gods. They would not have dignified false gods with the same name; they would not have described the true God so exclusively as *their* god, as the god of *their* country, or as the god of *their* fathers. In short, the one God meant for them no more than the first, the foremost, and the most perfect of his kind. In their view, the gods of the heathen were also gods; but among so many gods, only *one* could be the mightiest and wisest, and this mightiest and wisest god was their own Jehovah. So long as they found no reason to doubt that power and wisdom in which *their* god surpassed the gods of all other peoples, they remained loyal to him. But scarcely had they concluded that this or that neighbouring people, thanks to the protection of its god, enjoyed some benefit which they lacked, and which their Jehovah consequently could or would not grant them, than they secretly turned away from him and fornicated with the gods of the supposedly more fortunate people; and they did not return from them until they had paid for their lust through the loss of greater goods, by forfeiting more essential benefits. Only when they had learned, in Babylonian captivity, to make a little more use of their understanding, when they became better acquainted with a people who had worthier ideas of the one God, when for the first time the writings of their own lawgiver and prophets became more widely known among them, when they saw how many great and unrecognised truths were contained in these writings or could be read into them, when they recognised how, even according to these writings, their Jehovah possessed a more sublime unity than that which merely placed him at the head of all other gods – only then did they suddenly become a quite different people, and all

---

[15] Cf. *The Education of the Human Race*, §§14, 17, and 22 (pp. 220–2 below).

idolatry ceased among them. If this sudden change, which no one can dispute, cannot be explained by the nobler conception which they now formed of their own god, then nothing can explain it. One can become disloyal to a national god, but never to God, once one has recognised him.

As already suggested, let us take this further step beyond the objections of the fourth fragment, and add that, just as Moses himself had no conception of the infinite being at the start of his mission – would he otherwise have asked him his name?[16] – God descended to his level and *announced* himself to him not as the infinite God, but only as one of the particular gods with whom superstition had associated different countries and peoples. God was the god of the Hebrews; and when the Hebrews had had enough of their god, what was more natural than that they should try another god instead?

Even then – even if one could justifiably deny the ancient Israelites that great advantage, based rather on *tradition* than on *demonstration*, of having known the one true God – even then I would still feel able to justify God's ways with them.

From things such as these, at least, no conclusions can be drawn regarding the divinity of the books of the Old Testament. For this divinity must be proved by quite other means than through the truths of natural religion which appear in them. Truths, the clearest possible, the most sublime, the most profound truths of this kind, may be contained in any other book of equal antiquity, and we now have the evidence to prove it – evidence which gives the lie to many a learned deduction of the divinity of the Bible based in part on the claim that only the Old Testament teaches the oneness of God. Both in age and in worthy conceptions of God, the sacred books of the Brahmans must be a match for the books of the Old Testament, if the rest of them is anything like the samples which reliable men have only now brought to our attention.[17] For although the human understanding has undergone only a very gradual development, and truths which are at present so evident and intelligible to the most ordinary individual must once have seemed highly incomprehensible, hence directly inspired by the deity, and been considered worthy of acceptance only as such, there have nevertheless been privileged souls at all times

---

[16] Exodus 3.13.
[17] E.g. Alexander Dow, *The History of Hindostan* (1768).

and in all countries whose thoughts, by their own efforts, transcended the sphere of their contemporaries; they hastened towards the greater light, and even if they could not communicate their feelings to others, they could at least tell them about them.

Nothing derived from men of this kind – some of whom continue to appear from time to time, without always receiving just recognition – can be used as direct evidence of a divine origin. But if the presence of such evidence cannot prove this origin, neither can its absence disprove it; and books may very well come from God or be written by means of higher, divine inspiration even if only a few traces, or none at all, of the soul's immortality and of retribution in the afterlife are to be found in them. These books may even contain a religion of salvation – that is, a religion through whose observance a man can consider himself assured of happiness as far as his thoughts extend. For why should a religion not adapt itself to the limits of his longing and desires? Why should it necessarily have to enlarge their sphere? A religion of salvation such as this would certainly not be the Christian religion of salvation. But if the Christian religion could only appear at a certain time and in a certain area, did all the previous ages and all the other areas therefore necessarily have no religion of salvation at all? I will gladly concede to the theologians that the *salvational element* in the different religions must always have been the *same* – provided they will concede to me in turn that people need not therefore always have had the *same conception* of it. God might well wish to save the good people of all religions *in the same respect* and *for the same reasons*, without therefore having imparted to all of them the *same revelation* in that respect and for those reasons. –

Some time ago, a little essay was circulating in manuscript among a certain group of friends. It contained the outlines of a full-scale book, and was entitled *The Education of the Human Race*. I must confess that I have already drawn verbatim on some of the ideas in that essay.[18] So what is to prevent me from including here – or rather, what is more appropriate than that I should include here – the first part of that essay in its full context, which is so closely related to the content of our *fourth fragment*? I can answer for the indiscretion which I thereby commit, and I am convinced of the sincerity of the author's intentions. He is also

---

[18] See note 15 above.

not nearly as heterodox as he appears at first glance, as even the most scrupulous readers will concede if he should eventually see fit to publish the whole essay, or even its fully expanded version. But here, as promised, is the first part of it – on account of the relevant content made use of above.

The Education of the Human Race

> [Lessing here inserts paragraphs 1–53 of this work, without revealing his authorship. He issued the entire work three years later, again adopting the role of 'editor', as a separate publication. For the complete text, see pp. 218–40 below.]

And so the author arrives at the second great step in the education of the human race. The child's motives for obedience give way to the incomparably more stimulating prospects of the youth. Future honour, future prosperity replace the sweets and playthings of the present. But all these further speculations are irrelevant to our present topic, and I shall say no more; besides, a foretaste does not require the whole dish to be served.

V

On the contradictions in the story of the resurrection, so forcefully put to us by the fifth fragment, my thoughts are as follows.

§ The witnesses of Christ's resurrection were not the same people who transmitted the reports of these witnesses' statements to us. For even if the two are the same on one or other occasion, it is nevertheless undeniable that no single evangelist was present at each and every one of Christ's appearances.

§ Consequently, two kinds of contradiction are possible here: contradictions among the witnesses, and contradictions among the historians of these witnesses' statements.

§ Are contradictions present *now* among the witnesses? – These could only occur if an evangelist contradicted himself in reporting a particular occurrence which he had himself witnessed – or at least, if several evangelists gave mutually contradictory accounts of the same particular occurrence at which each had been present. I know of no such contradictions.

§ Were contradictions *originally* present among the witnesses? – Apparent ones; and why not? For experience confirms – and it cannot possibly be otherwise – that, among several witnesses, each will see, hear, and consequently report differently the same event occurring at the same time and place. For the attention of each will be differently attuned. I do not believe it is even possible for the same witness, who observed the same occurrence with complete and deliberate attention, to deliver the same statement about it at different times. For a person's recollection of the same thing will be different on different occasions – unless, of course, he has learned his statement by heart. But in that case, he will not say how he now remembers the thing in question, but how he remembered it at the time when he memorised his statement.

§ Were *true* contradictions present among the witnesses – that is, contradictions which no fair comparison or more detailed explanation can remove? – How are we to know? We do not even know whether the witnesses were ever properly examined. At least there is no longer any record of such an examination, and anyone who says that there were such contradictions has in this respect as much justification as someone who denies it.

§ Except that someone who denies it can cite in his favour a very legitimate presumption which his adversary cannot adduce – namely that the great legal action which depended on the credible statements of those witnesses was successful. Christianity triumphed over the heathen and Jewish religions. It is there.

§ And are we now to let this successful action be reopened two thousand years later in the light of the incomplete and discordant reports of those – to judge by the successful outcome – credible and unanimous testimonies? Certainly not!

§ On the contrary, it does not matter how many contradictions there are in the reports of the evangelists! – They are not contradictions of the witnesses, but of the historians, not of the statements, but of the reports of these statements.

§ But the Holy Spirit had a hand in these statements! – Quite so, in the sense that it impelled each evangelist to report the matter as he understood it to the best of his knowledge and conscience.

§ What if the matter were known, and necessarily known, in one way to one of them and in a different way to the other? – Should the Holy Spirit rather, at the moment when they began to write, have rendered their different impressions uniform, and by their very uniformity suspect, or should it have let them retain their diversity, on which nothing whatsoever now depends?

§ Differences, it is said, are not the same thing as contradictions. – But if they are not, they become so at second or third hand. What was a difference among the eyewitnesses becomes a contradiction among those who know the matter only from hearsay.

§ Only a continuous miracle could have prevented such corruptions of the oral accounts of the resurrection from arising during the thirty to forty years before the gospels were written. But what right have we to assume this miracle? And what compels us to assume it?

§ Anyone who wilfully submits to such a compulsion is welcome to do so. But he should also know what is then required of him: he must resolve all the contradictions which occur in the various reports of the evangelists, and resolve them in a simpler and more natural way than has happened in the usual gospel harmonies.

§ And he should not rely too heavily on this or that work which he may only know by its highly promising title. Ditton[19] certainly showed the truth of the Christian religion *demonstratively* by means of the resurrection. But he completely ignored the contradictions of the evangelists, either because he believed that these contradictions had long since been resolved in the most incontrovertible manner – which I doubt; or because he considered that his demonstration, despite all these contradictions, retained its full validity – which is also my opinion.

§ Thomas Sherlock, in his *Tryal of the Witnesses of the Resurrection*,[20] followed the same procedure. He confirms that the actual witnesses are completely trustworthy; but he does not address the contradictions in the reports of the evangelists.

§ Gilbert West[21] alone felt obliged to take some account of these contradictions in his plan. But anyone who is satisfied with his continual

---

[19] Humphrey Ditton, *A Discourse concerning the Resurrection of Jesus Christ* (1712).
[20] Thomas Sherlock, *The Tryal of the Witnesses of the Resurrection of Jesus* (1729).
[21] Gilbert West, *Observations on the History and Evidence of the Resurrection of Jesus Christ* (1747).

duplication of the same persons and phenomena must not be exactly difficult to satisfy.

§ Thus any man who asserts the infallibility of the evangelists' every word will find that plenty of work remains to be done here too. Let him make the attempt, and answer the ten contradictions which our fragment criticises. But let him answer them all. For merely to offer plausible resolutions of one or other of them and to pass the rest over with triumphant disdain is equivalent to answering none at all.

On the proof of the spirit and of power

... because of the prodigious miracles which may be proved by this argument among many others, that traces of them still remain among those who live according to the will of the Word.

Origen, *Against Celsus*[1]

To Director Schumann of Hanover[2]

Brunswick, 1777

Sir,

Who could be more eager than I to read your new work at once? – I hunger so greatly for conviction that, like Erysichthon,[3] I devour anything that looks remotely like food. – If you do the same with this pamphlet, we are two of a kind. I am, with the respect with which seekers after truth never fail to regard each other,

Yours etc. - - -

Fulfilled prophecies which I myself experience are one thing; fulfilled prophecies of which I have only historical knowledge that others claim to have experienced them are another.

---

[1] Origen, Church Father (c. 185–253), author of *Contra Celsum* [*Against Celsus*], a defence of Christianity against a lost treatise by the pagan Greek philosopher Celsus; Lessing's quotation is from 1.2 of that work.

[2] Johann Daniel Schumann, theologian and headmaster, had published *Über die Evidenz für die Wahrheit der christlichen Religion* [*On the Evidence for the Truth of Christianity*] in 1777 in an attempt to refute the 'Fragments' of Reimarus. This work is reproduced in B VIII, 355–435.

[3] Mythological figure condemned by the gods to insatiable hunger (see Ovid, *Metamorphoses* VIII. 739–884).

Miracles which I see with my own eyes, and have an opportunity to assess, are one thing; miracles of which I know only from history that others claim to have seen and assessed them are another.

This is surely incontrovertible? Surely there can be no objections to this?

If I had lived at the time of Christ, the prophecies fulfilled in his person would certainly have made me pay great attention to him. And if I had actually seen him perform miracles, and if I had had no cause to doubt that these were genuine miracles, then I would certainly have gained so much confidence in one who worked miracles and whose coming had been predicted so long before, that I would willingly have subordinated my understanding to his and believed him in all matters in which equally indubitable experiences did not contradict him.

Or, if I were to experience even now that prophecies concerning Christ or the Christian religion, prophecies of whose priority in time I had long been certain, were being fulfilled in the most incontrovertible way; if miracles were performed even now by believing Christians which I had to acknowledge as genuine miracles, what could prevent me from accepting this 'proof of the spirit and of power', as the apostle calls it?[4]

Origen was still in that position, and he was quite correct in saying that, in this proof of the spirit and of power, the Christian religion had a proof of its own which was more divine than any that Greek dialectics could offer. For at his time, 'the power to do miraculous things had not deserted' those who lived in accordance with Christ's precept;[5] and if he had undoubted examples of this, he had necessarily to acknowledge that proof of the spirit and of power if he did not wish to deny his own senses.

But if I, who am no longer even in Origen's position, who live in the eighteenth century in which miracles no longer happen, if I hesitate now to believe something because of the proof of the spirit and of power which I can believe on other kinds of evidence more appropriate to my time, why is this so?

It is because this proof of the spirit and of power no longer has either spirit or power, but has sunk to the level of human testimonies of spirit and power.

It is because reports of fulfilled prophecies are not fulfilled prophecies; because reports of miracles are not miracles. The *latter* – i.e. prophecies

---

[4] 1 Corinthians 2.4.   [5] Origen, *Against Celsus* I.2.

fulfilled before my eyes and miracles that happen before my eyes – have an *immediate* effect. But the *former*, i.e. reports of fulfilled prophecies and of miracles, have to act through a medium which deprives them of all their force.

To quote Origen to the effect 'that the proof of power is so called on account of the prodigious miracles which have taken place to confirm the teaching of Christ' is not very helpful if one omits to tell one's readers what Origen says immediately afterwards. For these readers will also consult Origen and discover to their astonishment that he demonstrates the truth of these miracles which occurred at the foundation of Christianity 'by this argument among many others', i.e. from the narrative of the evangelists *among many other things*, but primarily and specifically through the miracles which were still happening then.

If, then, the proof of the proof has now completely disappeared, and if all historical certainty is much too weak to replace this evident but now absent proof of the proof, how can I be expected to believe equally strongly, and with infinitely less cause, those same incomprehensible truths which people believed for the strongest reasons sixteen to eighteen centuries ago?

Or is what I read in reliable historians invariably just as certain as what I experience myself?

I am not aware that anyone has ever made such a claim. On the contrary, it is merely asserted that the reports which we have of these prophecies and miracles are as reliable as historical truths can ever be. – And of course, it is added, historical truths cannot be demonstrated; but one must nevertheless believe them as firmly as one believes demonstrated truths.

My response is as follows. *Firstly*, who will deny – and I do not do so – that the reports of these miracles and prophecies are as reliable as historical truths ever can be? – But then, if they are *only* as reliable as this, why are they suddenly made infinitely more reliable in practice?

And by what means? – By basing on them quite different things, and more of such things, than one is entitled to base on historically demonstrated truths.

If no historical truth can be demonstrated, then nothing can be demonstrated *by means of* historical truths.

That is, *contingent truths of history can never become the proof of necessary truths of reason.*

Thus I do not deny for a moment that prophecies were fulfilled in Christ; I do not deny for a moment that Christ performed miracles. But since the truth of these miracles has ceased entirely to be proved by miracles still practicable today, and since they are merely reports of miracles (however undisputed and indisputable these reports may be), I do deny that they can and should bind me to the least faith in the other teachings of Christ. I accept these other teachings for other reasons.

For *secondly*, what does it mean to consider a historical proposition true, or to believe a historical truth? Does it mean anything in the least different from accepting this proposition or this truth as valid? having no objections to it? being content if someone else bases another historical proposition on it or deduces another historical truth from it? reserving the right to assess other historical things in its light? Does it mean anything in the least different from this? Anything more? Consider this carefully!

We all believe that someone called Alexander lived who in a short time conquered almost the whole of Asia. But who, on the strength of this belief, would risk anything of great and lasting importance whose loss would be irreplaceable? Who, as a result of this belief, would permanently disavow all knowledge that conflicted with this belief? I certainly would not. I have at present no objection to raise against Alexander and his victories; but it might still be possible that they were based on a mere poem of Choerilus,[6] who accompanied Alexander everywhere, just as the ten-year siege of Troy is based on nothing more than the poems of Homer.

Consequently, if I have no historical objection to the fact that Christ raised someone from the dead, must I therefore regard it as true that God has a Son who is of the same essence as himself? What connection is there between my inability to raise any substantial objection to the evidence for the former, and my obligation to believe something which my reason refuses to accept?

If I have no historical objection to the fact that this Christ himself rose from the dead, must I therefore regard it as true that this same risen Christ was the Son of God?

That the same Christ to whose resurrection I can make no significant historical objection consequently proclaimed himself the Son of God, and that his disciples consequently regarded him as such – all this I most

---

[6] Choerilus of Iasus, an undistinguished poet who travelled with Alexander.

willingly accept. For these truths, as truths of one and the same class, follow quite naturally from one another.

But to make the leap from this historical truth into a quite different class of truths, and to require me to revise all my metaphysical and moral concepts accordingly; to expect me to change all my basic ideas on the nature of the deity because I cannot offer any credible evidence against the resurrection of Christ – if this is not a 'transition to another category', I do not know what Aristotle meant by that phrase.[7]

It will, of course, be said: 'But the same Christ of whom you must concede on historical grounds that he raised the dead, and that he himself rose from the dead, said himself that God has a Son of the same essence as himself and that he is this Son.'

This would be all very well, if the fact that Christ said this were not likewise no more than historically certain!

If I were pressed further and told: 'On the contrary! This is more than historically certain, for we are assured that it is the case by inspired historians who cannot err', the fact that these historians were inspired and could not err is unfortunately likewise only historically certain.

This, this is the broad and ugly ditch which I cannot get across, no matter how often and earnestly I have tried to make the leap. If anyone can help me over it, I beg and implore him to do so. He will earn a divine reward for this service.

And so I repeat what I said above, and in the same words. I do not deny for a moment that prophecies were fulfilled in Christ; I do not deny for a moment that Christ performed miracles. But since the truth of these miracles has ceased altogether to be proved by miracles still practicable today, and since they are merely reports of miracles (however undisputed and indisputable these reports may be), I do deny that they can and should bind me to the least faith in the other teachings of Christ.

Then what *does* bind me to them? – Nothing but these teachings themselves; whereas eighteen hundred years ago, they were so new, so alien, so incompatible with the whole range of truths then recognised, that nothing short of miracles and fulfilled prophecies was required before the mass of people would pay any attention to them.

But to make the mass pay attention to something means to help common sense to find the right track.

[7] Aristotle, *Posterior Analytics* 1.6–7.

It did find that track, and it still follows it; and what it brought to light on either side of the track is the fruits of those miracles and fulfilled prophecies.

And if I see these fruits ripening and ripened before me, am I not supposed to eat my fill of them? Because, while I did not deny or doubt the pious old legend that the hand which scattered the seed had to wash seven times in snails' blood before each throw, I simply disregarded it? – What does it matter to me whether the old legend is true or false? The fruits are excellent.

Suppose there were a great and useful mathematical truth which the discoverer had arrived at by way of an obviously false conclusion. (If there are no such truths, there very well could be.) Should I therefore deny this truth or decline to make use of it, and would I be an ungrateful denigrator of the discoverer if I were unwilling to argue – or indeed believed it quite impossible to argue – that, given his astuteness in other respects, the false conclusion through which he had hit upon the truth *could* not be a false conclusion? –

– I shall end with this wish: may all those whom the Gospel of St John divides[8] be reunited by St John's Testament! It is admittedly apocryphal, this testament – but not for that reason any the less divine.

---

[8] Divides: over the doctrine of Christ's divinity as expounded in John 1.1–14.

The Testament of St John

A dialogue

Brunswick, 1777

He and I

He. You were very quick off the mark with this pamphlet; but the pamphlet shows it.
I. Really?
He. You usually write more clearly.
I. For me, the greatest clarity was always the greatest beauty.
He. But I see that you can also get carried away. You begin to think you can refer constantly to things that not one in a hundred readers knows, and that you may yourself have discovered only yesterday or the day before –
I. For example?
He. Don't be so learned.
I. For example?

---

[1] St Jerome, Church Father (c. 347–420) and translator of the Bible into Latin; the quotation is from the preface to his *Commentaries on the Epistle to the Ephesians*.

He. Your riddle at the end. – Your Testament of St John. I couldn't find it either in Grabius or Fabricius.[2]

I. Does everything have to be a book, then?

He. Isn't this Testament of St John a book? – Well, what is it, then?

I. The last will of St John, the remarkable last words of St John, which he repeated again and again as he was dying. – They can also be called a testament, can't they?

He. Of course they can. – But I'm not so curious about them any more. – All the same, what were they exactly? – I'm not very well up on Abdias,[3] or wherever else they come from.

I. They actually come from a less suspect author. – Jerome has preserved them for us in his commentary on Paul's Epistle to the Galatians.[4] – You can look them up there. – But I hardly think you'll like them.

He. Who knows? – Just tell me what they are.

I. Out of my head? With whatever circumstances I can remember, or that seem to me probable?

He. Why not?

I. St John, the good St John, who wished never again to leave the congregation he had gathered together at Ephesus, to whom this single congregation was a large enough forum for his instructive wonders and wonderful instruction – John was now old, and so old that –

He. That pious simplicity thought he would never die.

I. Although everyone saw him draw ever closer to death from day to day.

He. Superstition sometimes trusts the senses too much, and sometimes too little. – Even when John had actually died, superstition still believed that John *could* not die, that he wasn't dead but sleeping.

I. How close superstition often comes to the truth!

He. But please continue. I don't want to hear you defending superstition.

I. As quickly but reluctantly as a friend tears himself away from the bosom of a friend to fly to the embraces of his lady, so did John's pure soul gradually but visibly part company with his equally pure but failing body. – Soon, his disciples could no longer even *carry* him to church.

[2] Johannes Ernst Grabe (Grabius), author of *Specilegium SS. Patrum, ut et hereticorum seculi post Christum natum I, II, et III* [*Gleanings on the Church Fathers, and on the Heretics of the First Three Centuries AD*] (1698–9); Johann Albert Fabricius, author of the *Codex apocryphus Novi Testamenti* [*Book of the New Testament Apocrypha*] (1703).
[3] Legendary sixth-century author of stories of the apostles.
[4] The passage in question is quoted in full at the end of this work: see pp. 93–4 below.

And yet John was unwilling to miss any assembly, and he never liked to let it pass without delivering his address to the congregation, which would rather have done without its daily bread than missed this address.

He. Which perhaps wasn't always based on careful study.

I. Do you prefer what is based on careful study?

He. It depends what it is.

I. John's address was certainly never that. For it always came entirely from the heart. For it was always simple and short, and it became simpler and shorter from day to day, until he finally reduced it to the words –

He. What words?

I. 'Little children, love one another!'

He. Good and short.

I. Do you really think so? – But one so quickly tires of the good, and even of the best, once it starts to become commonplace! – At the first assembly at which John *could* no longer say anything but 'Little children, love one another!', these words were extremely well received. They were still well received on the second, third, and fourth occasions, for it was said that the weak old man *couldn't* say any more. But when the old man now and then had good and cheerful days again and still said nothing more, but simply concluded the daily assembly with his 'Little children, love one another!', when they saw that the old man was not just *unable* to say more, but had *no intention* of doing so, the 'Little children, love one another!' became flat, empty, and meaningless. Brethren and disciples could scarcely listen to it any longer without becoming sick of hearing it, and they finally asked the good old man: 'But Master, why do you keep saying the same thing?'

He. And John – ?

I. John replied: 'Because the Lord commanded it. Because this alone, this alone, if it is done, is sufficient, quite sufficient.' –

He. So that's it? That's your Testament of St John?

I. Yes!

He. It's just as well you called it apocryphal!

I. In contrast to the canonic Gospel of St John. – But I still regard it as divine.

He. Much as you might call a pretty girl divine.

I. I've never called a pretty girl divine, and I'm not in the habit of misusing the word in this way. – What I here call divine, Jerome calls 'a sentiment worthy of John'.

He. Ah, Jerome!

I. Augustine tells us that a certain Platonist said that the opening of St John's Gospel, 'In the beginning was the word', etc., deserved to be inscribed in the most prominent place of every church in letters of gold.[5]

He. Certainly! The Platonist was quite right. – Oh, the Platonists! And for sure, Plato himself could not have written anything more sublime than the beginning of St John's Gospel.

I. That may well be so. – But although I can't make much of the sublime pronouncements of a philosopher, I think there's a stronger case for inscribing in the most prominent place of all our churches in letters of gold – the Testament of St John.

He. Hm!

I. 'Little children, love one another!'

He. Yes, yes!

I. It was by this Testament of St John that a certain 'salt of the earth'[6] used to swear. Now this salt of the earth swears by the Gospel of St John, and it's said that it has become a little damp since this change took place.

He. Another riddle?

I. He that has ears to hear, let him hear![7]

He. Yes, yes, I get the point.

I. What point do you get?

He. That's how certain people always get their heads out of the noose. – It's enough if they hold on to Christian love, and it doesn't matter what happens to the Christian religion.

I. Do you count me among these people?

He. You must ask yourself whether I'd be right in doing so.

I. Then may I say a word on behalf of those certain people?

He. If you feel so inclined.

I. But maybe I don't understand you either. – So is Christian love not the Christian religion?

He. Yes and no.

I. In what sense no?

He. For the doctrines of the Christian religion are one thing, and the practice which it claims should be based on these doctrines is another.

---

[5] Augustine, *The City of God* x. 29.   [6] Matthew 5.13.   [7] Matthew 11.15.

I. And in what sense yes?

He. In so far as the only true Christian love is that which is based on Christian doctrines.

I. But which of the two is more difficult? – To accept and confess the Christian doctrines, or to practise Christian love?

He. It wouldn't help you even if I admitted that the latter is far more difficult.

I. But why should it help *me*?

He. It's all the more ridiculous that those certain people I mentioned make the road to hell so tough for themselves.

I. How so?

He. Why take on the yoke of Christian love if it's not made either easy or meritorious by the Christian doctrines?

I. Yes, of course; we must simply let them take this risk. So all I ask is whether it is *wise* of certain other people to deny them the name of Christians because of the risk they take with their unchristian Christian love?

He. Cui non competit definitio, non competit definitum.[8] Did I invent that?

I. But couldn't we interpret the definition a little more broadly, in keeping with the saying of a certain good man: 'He that is not against us is for us.'[9] – You know who this good man was, don't you?

He. Very well. It's the same man who says on another occasion: 'He that is not with me is against me.'[10]

I. Yes, indeed! Certainly; that reduces me to silence. – Oh, you alone are a true Christian! – And as well versed in the Scriptures as the devil.

From St Jerome, *Commentaries on the Epistle to the Galatians* III.6 (on Galatians 6.10)

The blessed John the Evangelist, who remained in Ephesus to an advanced age and could scarcely be carried to church with the help of his disciples, could no longer put many coherent words together. At each assembly,

[8] 'He whom the definition does not fit does not possess the defined attribute' (basic principle of logic).
[9] Mark 9.40.
[10] Matthew 13.30 (both this and the previous reference are to sayings of Christ).

he used to say no more than this: 'Little children, love one another!' Eventually, the disciples and brethren who were present grew tired of always hearing the same thing, and said: 'Master, why do you keep on saying this?' He replied with a sentiment worthy of John: 'Because it is a precept of the Lord, and it is sufficient if this alone is done.'

A rejoinder

Rather to establish the point at issue than to put anything forward through the discourse.

Dictys the Cretan, *Diary of the Trojan War*[1]

Brunswick, 1778

I have all due respect for the pious man[2] who felt obliged by his conscience to defend the *story of the resurrection* against the fragment of my anonymous author. We all act in accordance with our understanding and abilities; and it is always touching when even the weak and decrepit Nestor is ready to accept Hector's challenge if no younger and stronger Greek is willing to face up to him.

Nor do I presume to act as *arbiter* of this combat and to throw my staff between the contestants if one or other of them delivers an all too vicious or dishonourable thrust. The arbiter of combats was a member of the judiciary; and I judge no one, so that no one may pass judgement on me.

But I must not forget what I owe to myself. There is a risk that my intention will be misjudged and my proposed solutions misinterpreted.

---

[1] Dictys the Cretan, supposed author of *Ephemeris belli Troiani* [*Diary of the Trojan War*], translated in the fourth century AD by Lucius Septimius from a lost Greek original of the second or third century.

[2] *A Rejoinder* is directed against *Die Auferstehungsgeschichte Jesu Christi* [*The Story of Christ's Resurrection*] (1777), published anonymously by Johann Heinrich Ress, a senior clergyman in Wolfenbüttel; Lessing later addresses him as 'neighbour', thereby revealing that he has discovered his identity. For relevant extracts from Ress's work, see B VIII, 475–503.

A brief word may avert this misfortune; and who will not allow me this word or pardon me for uttering it?

Lessing

Let us first give due consideration to the position which each of us occupies, so that we may have as fair a share as possible of light and weather. For it is not enough that we all fight with identical weapons. A ray of sunlight that strikes the eye of one party more than the other; a stiff breeze to which one is more exposed than the other – these are advantages of which no honest combatant will knowingly take advantage. – And in particular, may God preserve us from the deadly draught of covert calumny!

My anonymous author maintains that the resurrection of Christ is incredible *also because* the reports of the evangelists are mutually contradictory.

I reply that the resurrection of Christ may well be perfectly true *even if* the reports of the evangelists are mutually contradictory.

Now a third party comes along and says that the resurrection is entirely credible *since* the reports of the evangelists are not mutually contradictory.

Take careful note of this *also because*, this *even if*, and this *since*. It will be found that nearly everything depends on these particles.

I

As far as I can tell from the manuscripts, the anonymous author mounted nothing less than a full-scale onslaught on the Christian religion. There is not a single aspect, not a single angle, however well concealed, which he has not attacked with his scaling ladders. Of course he did not fashion all these ladders himself or with new materials; most of them have already been used in several assaults, and some have even suffered considerable damage, for in the besieged towns, there were also men who cast formidable rocks down upon the enemy. – But what does it matter? It is not the maker of the ladder who prevails, but the man who scales it; and even a dilapidated ladder may still support a bold and agile man.

When he came to the story of the resurrection, he consequently had to bring with him every objection which had been made to its historical credibility since time immemorial – or could have been made, if in fact a topic so thoroughly worked over as this was still open to objections which someone or other had not thought of over the last seventeen hundred years. And whatever objections have been made in the recent or more distant past, we can be confident that answers have also been given to them. But the anonymous author no doubt thought that it is one thing to *give an answer to* an objection, and another to *answer it.* He therefore mustered everything which might possibly be of service – old and new, familiar or less familiar, arguments both major and minor. And he was fully *entitled* to do so. For a soldier who has been defeated twenty times over may still play his part in the final victory.

But if – given the fact that I was not able or willing to publish anything but fragments from the work of this thorough and persuasive author (and one can be thorough and persuasive even if one is very far from the truth) – if, I say, someone *now* takes him to task with a scornful shrug of the shoulders and a half pitying, half irate expression, talks of reheated broth and laments the fate of theologians who still have to reply to objections answered long ago by faith and trust in their own teachers and their teachers' teachers: then I have to offer such persons the friendly advice to moderate their shrill tone while there is still time. For they might otherwise make themselves totally ridiculous when they finally discover the identity of the honest and respectable man whom they have mocked with such Christian charity, of the undisputed scholar whom they were so eager to reduce to an ignorant and malicious idiot.[3]

This is merely to do him justice as a *person*. The justice of his *cause* is a completely different matter. A man who, in good faith and with intelligence as well as modesty, attempts to demonstrate a falsehood which he himself believes to be true is worth infinitely more than one who, in a humdrum fashion and with vilification of his adversaries, defends the best and noblest truth out of prejudice.

Will a certain class of people never learn that it is absolutely untrue that anyone has ever wittingly and intentionally deluded himself? It is untrue, I say, for no less a reason than that it is impossible. So what do they mean by their accusations of malicious intransigence, deliberate obduracy, and calculated plans to whitewash lies which are known to be lies? What do they mean by it? What else but – No, for I must also give *them* the benefit

---

[3] This sentence betrays the fact that, despite his denials, Lessing knew who the author of the 'Fragments' was.

of this insight, and believe that *they too* cannot deliberately and knowingly pass false and slanderous judgement; so I shall hold my peace, and refrain from all recriminations.

Not the truth which someone possesses or believes he possesses, but the honest effort he has made to get at the truth, constitutes a human being's worth. For it is not through the possession of truth, but through its pursuit, that his powers are enlarged, and it is in this alone that his ever-growing perfection lies. Possession makes us inactive, lazy, and proud –

If God held fast in his right hand the whole of truth and in his left hand only the ever-active quest for truth, albeit with the proviso that I should constantly and eternally err, and said to me: 'Choose!', I would humbly fall upon his left hand and say: 'Father, give! For pure truth is for you alone!'

II

Once again: the blame is entirely mine if the anonymous author has not hitherto appeared as significant as he is. He should not be held to account for someone else's fault.

How can he help it if I discovered only fragments of his work, and selected only the present ones for publication? He himself, to show himself to his best advantage, might perhaps have selected quite different examples, or rather have refused to publish any examples of his work at all.

For how can one provide an example of an elaborate and complex machine whose smallest parts are designed to contribute to one single great effect? An exemplary instance or model can certainly be indicated. But who has ever offered a weight or a balance, a spring or a wheel as an example of a clock?

I do indeed feel that, in this respect – but only in this respect – I might have done better to keep my examples to myself. And why did I not do so? Because I did not yet feel as I do now? or because the quality of the examples themselves led me astray?

It was for the latter reason, to be frank, for the latter reason. I did not put forward a wheel or a spring as an example of a clock, but as an example of its own class. That is, I did indeed believe that, in the specific areas with which the published fragments dealt, nothing better or more thorough had yet been written than these particular fragments. I did indeed believe that, for example, the frequent contradictions of the evangelists which I recognised as genuine had never on any occasion been brought to light so circumstantially and deliberately as in the fragment on the story of the resurrection.

That is what I believed; and I still believe it. – But did I, or do I, therefore fully share the anonymous author's opinion? Did I, or do I, therefore have the same intention as he had?

Certainly not! – I accepted the premise, but I rejected the conclusion.

I accepted the premise because, after numerous sincere attempts not to accept it, I became convinced of how inadequate all gospel harmonies are. For looking at them as a whole, I am confident that, following the same rules as those on which they are based, I could reduce each and every different account of the same event, without exception, to no less a degree of unanimity. Where historians agree only on the main issue, the method of our gospel harmonists can easily cope with all the remaining difficulties. However unimaginable the challenge they pose, I will soon put them in order, and in each case cite precedents for my procedure in that of one or other famous harmonist. –

But I rejected my anonymous author's conclusion. – And whoever presumed to draw this conclusion in secular history? If Livy and Polybius and Dionysius and Tacitus[4] each report the same event – for example the same battle or the same siege – with circumstances so different that those described by one completely give the lie to those described by the others, has anyone ever denied the event itself on which they all agree? Have people never been willing to believe them until they have at least devised ways and means of confining these refractory differences of circumstance, like angry he-goats, in a narrow pen where they will have to refrain from butting each other?

The very image of our harmonising paraphrases of the evangelists! For unfortunately, the goats will still remain violent, they will still turn their heads and horns against each other and rub against and jostle each other. – But what does it matter? It is enough if the same number of quarrelling goats fits into the narrow pen as patient and docile sheep ever would.

---

[4] Four historians of the first centuries BC and AD.

Oh, what splendid concord! – And can Livy and Polybius, Dionysius and Tacitus not be credible historians without such a constantly ferment-ing, bubbling, and seething harmony? –

'Nonsense!', the free and open-minded reader will reply, refusing to let trifling sophistries wilfully deprive him of the use and pleasure of history. 'Nonsense! What do I care about the dust which the footsteps of each of them raise? Were they not all human? In one case, this or that historian was less well informed than a third! In another, one of them perhaps wrote down something for which he had no corroboration – at his own discretion! to the best of his belief! He just needed this one additional circumstance to establish a connection or round off a sentence. And so, there it is! – Can I expect the same number of footsteps to raise the same amount of dust?'

This, I say, is how a free and open-minded person who knows a little more about human limitations and the craft of the historian will think. – Cross yourself and say your prayers, you good and honest soul who have been led to expect I know not what degree of infallibility in the min-utest details of a good historian! Have you never read what one his-torian, indeed one of the most conscientious historians, says himself? 'As far as history is concerned, there is no writer who has not uttered some falsehood' (Vopiscus).[5] This does not, of course, apply to whole events or facts, but to the minor particulars which, perhaps quite in-voluntarily, the flow of his discourse elicits from him. What historian would ever have got beyond the first page of his work if he had been obliged to have the sources of all these minor particulars in front of him? Nordberg convicts Voltaire of falsehood a hundred times over with re-gard to such particulars, yet this does not begin to account for Voltaire's novel-like mode of writing history.[6] If one keeps as tight a rein as this, one can perhaps piece together a chronicle, but certainly not write a history.

If, then, we treat Livy and Dionysius and Polybius and Tacitus openly and generously enough not to put their every syllable on the rack, why should we not do the same with Matthew, Mark, Luke, and John?

---

[5] Flavius Vopiscus (fourth century), author of lives of the Roman emperors, from which Lessing's quotation is taken.

[6] The Swedish historian Göran Andersson Nordberg, author of a *History of Charles XII* and military chaplain to that monarch, convicts Voltaire of numerous inaccuracies in the latter's *Histoire de Charles XII*.

I have already stated my opinion that their special advantage of writing under the immediate inspiration of the Holy Spirit makes no difference here. Those who insist that it does make a difference betray their real concern: it is not with the credibility of the resurrection, which might suffer if contradictions between the gospels were irresolvable, but with the notions of divine inspiration which they have previously assimilated – i.e. not with the gospels, but with their own dogmatics.

And yet, even if one assumes the crudest notions of divine inspiration, I believe I can prove that, even if the evangelists did receive mutually contradictory accounts of this or that minor circumstance concerning the resurrection – for they could so easily have received such accounts, and it is almost impossible that they did not do so, given that they wrote so much later and had witnessed little or nothing of the events in question – I believe I can prove, I say, that the Holy Spirit had of necessity to leave them with these contradictory accounts.

The orthodoxist (not the orthodox believer, who will take my side here; and I am not the first to make this distinction between orthodox and orthodoxist) – the orthodoxist will in fact say himself that it is not out of keeping with the wisdom of the Holy Spirit to allow *apparent* contradictions to enter into the narratives of the evangelists, so that any suspicion of collusion, which an all too obvious unanimity might arouse, would be less likely to fall on them.

Quite so! But why only *apparent* contradictions? – Then the Holy Spirit must in fact have used only an *apparent* means to deflect that suspicion from the evangelists! For what are *apparent* contradictions? Are they not contradictions which can ultimately be reduced to perfect agreement? – So we are back once more with that perfect agreement which the Holy Spirit wished to avoid because it smacks so much of collusion. The only difference would be that, in this case, the evangelists managed to conceal their collusion in a masterly fashion. They confused and complicated and truncated their narratives to avoid the appearance of writing in accordance with a provisional agreement. But they confused and complicated and truncated their narratives in such a way that they could not be accused of any contradictions either. Our immediate successors, they thought, who might yet manage to discover that all the streams flow from the same source, can be prevented from doing so by the labyrinthine character of our narratives. And once such investigations are no longer possible, people will soon find the way through our labyrinth, and our covert agreement will become a new proof of our veracity.

I wager a million years of my eternal bliss that this is not how the evangelists thought! But the fact that such sophistries can occur to anyone, that one is obliged to consider such things as possible – what is more obviously conducive to this than our elaborate gospel harmonies?

Should it not first have been asked whether, in the whole wide range of history, a single example can be found of an event related by several people who have neither drawn on a common source nor followed one another's versions (if they choose to go into similar *detail* concerning minor circumstances such as those with which we find the story of the resurrection embellished), without the most obvious and irresolvable contradicions? I defy the world at large to show me a single such example. But the above conditions must be properly observed: the event must be related by several people who have neither drawn on a common source nor followed one another's versions. – I am as convinced of the impossibility of such an example as I am of my own existence.

But if such an example has never been found, and never will or can be found, in the whole endless history of the world, why should we expect the evangelists in particular to have furnished this example?

Because the Holy Spirit moved them? Is that the reason? – Because poor mortals are, of course, subject to error, but not the Holy Spirit? Is that the reason?

Never! never! – For in order to show itself for what it is, the Holy Spirit could do absolutely nothing which *could* just as well be the product of the most subtle charlatanry – which even *could* be of this nature. It is not what the Egyptian sorcerers could do (actually or only apparently) in imitation of Moses which confirmed his divine mission, but what Moses alone could do.[7]

As far as I am aware, it has not yet occurred to any orthodox believer to claim that the Holy Spirit's influence rendered the evangelists omniscient. That is, what the evangelists did not know before this influence they did not know under and after this influence either. But if they did not learn anything *more* through the Holy Spirit's influence, they did not learn anything *better* either. For one cannot learn anything *better* without

---

[7] See Exodus 7–11.

learning something *more*, because all our false judgements arise only because we do not have sufficient grounds for making them, and instead
resort to assumptions in place of genuine reasons.

The Holy Spirit gave quite enough assistance if it prompted only those
individuals to write in whom it detected the fewest and least significant misconceptions, and if it watched over the writings only of those
who made no necessary link between these few insignificant misconceptions of past events and their own teachings. If common sense is not
satisfied with this, it will soon have such a surfeit of the whole business that it would rather have nothing at all. In this respect, it may be
said that no one has created more unbelievers than the so-called true
believer.

The new religion was, however, based on the belief *of that time* in the
resurrection of Christ, and this belief had in turn to be based on the credibility and unanimity of the eyewitnesses. But we who are alive today no
longer have these eyewitnesses among us; we only have historians' reports
of these eyewitnesses' statements, and only the general conclusion drawn
from these statements could be authentically preserved by these historians. And are we nevertheless supposed to accept that our present belief in
the resurrection of Christ is not adequately supported if it is based only
on that general conclusion, and not also on complete agreement between
the historians' reports of the statements from which that conclusion is
drawn? – If so, we are indeed in a fine position today!

Nevertheless, I am very much inclined to maintain that we who live
today are also better off in this respect than those in whose time the
eyewitnesses were still present. For the loss of the eyewitnesses is amply
compensated by something which the eyewitnesses could not have. They
had before them only the foundation on which, convinced of its reliability,
they dared to erect a great edifice. And we – we have this great edifice
itself standing before us. – What fool will burrow out of curiosity in the
foundations of his house merely to convince himself that they are sound? –
The house first had to settle, of course, at this or that point. – But now that
the house has stood for so long, I know more surely that the foundation
is sound than those who saw it laid ever could.

A simile which occurs to me here can do no harm. Let us suppose that
the Temple of Diana at Ephesus still stood before us in all its splendour,
and that it was discovered from ancient reports that it rested on a base

of charcoal;[8] perhaps even the name of the wise man who recommended such a strange foundation was still remembered. A foundation of charcoal! Of brittle and friable charcoal! But I could soon get over this problem; I might even realise that Theodorus[9] was perhaps not entirely mistaken in judging that charcoal, once it has lost the character of wood, would resist the destructive effects of moisture. Should I therefore, despite this reasonable a priori assumption, doubt the entire historical report just because the various historical authorities disagreed, for example, on the nature of the charcoal itself? Because Pliny, for example, spoke of olive-wood charcoal, Pausanias[10] of alder, and Vitruvius[11] of oak? Oh, what idiots would consider this contradiction, such as it is, an adequate reason for excavating the foundations at twenty different places, only to discover a piece of charcoal in whose fire-ravaged texture one could equally well detect olive-wood, oak, or alder! Oh, what arch-idiots would rather quarrel over the inconclusive texture of charcoal than admire the grand proportions of the temple!

I praise that which is above the earth, and not what lies hidden beneath it! – Forgive me, dear architect, if all I wish to know of the latter is that it must be good and sound. For it bears its load, and has done so for so long a time. If no wall, no column, no door or window has yet shifted from its correct angle, this correct angle certainly offers tangible proof that the foundation is stable – but it does not therefore constitute the beauty of the whole. It is on this, on this that I wish to feast my eyes; this, this, is what I will praise you for, dear architect! I will praise you, even if it were possible that the whole beautiful mass had no foundation at all, or rested merely on soap-bubbles.

How strange that people are so rarely satisfied with what they have before them! – The religion which triumphed over the pagan and Jewish religions through the message of the risen Christ is *there*. And are we to suppose that this message was not credible enough at the time when it triumphed? Am I to believe that it was not considered credible

---

[8] See Pliny, *Natural History* XXXVI.21.
[9] Theodorus of Samos (sixth century BC), sculptor and architect.
[10] Pausanias (second century AD), author of the *Description of Greece*; the reference is to Book IV (on Messenia).
[11] Vitruvius (first century BC), author of *De architectura*, the most celebrated ancient treatise on architecture.

enough then, because I can no longer prove its complete credibility now? –

It is much the same with the miracles through which Christ and his disciples propagated their religion. – However dubious and suspect the present accounts of them may be, they were not performed for us Christians who live today. It is enough that they had the power of conviction they required, and the proof that they had it is the enduring miracle of the religion itself. The miracle of this religion must render probable the miracles which are said to have occurred when it was first founded. But to base the truth of the religion on the historical probability of these miracles – is this right, or even well advised? – Let it be clearly stated: if I am ever capable of such right and well-advised thinking as this, my understanding has deserted me. My understanding tells me so now. And if ever I have an understanding other than this, I can never have had one in the first place.

The miracles which Christ and his disciples performed were not the building, but the scaffolding. The scaffolding is dismantled as soon as the building is finished. Anyone who thinks he can demonstrate the excellence of the building from the dismantled scaffolding because the old builders' estimates suggest that the scaffolding must have required as great a master as the building itself must have little interest in that building. – He may be right! – But I would not lend or wager the smallest sum on the strength of this assumption, let alone allow this prejudice concerning the scaffolding to deter me in the least from judging the building itself by the recognised rules of good architecture. –

When will people stop trying to suspend no less than the whole of eternity from a thread of gossamer? – No, scholastic dogmatics never inflicted such deep wounds on religion as historical exegetics now inflicts on it every day.

What? Is it not the case that a lie can be demonstrated beyond doubt by historical means? That those thousands upon thousands of things which neither reason nor history gives us any cause to doubt might sometimes include things which never happened? Is it not true that an infinite number of events were true and incontestable even if history has left us too little and too insignificant evidence for us seriously to believe in them?

Is all this not true? – But if it is true, where does this leave all the *historical* proofs of the truth of Christianity? – No matter where! Would it really be a great misfortune if they were finally returned to that corner of the arsenal where they still stood *fifty* years ago?[12]

III

Since I hold this view of historical truth, which is neither the product of scepticism nor conducive to it, my exhortation was certainly not meant seriously when I wrote in my *Counter-Propositions*: 'If any man wishes to assert the infallibility of the evangelists' every word, he will find that plenty of work remains to be done here too' (i.e. in the story of the resurrection). I did, admittedly, add: 'Let him make the attempt, and answer the ten contradictions which our fragment criticises.'[13] Such a tone can also serve as a deterrent, however, and that was how I intended it. For I continued: 'But let him answer them all, those criticised contradictions. Merely to offer plausible resolutions of one or other of them and pass over the rest with triumphant disdain is equivalent to answering none at all.'

Now I never expected anyone to act in response to my exhortation, or to be deterred from acting by my warning. My conscience testifies that I am incapable of such vanity. All that I can reproach myself with here is that it does somewhat perturb me if the response to my exhortation to do something is not to do it, and the response to my warning against doing something is to do that very thing.

But if I am perturbed, it is really not out of pride; nor is it out of impatience at hearing yes instead of no and no instead of yes from my good neighbour.[14] I simply cannot readily imagine that I have understood him properly, or that he has properly understood me. – So I shall listen to him once more – and thereafter never again. –

Can it really be so, dear neighbour, can it be so? – You have undertaken to answer all the criticised contradictions? to answer all of them satisfactorily? – And you really believe that you have now achieved no less than you intended? –

This is the friendly question I would put to my neighbour in private if I knew who he was, if I were reliably informed of his name, and if I

[12] Lessing probably refers to the work of Siegmund Jakob Baumgarten (1706–57), who attached greater importance than his Lutheran predecessors to historical evidence as a means of 'proving' the truth of revelation; Lessing's next major adversary, J. M. Goeze, was a pupil of Baumgarten.
[13] See p. 82 above.
[14] Neighbour: see note 2 above.

could hope to make his acquaintance through openheartedness and love of truth. But I do not know his name, although he knows mine.

He knows it, although he does not mention it. He has left my name completely out of this controversy, and has made not a single prejudicial reference to me. He has taken me for what I am, a custodian of valuable books who is unconcerned (as such people generally are!) whether or not the rare material which he brings to light is also in every respect good, provided that it is rare. This is what he takes me for, and I thank him sincerely at least for not taking me for anything worse.

But I also regret that, in dealing with his reaction to a supposed challenge, I cannot preserve that distance which he so kindly wished to allow me to keep. I cannot do so for the following reason.

If it is true that my anonymous author was as ignorant as he was malicious; if it is true that all his objections had already been made and all the contradictions he criticised had already been criticised on countless occasions, but also no less frequently refuted and answered; if it is true that he found diametrically opposed assertions in the story of the resurrection simply because he *wanted* to find them, and not because he had the misfortune really to consider them as such; if it is true that one need only take his diatribe in one hand and the Bible in the other in order to do justice to both; if all this is true – then I, his unsolicited editor, am not just as culpable, but far more culpable than he. (The verdict is a just one! I deliver it on myself and duly stand condemned!)

And this, this is how I was supposedly content even to *appear*? (That I actually *was* what I appeared to be is not an issue, for only one person needs to know that I was *not*, and that person knows it already.) I must therefore have been ignorant of the fact that the world pays more attention to how one appears than to what one is, although I still have to live with that world, and wish to do so.

Perhaps my anonymous author wrote his material in a fit of fever, and although God restored his powers of cool and sound reflection, he was prevented from destroying this trash altogether. Then I come along, I who could and should know very well what the anonymous author was unable to grasp in his feverish state, namely that his entire work was nothing but old threshed straw, long since fit for the flames; I come along and commit a sin which I did not even have the wit to plan and work out properly, I commit a sin so that none of the poor devil's work might be lost, purely for the sake of committing it and causing offence. – If I say that I accepted only his premise but denied his conclusion, this does not make my case one whit better. For those whom I offend consider it just as important to deny the premise as not to admit the conclusion; indeed, they only believe the conclusion *because* and *in so far* as the opposite of the premise is correct.

But what? Because I see and am convinced that my anonymous author is not being treated with due fairness; because I find that others make it as easy for themselves to refute him as I consider it difficult; because I notice that he is being surreptitiously dealt the cards which others think they can most readily trump – must I therefore become his champion? I shall certainly do no such thing! Anyone who resorts to tricks of that kind and can believe he has won his money rather than stolen it can believe it if he will! The onlooker who has watched his fingers too closely does well to remain silent.

Silent? – But what if he has put his money on the cheated player's hand? – In that case, he certainly cannot remain silent without wilfully forfeiting his money. He then has a tricky problem. He must look to his mettle, and at least place no further stakes. – –

I shall therefore confine myself, throughout the rest of this rejoinder, solely to that aspect of the anonymous author's assertions with which I can agree, namely his remarks on the contradictions in the story of the resurrection as reported by the evangelists.

Of these, I have maintained and continue to maintain that I have nowhere found them so forcefully enumerated and so clearly analysed. If I am wrong, I should like to know which author or book makes the same points, and makes them equally well. My amazement at not having encountered such a work can only be surpassed by the amazement I would feel if I were also shown a work in which all these objections were answered, and of which I knew equally little. I still know as little of such a work. For I shall now show, with my good neighbour's permission, that at least his dialogues, as of yesterday and today, do not constitute the work in question.

How far my patience will accompany me along this road I really still do not know myself. Right to the end, through all *ten* contradictions and their supposed resolutions? We shall see! I scarcely think it possible. But what is the need? For if I show that just one single contradiction cannot be resolved either by the answer supplied or by any other possible answer, I shall, in keeping with my provisional declaration, have done enough.

Where one contradiction is present, there may be a hundred; all that matters is that even a thousand do not prove what my anonymous author wished to prove *by them*. – So, without further ado, down to business! Anything else I might say will be said in due course.

[In the remainder of this work, Lessing proceeds to demolish in detail Ress's attempts to resolve each of the ten contradictions which Reimarus had identified in the four evangelists' accounts of the resurrection of Christ.]

A parable

– which may prepare a easy morsel for the mouth.

(An ancient etymologist)[1]

with a small request and, if necessary, a challenge

To Pastor Goeze in Hamburg[2]

Brunswick, 1778

Venerable Man,

I would say 'Venerable Friend' if I were a person who, by publicly advertising his friendships, disingenuously sought to predispose others in his favour.[3] On the contrary, I am one who has no wish to cast an unfavourable light on any neighbour by informing the public that he stands – or stood – with that neighbour in one of those closer relationships which the world is accustomed to describe as friendship. –

---

[1] Source unknown (or invented by Lessing). The Latin original, as quoted by Lessing ('quae facilem ori paret bolum') incorporates an untranslatable pun on the resemblance between *paret bolum* ('prepares a morsel') and *parabola* ('parable').

[2] Johann Melchior Goeze (1717–86), Chief Pastor at the Church of St Catharine in Hamburg, defender of Lutheran orthodoxy and prolific controversialist. The works of Goeze to which Lessing here responds are reproduced in B IX, 11–35.

[3] Lessing, who shared some of Goeze's scholarly interests, had been friendly with him during his own period in Hamburg (1767–70).

For I would certainly be entitled to describe as a *friend* a man who went out of his way to oblige me, of whom I got to know a side whose existence many are unwilling to recognise, and to whom I am still obliged, if only because his vigilant voice has so far sought to spare my name.

But as already noted, I seek to gain as little through my friends as I would wish them to lose through me.

So simply: *Venerable Man!* I beg you to be so kind as to devote some reflection to the following trifle. But I urge you in particular to state your response to the subsequent request, not just as a polemicist but also as an honest man and a Christian, as soon as possible.

Yours etc.

The parable

The wise and active king of a big, big empire had in his capital a palace of quite immeasurable dimensions and quite extraordinary architecture.

Its dimensions were immeasurable because in it, he had gathered around him all those whom he required as assistants or instruments of his government.

Its architecture was extraordinary because it violated virtually all accepted rules; but it was pleasing, and it served its purpose.

It was pleasing – especially through that admiration which simplicity and grandeur arouse when they seem rather to scorn opulence and embellishment than to be deficient in them.

It served its purpose – through durability and convenience. After many, many years, the whole palace was still as complete and immaculate as when the builders finished their work – from outside somewhat perplexing, from inside full of light and coherence.

Those who claimed to be experts in architecture were particularly offended by the external elevations, which were interrupted by few windows; these were large and small, round and rectangular, and scattered here and there. But there were all the more doors and gates of various shapes and sizes.

They could not comprehend how sufficient light could reach so many rooms through so few windows. For few could grasp the fact that the principal apartments received their light from above.

They could not comprehend why so many different kinds of entrance were needed, for a large portal on every side would, they thought, be much more appropriate and would serve the same purposes. For few could grasp the fact that all who were summoned to the palace could, through the many small entrances, reach the point where they were needed by the shortest and surest route.

Thus various kinds of conflict arose between the supposed experts, in which the most heated participants were generally those who had had least opportunity to see much of the palace from within.

There was also something which, at first glance, might have been expected to ensure that the conflict would be very simple and short, but which in fact did most to complicate it, furnishing it with the richest material for further controversy of the most obdurate kind. For it was believed that various old plans drawn up by the palace's original architects had survived, and it happened that these plans were annotated with words and symbols whose language and significance were as good as lost.

Each person accordingly explained these words and symbols as he saw fit. Each accordingly constructed from these old plans a new plan of his own devising, and this or that individual was often so obsessed with his new plan that he not only swore by it himself, but either persuaded or compelled others to swear by it too.

Only a few people said: 'What do we care for your plans? This plan or the next one – to us they are all the same. It is enough that we realise every moment that the most benevolent wisdom pervades the entire palace, and that nothing but beauty and order and prosperity radiates from it throughout the entire country.'

They often had a poor reception, these few! For sometimes, if they good-humouredly offered more detailed comments on a specific plan, they were denounced by those who supported it as despoilers of the palace itself.

But they paid no heed to this, and so became best qualified to associate with those who worked inside the palace and had neither time nor inclination to become involved in quarrels which they regarded as baseless.

Once, when the conflict over the plans was not so much settled as quiescent – once, at midnight, the watchmen's voices suddenly rang out with cries of 'Fire! Fire in the palace!'

And what happened? Everyone leapt out of bed and, as if the fire had broken out not in the palace but in their own homes, they rushed to what they saw as their most valuable possession, namely their plans. 'My plan must be rescued!', each of them thought. 'The palace cannot burn down in any truer sense than as it is depicted here!'

And so each ran out into the street with his plan, and there, instead of hurrying to save the palace, each wished first to show the rest by means of this plan where the fire presumably lay. 'Look, neighbour, the fire is here! This is where it can best be tackled! – You mean here, neighbour, here! – What are the two of you thinking of? This is where it is! – What would it matter if it were there? The fire is surely here! – Tackle it there if you wish. I won't tackle it there. – Nor will I there! – Nor will I there!'

If it had been left to these tireless squabblers, the palace might well have burned down – if there had been a fire. – But the terrified watchmen had mistaken the northern lights for a conflagration.

The request

A pastor is one thing, and a librarian is another. Their designations do not sound as different as their duties and obligations are.

I think, on the whole, that the relationship of the pastor and the librarian is like that of the shepherd and the botanist.

The botanist wanders over mountains and valleys and scours forests and meadows to discover a herb which Linnaeus[4] has not yet named. How heartfelt his delight when he finds one! How little he cares whether this new herb is poisonous or not! He thinks that, even if poisons have no use – and who is to say that they might not be useful? – it is nevertheless useful for them to be known.

But the shepherd knows only the herbs on his pasture, and he values and protects only those which are most agreeable and beneficial to his sheep.

The same applies to us, Venerable Man! – I am a keeper of valuable books, and I have no wish to be the dog which guards the hay[5] – though I certainly would not care to be the stable lad who carries the hay to every hungry horse's manger either. Now if I find among the treasures with which I am entrusted something which I believe is unknown, I announce my discovery – initially in our catalogues, and then gradually, as I find that it helps to fill this or that gap or to correct this or that error, also to the public. In so doing, I am quite indifferent as to whether one person

---

[4] Linnaeus: the Swedish botanist Carl von Linné (1707–78), founder of the binomial system of plant and animal taxonomy.
[5] The reference is to Aesop's fable of the dog in the manger.

calls it important or another unimportant, whether it benefits one or harms the other. Useful and harmful are as relative concepts as large and small.

You, on the other hand, Venerable Man, evaluate all literary treasures only according to their potential influence on your congregation, and you would rather be over-solicitous than over-negligent. What does it matter to you whether something is known or unknown? What matters is whether it might offend even one of the humblest parishioners who are entrusted to your spiritual care.

Quite rightly so! I praise you for it, Venerable Man. But because I praise you for doing your duty, do not chide me for doing mine – or, what amounts to the same thing, for believing that I am doing mine.

You would tremble at the prospect of your death if you had the slightest share in publicising the fragments in question. – I shall perhaps tremble *in* the hour of my death, but I shall never tremble at the *prospect* of it, least of all because I have done what intelligent Christians now wish the ancient librarians at Alexandria, Caesarea, and Constantinople had done with the writings of Celsus, Fronto, and Porphyry,[6] had they been in a position to do so. As someone familiar with such matters says, many a friend of religion would now willingly give a pious Church Father in exchange for Porphyry's writings.

I do hope, Venerable Man, that you will not reply: 'Those old enemies of religion certainly deserved to have their writings more carefully preserved. But why preserve those of modern writers who, seventeen hundred years later, cannot in any case say anything new?'

Who knows whether this is so without giving them a hearing? Who among our successors will believe it without seeing them? Besides, I am firmly convinced that the world and Christianity will survive long enough for the religious writers of the first two millennia of the Christian era to become just as important to the world as the writers of the first two centuries are to us now.

Christianity proceeds on its eternal and gradual course; and eclipses do not deflect the planets from their orbits. But the sects of Christianity are its phases, and these cannot remain static unless all of nature comes

---

[6] On Celsus, see note 1 on p. 83 above; Fronto (second century) and Porphyrius (third century) were likewise authors of lost anti-Christian works.

to a standstill and sun and planets and observer remain tied to the spot. God preserve us from this terrible stagnation!

So, Venerable Man, please at least be less severe in your disapproval of the fact that I was honest enough to rescue from destruction and bring to light both the very un-Christian fragments and a very Christian work by Berenger of Tours.[7]

But this is not yet the request, Venerable Man, which I have to put to you. I do not ask of certain people anything which I would not in any case be justified in demanding of them. And you can of course react to this request in whatever way you please.

No, my actual request is such that you cannot readily refuse to grant it. You have done me an injustice; and nothing is more incumbent on an honest man than to make good an injustice he has done, even if he did not intend to do it.

This injustice consists in the fact that you were unfortunate enough to interpret a passage I wrote in a sense quite at variance with its context. For your head was more heated than clear. I shall explain myself by means of a simile.

If a carter, stuck fast with his heavy load on an unsurfaced road, finally says, after various fruitless attempts to free himself, 'if all the traces snap, I shall have to unload', would it be fair to conclude from these words that he really *wanted* to unload, that he deliberately employed the weakest and most fragile traces as a pretext for unloading? Would it not be unjust for the shipper consequently to demand compensation from the carter for any damage sustained, including all externally invisible damage, which could just as easily have been caused by the packer?

I am this carter; and you are the shipper, Venerable Man. I said that, *even if* we were not in a position to counter all the objections which reason is so intent on making to the *Bible*, *religion* would nevertheless remain unshaken and unharmed in the hearts of those Christians who have attained an inner feeling for its essential truths. In support of this, I wrote that passage which was subjected to so uncharitable an extension by you. I supposedly said that no answer can possibly be given to the

---

[7] In 1771, Lessing had published an account of a previously unknown work by Berenger of Tours (1010–88) which he had newly discovered in the Wolfenbüttel library; his presentation of Berenger, condemned as a heretic by the Catholic Church, as a precursor of Luther was warmly received by German Lutherans.

objections to the Bible, and that it is utterly futile to try to answer them. I supposedly advised the *theologian* to seek, the sooner the better, the last infallible refuge of the *Christian*, so that a weak but vainglorious enemy might triumph all the sooner.

That is not a true representation of my thoughts, Venerable Man. Nevertheless, it cannot have been your *intention* to give such a false representation of them. Confident in the rightness of your cause which you imagined that I, too, was attacking, you were overhasty: you jumped to conclusions.

Venerable Man, those who most readily jump to conclusions are not the worst people. For they are for the most part equally ready to acknowledge their overhastiness, and an admission of overhastiness is often more instructive than cold, calculated infallibility.

I therefore expect, Venerable Man, that in one of the next instalments of your *Voluntary Contributions*,[8] you will not fail to make an as good as voluntary declaration to this effect: that there nevertheless remains a certain sense in which the passage you attacked in my work appears very innocent; that you overlooked this sense; and that you have no further cause for not considering this overlooked sense, now that your attention has been drawn to it by me, as representing the intention of my work.

Only a declaration such as this can put paid to the suspicion which you, Venerable Man, seem to wish to cast on my intentions. Only after such a declaration can I again take an interest in whatever other objections you care to raise against me. But without such a declaration, Venerable Man, I must leave you to write – in the same way as I leave you to preach.

The challenge

Herr Pastor,

I thought I had taken leave of you with the foregoing conciliatory pages, and I was already looking forward to the *Voluntary Contribution* in which your holy fist would once more brandish the Christian banner over my head.

---

[8] *Voluntary Contributions* [*Freywillige Beyträge*] was the title of a Hamburg periodical of conservative religious leanings, to which Goeze regularly contributed.

But while either the press worked too slowly for me or I for it, I received numbers 61 to 63 of the said *Contributions* – and I am dumbfounded!

Did the same man write this? How is posterity, to which the *Voluntary Contributions* will doubtless descend, to explain so sudden a transition from white to black? – 'Was Goeze', posterity will say, 'was Goeze a man who could in the same breath mutter sour-sweet compliments between his teeth and shout slanderous insults at one and the same writer? Did he play both the cat which circles round the hot broth and the boar which charges blindly on to the spear? This is inconceivable! In number 55, his zeal is still so moderate and quite impersonal; he names neither the sack nor the donkey which his stick belabours. And suddenly, in number 61, Lessing's name appears from start to finish. Does Lessing have to be pinched every time he gets cramp in his orthodox fingers? In number 55, Goeze will scarcely dip into the water; and then, *splash!* This is incomprehensible! It must be that, between numbers 55 and 61 of this invaluable journal as we have it today, all those issues which would explain this sudden plunge are missing.'

That is what posterity will say, Herr Pastor. But what do we care for posterity, Herr Pastor, which will perhaps *not* say this? It is enough that you know best how mistaken posterity would be; and I strike this note only to apologise to the *contemporary* world – that is, to the world which *both* of us inhabit – in case the tone in which I take leave to address Herr Pastor Goeze in future should seem to deviate too far from the tone which I have hitherto considered more appropriate.

For frankly, Herr Pastor, the importunate thrusts you direct at me are gradually becoming excessive! Don't expect me to list all of them, for it would only gratify you to see that I had felt them all. I will simply inform you of the consequences.

I absolutely refuse to be decried by you as a man who is less well disposed towards the Lutheran Church than you are. For I am aware that I am far better disposed towards it than one who would have us believe that every tender sentiment he feels for his lucrative office, or the like, is holy zeal for the divine cause.

Can you, Herr Pastor, can you really have the slightest spark of Luther's spirit? – You, who are not even capable of grasping Luther's doctrinal system in its entirety? – You who, with tacit approval, allow one side of the Lutheran edifice which had sunk a little to be jacked up well beyond the horizontal by unwashed and doubtless perfidious hands? – You, who persecute and stone the honest man who – albeit unasked, but with sincere intent – calls out to the men at the jack 'Don't raise it any higher there, or the building will collapse here!'

And why? – Because this honest man also believed that the written advice of an anonymous architect to demolish the building completely should be – approved? supported? implemented? set in train by himself? – No! – merely that this advice should not be suppressed.

O sancta simplicitas![9] – But I have not yet reached *that* point, Herr Pastor, where the good man who uttered these words could *do no more* than utter them. – Let us first be heard and judged by those who can and will hear and judge us!

If only *he* could do it, he whom I would most wish to be my judge! – Luther, you! – Great, misunderstood man! And no more seriously misunderstood than by the short-sighted bigots who, with your slippers in their hand, trudge along the path you opened up, raucous but indifferent! – You redeemed us from the yoke of tradition; but who will redeem us from the more intolerable yoke of the letter? Who will at last bring us a Christianity as you would teach it *now*, as Christ himself would teach it? Who – –

But I forget *myself*. And I would forget *you* even more, Herr Pastor, if, after words such as these, I were to say to you in confidence: 'Herr Pastor, until that time comes, which neither you nor I will live to see, until then – though it will most certainly come! – would it not be better if people like us kept silent? if people like us simply remained wholly passive? What one of us wishes to keep back, the other might claim to detect in any case, so that the one would do more to further the other's intentions than his own. What if we were to let the duel which I still have to fight with you, Herr Pastor, be the first and the last? I am prepared to waste not one more word with you than I have already wasted.'

But no – you will not wish for this. Goeze has let none of his opponents have the last word, although he has always uttered the first word himself. He will regard what I *must* say in my defence as an attack. For it is not for nothing that he is now the *sole* heir to the late Ziegra's journalistic platform.[10]

[9] 'O sacred simplicity!', words uttered by the Czech religious reformer Jan Hus (c. 1370–1415) as he saw a peasant adding fuel to the fire by which Hus was burned at the stake.
[10] Christian Ziegra had edited the *Voluntary Contributions* (see note 8 above) until his death in January 1778.

I complain – for you see, Herr Pastor, it will be impossible for me not to kick against your goads, and I fear that the furrows which you are determined to make me plough on God's acre will become ever more irregular.

It is not as if I wished to hold against you or, if I could, to deny you, every malicious innuendo, every (God permitting) poisonous bite, every comic outburst of your tragic pity, every teeth-gnashing sigh which bewails the fact that it is only a sigh; or every dutiful pastoral incitement of the secular authorities with which you will henceforth lard and season the *Voluntary Contributions* you will launch against me. I am not so unreasonable as to ask any bird on earth for a single feather other than its own; besides, *palliatives* of this kind have long since lost their credibility.

No, there is only one thing which I shall not be able to tolerate: namely your pride, which questions the reason and learning of everyone who employs reason and learning in ways other than you do. In particular, my anger will boil over if you continue to treat my anonymous author, whom you know only from disconnected fragments, so much like a schoolboy or miscreant. For man against man (not cause against cause), this anonymous author was of *such* consequence that, in all varieties of learning, seven Goezes would not amount to one-seventh of his weight. On this, Herr Pastor, you may take my word.

And so I can be brief with my knightly *challenge. Write, Herr Pastor, or get others to write, as much as the topic will stand; I shall write too. If I fail to correct you on the smallest thing concerning me or my anonymous author in which you are not in the right – then I can no longer hold a pen.*

Axioms
(if there are any in matters such as this)

> . . . to those who, by their acumen, are able to perceive that the concept
> of the predicate is indivisibly linked to that of the subject.

> Christian Wolff, *Philosophia rationalis sive logica* [1728]

Against Pastor Goeze of Hamburg[1]

Brunswick, 1778

This sheet – or however many sheets there may be – which I sit down to write is likely to prove a laborious task, because I scarcely know *for* whom I am writing. I only know *against* whom, and I have so little hope that it will also be *for* the person *against* whom it is directed that I scarcely dare transform this hope into a wish.

With reference to a passage that I am conscious of having written with deliberation and good intentions, Herr Pastor Goeze of Hamburg has made, and published in two different newspapers, certain remarks which label me rather as an opponent of the Christian religion.

I will not repeat here that passage as I wrote it.[2] There is all the less need to do so since I wish to rearrange its individual sentences, which I allegedly 'set down like simple axioms', in a somewhat different order. Perhaps this minor change alone will enable my opponent to understand

---

[1] The article by Goeze to which Lessing here replies is reproduced in B IX, 11–20. It had appeared in two separate publications in Hamburg and Altona.

[2] Lessing refers to the third and fourth paragraphs of his own 'counter-propositions' to the 'Fragments' of Reimarus: see p. 63 above.

me better, especially when he finds that his own objections have helped me to explain myself more adequately. Perhaps this minor change alone will enable my sentences fully to achieve that status [of axioms] which they had not yet attained. For who does not know that axioms are sentences whose words only need to be properly understood for there to be no doubt as to their truth?

At the very beginning of his work, the Pastor is horrified that I am not entirely happy with either the rebuttals or the defences of the Christian religion which have hitherto been put forward. He is horrified: but if I can once induce him to take a proper look at the thing which fills him with such alarm, he should, I hope, be able to pass it by with less anxiety.

If I were a hypocrite, I would only need to put the entire blame for my frustrated expectation on past rebuttals of religion. The Pastor will readily concede that these, without exception, are completely misplaced and mistaken. I might say, for example: 'The defence tends to match the attack. How can the theologian help it if attacks on his good cause are not mounted from any other angle, or with better weapons? Once the fortifications are attacked from a higher level, means will be devised to protect them from that quarter too.'

But I disdain all evasions, and anything that even resembles an evasion. I have said it before and I say it again, that even in their own right, defences of the Christian religion have not hitherto been written with anything like the knowledge, love of truth, and gravity which the importance and dignity of the subject demand.[3]

This general pronouncement of mine was indeed based on induction, indeed as complete and carefully considered an induction as I was able to implement in my present circumstances.

'Well, let us first see this induction for ourselves!', my opponent cries out to me, already in a tone of triumph.

Dear Herr Pastor, I do very much wish you had not made this unreasonable demand in print. It is truly a pulpit demand, and you doubtless know how one replies to a demand of this kind – with a similar counter-demand.

If I say that all mercury evaporates over a flame, must I satisfy someone who takes exception to the generality of my assertion by bringing together all the mercury throughout nature and evaporating it before his eyes? Until I am in a position to do so, I would rather simply reply: 'Dear friend, all

[3] See p. 64 above.

the mercury I have so far held above a flame really did evaporate. If you know of some which does not evaporate, do bring it here so that I can examine it, and I shall be most grateful.'

To examine closely all the countless works, large and small, which have been written even since the beginning of this century to demonstrate the truth of Christianity – what an imposition! If the Pastor really meant it seriously, and did not merely wish to make fun of me and rejoice at my embarrassment at having either to retract my claim or submit to an endless task, very well – let him prove it by a trifling gesture which will cost him only a word.

Simply this: let him name the work with which I am to make my first experiment in evaporation. He need only name it, for I am ready. If it is one with which I am already familiar, I have nothing to fear. If it is one I do not know and my experiment fails, so much the better: I am happy to accept a minor humiliation in exchange for a major lesson.

But I must make one prior condition. He must not assume that a person who doubts *certain* proofs of something also doubts the thing itself. The least suggestion to that effect is murderous. How can I help it if attempts have been made in recent times to elevate secondary proofs to a level of certainty and self-evidence of which they are absolutely incapable? How can I help it if people are no longer willing to let the whole matter remain within the modest confines in which all earlier theologians considered it secure enough? Or is the Pastor so unfamiliar with the history of dogmatics that he does not know of these changes? How does he in particular come to oppose a man who is merely dissatisfied with them? In other respects, he is certainly no friend of theological innovations. Why does he wish to defend only these particular changes against me? Because I have not expressed myself throughout in the theological jargon to which *he* is accustomed? I am an amateur of theology, not a theologian. I have taken no oath on any particular system. I am not obliged to speak any language other than my own. I feel pity for all the honest men who are not so fortunate as to be able to say the same. But these honest men must not seek to bind the horns of other honest men with the same rope which ties *them* to the manger. Otherwise, my pity is at an end, and I can only despise them.

So much for that abomination which the Pastor encountered at the start of his investigation. Now to the actual passage which I find myself compelled to defend against the Pastor's misinterpretations – not, as already mentioned, in the same order as before, but nevertheless in its full wording and complete sense. The logical order of our thoughts is not always that in which we communicate them to others; but it is the order which an opponent must seek above all to identify if his attack is to be an equitable one. And so the Pastor should have begun with the third of my propositions, as follows.

<h2 style="text-align:center">I (3)[4]</h2>

The Bible obviously contains more than what pertains to religion.

I have no reason to regret having written this. But nothing in the world could persuade me to reply to it as Pastor Goeze has done. He replies:

> This sentence contains two propositions. Firstly, that the Bible contains what pertains to religion, and secondly, that the Bible contains more than what pertains to religion. In the first proposition, the editor admits what he had denied in the previous sentence. If the Bible contains what pertains to religion, it objectively contains religion itself.

I am shocked! I allegedly denied that the Bible *contains* religion? I? But where? In the immediately preceding sentence? Surely not by saying 'The Bible *is* not religion?' By this?

My dear Herr Pastor, is this how you dealt with all your past adversaries? Is *to be* the same thing as *to contain*? Are the two propositions 'the Bible *contains* religion' and 'the Bible *is* religion' completely identical? Surely no one in Hamburg will deny me the whole difference between *gross* and *net*? In Hamburg, where so many goods have their specific *tares*, would no one allow me a modest tare on so valuable a commodity as the Holy Writ? – Well, well; the Pastor is not really so *uncommercial* as this, for he continues:

> The second proposition can be conceded, if a distinction is made between what pertains essentially to religion and what pertains to the elucidation and confirmation of the central principles which actually constitute the essence of religion.

---

[4] The roman numeral refers to the present order of Lessing's ten 'axioms', the arabic numeral to their original order in his 'counter-propositions' to the 'Fragments' (see note 2 above).

Good! So we are in fact dealing with the *gross* amount. But what if that were also to include completely unnecessary *packaging*? – What if there were a good deal of material in the Bible which simply does not serve to elucidate or confirm even the least significant religious principle? What other theologians, *including good Lutherans*, have asserted of entire books in the Bible, I may surely assert of individual items in this or that book? One must be at least a rabbi or a preacher to work out any possible meaning or wordplay whereby the *hajiemim* of Anah,[5] the Cherethites and Pelethites of David,[6] the cloak which Paul left behind at Troas,[7] and a hundred other such things can be in any way linked to religion.

Thus the proposition 'The Bible contains more than what pertains to religion' is true without qualification. Its proper use can also be infinitely more advantageous to religion than its misuse can be harmful. Misuse of anything is deplorable, and I have no objection to precautions being taken to protect oneself against it. But this ought to be done in a more appropriate manner than in the Pastor's following addendum:

> But if this proposition should be prejudicial to the Bible, it is totally invalid – as invalid as if I were to say that Wolff's system of mathematics contains annotations, and these annotations detract from its worth.

As already indicated, this proposition of mine should not be prejudicial to the Bible. It should rather relieve it at one stroke of countless objections and mockeries and restore to it the forfeited rights of ancient documents, which are worthy of respect and conservation.

As for your example, Herr Pastor, I am more content with it than you think. Of course the annotations in Wolff's *Elements of Mathematics* do not reduce the value of that work. But they do mean that not everything in the work is demonstrated. Or do you think that the annotations must be just as certain as the theorems? It is not so much that the annotations *could not* also be demonstrated as that they *need not* be demonstrated here. It would be a waste of demonstrations if one were to supply them for all those minor points which may or may not be included in an annotation. – A similar waste of divine inspiration is equally pointless, but infinitely more vexatious.

[5] Genesis 36.24.   [6] 2 Samuel 8.18 and 20.7.   [7] 2 Timothy 4.13.

II (4)

It is merely a hypothesis that the Bible must be equally infallible in this additional respect.

No? Then what is it? 'An indisputable truth'. Indisputable? But it has so often been disputed! And so many still dispute it today – so many who also claim to be Christians, and who are Christians! Not, of course, Wittenbergian Lutheran Christians, or Christians by the grace of Calov,[8] but nevertheless Christians, and even Lutheran Christians, by the grace of God.

But what if Calov and Goeze were right? Goeze, at least, presents such a splendid dilemma! He says:

> Either this additional material is inspired, or at least approved, by God, or not. If the former, it is just as infallible as the essential elements. But if one assumes the latter, the former proposition cannot be relied on either.

If this dilemma is correct, it must also be valid if we substitute for 'this additional material' some other subject to which the same dual predicate seems applicable. For example, 'Either *moral evil* owes its existence to God, or is at least approved by him, or not. If the former, it is just as divine, and therefore just as good, as the good itself. But if one assumes the latter, we cannot know whether God created and approved the good either. For evil is never without good, and good is never without evil.'

What do my readers think? Shall we retain both dilemmas, or reject them both? I am resolved to reject them. For what if God, in his inspiration, had treated those human additions which were themselves made possible by that inspiration in the same way as, in his creation, he treated *moral evil*? What if, once this or that miracle had taken place, he left what had produced the miracle to run its natural course? What does it matter that, in this case, the boundaries between human additions and revealed truths can no longer be defined so precisely? After all, the distinction between moral evil and moral good is equally indeterminable. But do we therefore have no feeling whatsoever for good and evil? Would therefore no revealed truths whatsoever be distinguishable from human additions?

---

[8] Abraham Calov (1612–86), orthodox Lutheran and professor at Wittenberg, who defended the infallibility and literal truth of Scripture.

For does a revealed truth have no internal distinguishing marks at all? Has its direct divine origin left no trace in and upon it other than that historical truth which it shares with so many absurdities?

These, among others, are the objections I might raise to the Pastor's conclusion. But he seeks to prove his point not so much by means of conclusions as by similes and Scriptural quotations.

But these latter, the Scriptural quotations, will surely be indisputable? If only they were! How glad I would be to forget that eternal circle whereby the infallibility of a book is demonstrated by a passage within it, and the infallibility of the passage is demonstrated by that of the book itself! But these passages are so far from indisputable that I must conclude that the Pastor selected the most doubtful passages of all for me, in order to save the more telling ones for a better occasion.

When Christ says of the Scripture that *it bears witness to him*, did he mean to say that it bears witness *only* to him? How can these words possibly indicate that all the books of the Bible are homogeneous, both in content and inspiration? Could not the Scripture bear witness to Christ equally well even if its inspiration extended only to what it explicitly designates as the words of God or of the prophets?

And the 'all Scripture' of Paul![9] – I need not remind the Pastor whom he has to satisfy concerning the true explanation of this passage before he proceeds to make such unquestioning use of it. Another reading gives Paul's words quite a different sense, and this reading is just as grammatical, just as appropriate to the context, and has the support of just as many old and new theologians as the reading approved in the commonest manuals of Lutheran dogmatics, so that I cannot see why the latter should remain absolutely binding. Luther himself did not follow this reading in his translation, but rather the former one. He did not accept the 'and'; and it is bad enough if this variant – i.e. the inclusion or omission of 'and' – renders the central text on the epistemological basis of all theology so highly uncertain.

And finally, the 'sure word of prophecy'![10] – Where is the evidence that the 'word of prophecy' was meant to include all the historical words as

---

[9] 2 Timothy 3.16: alternative readings of this passage support either the literal inspiration of all Scripture ('All Scripture is given by inspiration of God, and is profitable ... [etc.]') or the view that its divine inspiration is manifest only in so far as it has profitable effects ('All Scripture given by inspiration of God is profitable ... [etc.]').
[10] 2 Peter 1.19–21.

well? Where is it? The historical words are the *vehicle* for the prophetic word. But a vehicle should not and cannot have the strength and nature of the medicine it contains. What objection does the Pastor have to this interpretation? I know that it is not his interpretation and not that of Wittenberg. But if that is all that Germany needed to be told via two different newspapers, why did he not make things much easier for himself and for me? Why did he not declare comprehensively, and in a nutshell, that my entire passage flatly contradicts the compendia of Wittenberg orthodoxy? I might have replied equally succinctly: 'I most heartily agree!'

III (1)

The letter is not the spirit, and the Bible is not religion.

If it is true that the Bible contains more than what pertains to religion, who can prevent me from calling it, in so far as it contains both elements and in so far as it is merely a book, *the letter*, and from describing its better part, which either is, or relates to, religion, as *the spirit*?

Anyone who accepts the inner testimony of the Holy Spirit is indeed entitled to designate it thus. For since this testimony can only express itself more or less in those books and passages of Scripture which aim more or less at our spiritual improvement, what is more reasonable than to call only those books and passages 'the spirit' of the Bible? I even think it would be verging on blasphemy to assert that the power of the Holy Spirit manifests itself as much in the genealogical tables of Esau's descendants in Genesis as in the Sermon on the Mount in St Matthew's Gospel.

This distinction between the letter and the spirit of the Bible is basically the same as that which other theologians, *including good Lutherans*, have long since made between the Holy Writ and the word of God. Why did Pastor Goeze not first pick a quarrel with them before branding a poor layman as a criminal for following in their footsteps?

IV (2)

Consequently objections to the letter, and to the Bible, need not also be objections to the spirit and to religion.

It is quite certain that a consequence is of the nature of the principle from which it is drawn. The principle is in part conceded and in part demonstrated. If objections to contingent elucidations of the main doctrines of the Christian religion are not objections to the main doctrines themselves, it is even less likely that objections to those Biblical matters which are not even contingent elucidations of religion can be objections to religion itself.

Thus I only need to reply here to the example the Pastor cites. It is of course true that, if a country's *constitution* contains no more and no less than that country's *civil order*, any subject who makes wilful objections to the constitution has also wilfully attacked the civil order. But if so, what is the point of having two quite distinct terms? Why are both not described either as the civil order or as the constitution? The fact that one is *called* something different from the other is an obvious indication that the one also *is* something different from the other: for there is no such thing as perfect synonyms. But if the one is different from the other, it is quite untrue that challenges to the one are necessarily also challenges to the other. For however small the circumstance which gave rise to the two distinct names, the objection may also apply only to this small circumstance, and what the Pastor so contemptuously describes as an antithesis is a complete justification [of the objection]. I shall explain myself by means of an example from his own home territory. Does not the collection of Hamburg laws compiled by Councillor Klefeker[11] – I do not know whether it was ever completed – contain the most complete and reliable constitution of the city of Hamburg? And could it not well be given this title? But if it did have this title, could I make no objection to this work without opposing the authority of the laws of Hamburg themselves? Might not my objection concern the historical introductions with which Herr Klefeker prefaced each class of laws? Or have these historical introductions acquired the force of laws just because they were printed in the same volume as the laws themselves? How does the Pastor know that the historical books of the Bible are not meant to be introductions of roughly the same kind? Perhaps God had as little need to inspire, or even merely to approve, these books as the citizens and Council had to grant those introductions their special protection. It was enough that Klefeker was given access to all of the city's archives! If he did not use them carefully enough, let someone

---

[11] Johann Klefeker, editor of the *Sammlung der Hamburgischen Gesetze und Verfassungen* [*Collected Laws and Constitutions of Hamburg*] (1765–74).

else make better use of them, and all is well. It would, on the other hand, be a gross misuse and futile waste of the legislative power if any attempt were made to lend its authority equally to two such disparate things as the laws and the history of the laws.

V (5)

Religion also existed before there was a Bible.

To this, the Pastor replies 'But not before there was a revelation'. – What he means by this is beyond my comprehension. Of course a revealed religion cannot exist before it is revealed. But it certainly can exist before it is written down. That is all that was meant. All I wish to say is that the religion existed before the least syllable of it was recorded in writing. It existed before there was a single book of that same Bible which is now equated with religion itself. What, then, is the point of this misguided question other than to throw my own thinking off course? – I have nothing further to reply to this.

VI (6)

Christianity existed before the evangelists and apostles wrote about it. Some time elapsed before the first of them wrote, and a very considerable time before the whole canon was established.

'All this', says the Pastor, 'I can now grant to the editor.' – *Can?* Why only *can?* – He *must* grant me this.

But if he must grant me this, he must at the same time concede that the oral revelation of Christianity was much earlier than the written record, and that it was able to survive and spread without this record. I claim no more than this, and I again have no idea why he asks me the question 'Did Christianity then exist before Christ and the apostles preached it?'

This question is designed to render the above proposition [VI (6)] unfit for its purpose, which is contained in the following proposition [VII (7)] below. We shall see.

I should also like to ask one or two provisional questions here, simply for information and in order to grasp the complete sense of the Pastor's remarks. – If, as he says, as long as Christ and the apostles were preaching, and as long as the extraordinary gifts of the Holy Spirit were active in the congregations, the propagation of the Christian religion could be *better* sustained by oral instruction than by the written word,

did the use of written records begin only after those extraordinary gifts came to an end, or did it begin earlier? If it began earlier, and if it is undeniable that these gifts did not end with the apostles but lasted for further centuries, did the gifts gain their authority from the Scriptures during this time, or the Scriptures from the gifts? The former makes no sense, and if the latter is the case, are *we* not in the highly unfortunate position of having to believe, *without* the evidence of the gifts, those same Scriptures which the first Christians believed on that evidence? But if, on the other hand, the use of the Scriptures did not begin until the miraculous gifts ceased, where can we find the evidence that the Scriptures not only *replaced* the miraculous gifts, but were *meant* to replace them?

And yet it is clear from history that this was certainly the case. It can certainly be demonstrated that, as long as the miraculous gifts – and especially the direct illumination of the bishops – were in operation, much less weight was attached to the written word. It was even a crime not to give credence to the bishop except on the strength of the written word. And there were good grounds for this, for the 'implanted gift of teaching'[12] which the bishops possessed was the same as that of the apostles; and when bishops quoted the written word, they naturally quoted it as confirmation, but not as the source, of their opinion.

This brings me back to the intention I followed in first putting forward the above proposition and the one immediately before it. It is as follows.

VII (7)

Thus, however much may depend on these writings, it is impossible for the whole truth of the Christian religion to be based on them.

That is, if it is true that the religion of the Old and New Testament had already been revealed for some time before the least syllable of it was recorded in writing, and that an even longer time elapsed before all the books which we now include in the canon of the Old and New

---

[12] Quotation from the so-called *Epistle of Barnabas* (c. AD 130) IX.9.

Testament were completed, that same religion must also be conceivable without these books. I say 'without these books', not 'without the content of these books'. Whoever makes me say the latter instead of the former makes me talk nonsense, in order to attain the great and holy distinction of refuting nonsense. So I again repeat 'without these books'. Besides, no orthodox believer has yet maintained, so far as I know, that the religion was first revealed in one of these books, or revealed there originally and gradually developed as the remaining books were added. On the contrary, learned and thoughtful theologians unanimously admit that sometimes more, sometimes less, of this religion was recorded *as the occasion arose.* – And if this more or less *was already true before* the occasion arose to record it, can it only be *true for us now because* it was recorded in writing? –

The Pastor does try at this point to get round the difficulty by means of a distinction, by claiming that the truth of religion is one thing, and our conviction of this truth another. He declares:

> The truth of the Christian religion does indeed rest upon itself; it is founded on its consonance with the qualities and will of God, and on the historical certainty of the facts on which its doctrines are partly based. But our conviction of the truth of the Christian religion nevertheless rests solely and exclusively on these Scriptures.

But if I understand these words correctly, either the Pastor is saying something very unphilosophical or he contradicts himself and is entirely of my opinion. It is also possible that he had to express himself so unphilosophically in order not to appear too obviously to share my opinion. For let us reflect for a moment! If the truth of the Christian religion rests *in part* – he did not, of course, explicitly include the latter words, but his sense necessarily requires them – if, I say, it rests *in part* on itself, i.e. on its consonance with the qualities and will of God, and *in part* on the historical certainty of the facts on which some of its doctrines are based, does not this double basis also give rise to a double conviction? Does not each of the two bases require its own separate conviction? What need does either of them have to borrow its conviction from the other? Is it not indolent frivolity to give the one the benefit of the other's conviction? Is it not frivolous indolence to try to make the conviction of one extend to both? Why should I *believe* things which I *must consider true* because they are consonant with the qualities and will of God, *merely* because other things, which were at one time associated with them in time and space, are historically demonstrated?

Let us take it as given that the books of the Bible furnish proof of all the facts on which the Christian doctrines are in part based; books can furnish proof of facts, and why should these books not do so? It is enough that not all of the Christian doctrines are based on facts. The rest are based, as already conceded, on their inner truth; and how can the inner truth of any proposition depend on the authority of the book in which it is put forward? That is a manifest contradiction.

I still cannot overcome my amazement at a question which the Pastor asks with such confidence as to assume that only *one* answer is possible. 'Would any trace remain in the world', he asks, 'of Christ's actions and teachings if the New Testament books had not been written and handed down to us?' – God preserve me from ever thinking so little of Christ's teachings that I might dare to answer this question with an outright 'no'! No; I would not repeat this 'no', even if an angel from heaven dictated it to me, let alone if it is only a Lutheran pastor who tries to put it into my mouth. – If everything that happens in the world leaves traces in the world behind it, even if we cannot always detect them immediately, can it be, divine philanthropist, that only your teachings, which you did not write down, which you commanded should be preached, have had no effects at all which might betray their origin – even if they were *only* preached? Could your words only become words of life when they were transformed into dead letters? Are books the only way of illuminating and improving mankind? Is oral tradition nothing? And if oral tradition is subject to a thousand deliberate and involuntary falsifications, are books not subject to them too? Could God not have preserved the oral traditions from falsification by the same exercise of his direct power as we say he employed in order to preserve the books? – Oh, what a man, almighty God, who purports to be a preacher of your word and so boldly claims that you had only one way of attaining your end, the way which you were pleased to reveal to him! Oh, what a theologian, who, apart from this one way which he can see, flatly denies all other ways because he cannot see them! – Let me never, merciful God, become so orthodox, so that I should never become so presumptuous! –

How many small pieces of information and concepts *without* whose help we would scarcely understand and interpret the New Testament writings in quite the *same* way as we do *with* their help have not in fact been passed down to the present day through oral tradition alone? This applies not only to the Catholics, who acknowledge the fact, but also to the Protestants, although few of them admit it.

The Apostles' Creed obviously arose out of an orally transmitted set of doctrines rather than by direct derivation from Scripture. If the latter were the case, it would certainly be on the one hand more comprehensive, and on the other, more specific. That it is not derived from Scripture is less easy to explain by the hypothesis that it was intended only as a form of words for baptism than if we assume that it contains the orally transmitted faith which was current at the time of its composition, when the books of the New Testament had not yet been so thoroughly sifted through, and the need for such thorough scrutiny had not yet been recognised.

But where am I going? – To the point where the Pastor can more easily make the sign of the cross behind my back and shout a curse after me rather than follow in my footsteps. – So I shall resume where I left off.

VIII (8)

If there was a period in which it (the Christian religion) *was
already so widely disseminated, and in which it had already won over so
many souls – but without a single letter of that material which has come down
to us having yet been recorded – then it must also be possible for everything
that the evangelists and apostles wrote to be lost once more, and for the
religion they taught to continue to exist.*

It is not a mocking parody but genuine seriousness on my part if I now turn some of the Pastor's words back against him and say, 'For all the respect I have for the Pastor's other skills and services to theological literature, I can only describe what he says against this proposition either as highly dangerous *heterodoxy* or highly malicious *defamation*.' – Let him choose which! He can even have both!

Firstly, then, his comments from the point of view of defamation. – 'A sophism we can *lay our hands on*!', he cries. Surely not! (unless for a man whose hands are more perceptive and orthodox than his head). He continues:

> For if, instead of the words 'without a single letter of that material which has come down to us having yet been recorded', we substitute 'without a single word of that material which has come down to

us having yet been preached', the falsity of this statement at once becomes obvious.

Excellent! – Where is the writer whom I cannot convict of a sophism or blasphemy if I may first substitute other words for his own? – Other words? Only other words? If only our fair-minded and Christian Pastor had been content with this! But for my good words, which at least have a sense – if not a true sense –, he substitutes words which make no sense at all. I say: 'The Christian religion existed before anything of the Christian religion was written down.' I am supposed to have said: 'The Christian religion existed before the Christian religion was preached or revealed.' That is, I am supposed to have said: 'The Christian religion existed before the Christian religion existed.' Have I escaped from the madhouse to say or write such things as this?

The Pastor then proceeds to remonstrate with me about things which I have never doubted. And why? To what end? So that his newspaper readers may think that I do in fact doubt them? – Admirable! Most worthy of him!

But when he once more raises the question, 'How then can we know the doctrines and deeds of Christ and his apostles?' and himself replies '*Only* from the writings of the evangelists and apostles', I must again protest against this 'only' – with the reminder that the majority of Christians find this 'only' equally unacceptable. Or are the Catholics not Christians? Would I not be a Christian if I inclined to the view of the Catholics in this matter? It is ungracious enough of many Protestants to present their proof of the truth of Christianity as if the Catholics had not the least share in it![13] I would have thought that, just as that alone can count *against* Christianity which neither Catholic nor Protestant can rebut, so also must that alone count as *part* of Christianity which is common to both Catholics and Protestants. At least, it ill befits a theologian of either party who knows that a given proposition is supported by the other party to condemn that proposition in the mouth of a third party who makes no claim to be either Catholic or Protestant, and to condemn it as completely denying the whole Christian religion.

---

[13] As Lessing admitted in his letter of 9 August 1778 to Elise Reimarus, his strategy here was to play off the Catholics – who, together with Lutheran and Calvinist delegates, advised the Aulic Council of the Holy Roman Empire on religious affairs – against the Protestants, in order to thwart Goeze's attempts to persuade the imperial authorities to silence him.

And this is where the Pastor's heterodoxy begins. What? The Christian religion itself would be lost if it were possible for the writings of the evangelists and apostles to be lost? What? So was no reliable set of doctrines extracted from these writings which might be preserved in other writings? So is someone who derived his entire faith from such an extract not a Christian? So is no one cured unless he swallows the container along with the medicine? – Just watch, for I shall soon be accused of saying that not just the writings of the evangelists and apostles, but also everything that was ever extracted from them might be lost, yet the Christian religion would still continue to exist. – Then I shall be accused of saying that the Christian religion could continue to exist even if it were lost.

Nevertheless, it is only necessary to recall the intention I followed in writing the whole passage to which the Pastor takes such exception. My aim is to reduce to their true significance objections to the less important part of the Bible. That is my intention. And only with this in mind do I say that anyone whose heart is more Christian than his head will not be in the least troubled by these objections – because he *feels* what others are content to *think*, and because he could, if necessary, dispense with the entire Bible. He is the confident victor who leaves the fortresses aside and occupies the country. The theologian is the timorous soldier who beats his head against the frontier fortresses and consequently scarcely catches sight of the country at all.

Incidentally – at the beginning of the last century, a Lutheran preacher from the Palatinate, having been deprived of his office, resolved to emigrate with his family, which consisted of adopted children of both sexes, to one of the colonies in British America. The ship in which he made the crossing was wrecked on a small uninhabited island of Bermuda, and almost all of those on board, apart from the preacher's family, were drowned. The preacher found this island so agreeable, so healthy, so rich in everything necessary for sustaining life, that he gladly resigned himself to ending the days of his pilgrimage on its shores. The storm had washed ashore, among other things, a small chest which contained, along with all kinds of equipment for his children, a Lutheran catechism. This catechism, in the complete absence of all other books, obviously became for him a most precious treasure. He continued to instruct his children from it until he died. The children in turn instructed their children from it until they died. Not until two years ago was another English ship, with an army chaplain from Hesse on board, forced to land on this island.

The chaplain – I might have it from his own letters – went ashore with some sailors to collect fresh water, and was not a little astonished when he suddenly found himself, in a bright and peaceful valley, among a cheerful naked community whose language was German – indeed, a German in which he fancied he heard nothing but expressions and turns of phrase from Luther's catechism. This made him curious; and lo and behold! he found that the community not only spoke Luther's language, but also shared Luther's faith, as orthodox a faith as that of any army chaplain – except for a few details. The catechism had, of course, become worn out over the one-and-a-half centuries, and all that remained of it was the boards of its cover. 'In these boards', they said, 'lies all our knowledge.' – 'It once lay here, dear friends!', said the chaplain. – 'It is still there, still there!', they said. 'It is true that we cannot read ourselves, and we scarcely know what reading is; but our fathers heard their fathers read aloud from it. And they knew the man who cut the boards. The man's name was Luther, and he lived soon after Christ.'

Before I continue my story, Herr Pastor, were these good people Christians or not? They believed most fervently in a supreme being; that they were poor sinful creatures; that this supreme being had nevertheless taken steps, through another equally exalted being, to grant them eternal happiness after this life. – Herr Pastor, were these people Christians or not?

You must necessarily say that they were not. For they had no Bible. – Merciful God! Unmerciful priest! – No, I shall tell you nothing more of this amiable, cheerful, happy community.

Let us instead chat for a moment about something which it is far more excusable not to understand properly. The Pastor seeks to prove that my proposition 'is in any case plainly at variance with experience and history'. But what he puts forward in this connection is so vacuous and superficial that he should not allow himself tirades of this kind – except perhaps in his sermons. Just listen to what he says:

> From the ninth century onwards until the beginning of the fifteenth century, there was a period during which the writings of the evangelists and apostles were almost lost. Who, apart from a few scholars, knew the Bible? Until the invention of printing, it was confined, in manuscripts and translations, to the monasteries.

Why should there have been fewer copies of the New Testament from the ninth to the fifteenth century than from the fifth to the ninth? Why were there fewer from the fifth to the ninth century than from the first to the fifth? Quite the reverse! The codices of the New Testament writings multiplied with the passage of time. Such codices were scarcest precisely in the first and second centuries – so scarce that entire large communities possessed only a single codex which the presbyters of the community kept under lock and key, and which no one was even allowed to read without their express permission. Does the Pastor presume to demonstrate that this was the case in the period he specifies? In my humble opinion, there were more copies of the Bible in Germany alone during this period than there were in the entire world during the first two centuries – except, perhaps, for the basic text of the Old Testament. Or does he wish to suggest that the Bible began to be taken out of the hands of the common man in the ninth century? He must indeed think so, for he continues:

> The mass of people learned nothing of it except what the Roman clergy told them, and they told them nothing except what they might learn without prejudice to the clergy's interest. What was the character of the Christian religion at this time with regard to the mass of people? Was it anything more than a glorified paganism?

The strict truth is that, even before the ninth century, the Bible had never been in the hands of the common man. The common man had never learned anything more of it than what the clergy chose to tell him. So religion ought to have declined much earlier, were it not the case that it could survive even without direct access to the Bible. I might add with Irenaeus that 'many barbarian nations who believe in Christ follow this [traditional order], for without paper and ink, they have salvation written in their hearts by the Holy Spirit'.[14] Finally, if the Christian religion declined so much between the ninth and the fifteenth century only because the Scriptures were nearly lost, why did it not recover more generally after the Scriptures were so to speak rediscovered through printing? Has the Roman Church abandoned a single one of its old doctrines since then? Are there not men like Middleton[15] who even now regard it as no better than a modified paganism? I am sure that even the Pastor himself holds this edifying opinion. – But wasn't there the Reformation? Don't we have

---

[14] Irenaeus of Lyons, Church Father and author of *Adversus haereses* [*Against Heresies*]; Lessing's quotation is from III 4.2 of that work.
[15] Conyers Middleton, author of *A Letter from Rome, Showing the Exact Conformity between Popery and Paganism* (1729), to which Lessing here alludes.

it alone to thank for the unhindered and more frequent use of the Bible? –
Even that is not entirely beyond doubt. For the Reformation came about
not so much because people *began* to make better use of the Bible as
because they *stopped* making use of tradition. Besides, we owe not only
the Reformation to the unhindered and more frequent use of the Bible,
but also Socinianism.[16]

Such, at least, are my thoughts, however surprising the Pastor may
find them. I am not even surprised that he is surprised. May heaven
long preserve us in this same relationship, whereby he is surprised and I
am not.

IX (9)

The religion is not true because the evangelists and apostles taught it; on the
contrary, they taught it because it is true.

Any sharp-witted distinction can be turned into an antithesis by someone
who has the least control over language. But since not every antithesis is
based on a sharp-witted distinction, and what ought to be a devastating
flash of sharp-wittedness is often only the summer lightning of wit –
especially among our dear poets –, the term 'antithesis' has become a
trifle suspect. Now this is very convenient for those gentlemen who have
I know not what natural aversion to all sharp-wittedness, especially if it is
not couched in their mundane terminology. 'Antithesis! Antithesis!', they
cry, and all is thereby refuted.

'This antithesis also says nothing!', says the Pastor who has much to
say:

> For if the evangelists and apostles are men who spoke and wrote as
> the Holy Spirit moved them, the Christian religion is true because
> the evangelists and apostles, or actually God himself, taught it. The
> second proposition is simply superfluous.

Well, then! I must heap up the measure of my sins and reinforce one
antithesis with another. Even what God teaches is not true because God
is willing to teach it; on the contrary, God teaches it because it is true.

Is the second proposition superfluous here too? – Yes, if we did not
know what a fine conception these gentlemen have of the will of God!

[16] Socinianism: see note 2 on p. 38 above.

If we did not know that, in their view, God can will something simply because he wills it. But even that might still, in a certain sense, be said of God, so that I scarcely know how to put their nonsense into words.

X (10)

The written records must be explained by its [i.e. the religion's] *inner truth, and none of the written records can give it any inner truth if it does not already have it.*

The first word which the Pastor says in reply to this is 'Good!'. I was delighted to hear it. But he qualifies this 'good' with a 'but' – and it is the most singular 'but' imaginable. All at once, nothing is good any more – not even what we already have from his own mouth.

For he has already informed us that the inner truth of the Christian religion is based on its consonance with the qualities of God (see §VII above), and now he suddenly knows not a word of this inner truth. Instead, he either puts only *hermeneutic* truth in its place, or at least declares that hermeneutic truth is the only test of inner truth. As if inner truth needed any test at all! As if inner truth were not rather the test of hermeneutic truth!

Just listen. I shall turn the Pastor's supposed refutation, and my reply to it, into a kind of dialogue, which might be called a 'pulpit dialogue'. For while I interrupt the Pastor, the Pastor does not consider himself interrupted. He continues to speak, without caring whether our words complement each other or not. He is wound up, and so he must run on. So: *A Dialogue and No Dialogue*:[17]

He. Good; but anyone who wishes to explain the written traditions to me by means of their inner truth must convince me *beforehand* that he has a correct and well-founded conception of their inner truth himself. –
I. Beforehand? Why beforehand? Whoever does the one, also does the other. If someone explains to me the inner truth of a revealed proposition (I say explains, not *seeks* to explain), he surely proves quite adequately that he has a correct conception of this inner truth himself.
He. – and that he does not make an image of it to suit his own intentions.

---

[17] In this 'pulpit dialogue', the words of 'He' are taken verbatim from the polemic of Goeze to which Lessing is here replying (B IX, 19).

I. If his intentions have no inner goodness, the religious propositions which he wishes to impart to me will have no inner truth either. The inner truth is not a wax nose which any rogue can shape to fit his face as he pleases.

He. But where will he get his knowledge of the inner truth of the Christian religion from, –

I. Where will he get the inner truth from? From itself. That is why it is called the *inner* truth, the truth which requires no external confirmation.

He. – except from the written traditions, or from the writings of the evangelists and apostles, –

I. What must we take from these? The inner truth? Or our earliest historical knowledge of this truth? The former would be as strange as if I were to regard a geometric theorem as true not because of its demonstration, but because it appears in Euclid. That it appears in Euclid can be as reliable a presumption of its truth as one wishes. But it is one thing to believe truth on an assumption, and another to believe it for its own sake. The two may perhaps lead to the same thing in practice – but does this make them the same thing? – Is it then only the historical knowledge of inner truth that we are supposed to be able to derive solely and exclusively from the writings of the evangelists and apostles? But the majority of Christians assure us that there is another source of this historical knowledge, namely the oral tradition of the Church. And it is certainly incontrovertible that the oral tradition was once its only source, and that it is impossible to name any age in which it ceased entirely to be a source, as distinct from becoming only a secondary source. But be that as it may, I shall speak only as a Protestant here, and I am content to let the New Testament writings be the sole source of our historical knowledge of religion. Has the first and only source never flowed for seventeen centuries? Did it never overflow into other writings? Did it never overflow into other writings in its original purity and efficacy? Must all Christians without exception draw from the source itself? May no Christian whatsoever be satisfied with the nearer and more accessible depths into which it has overflowed? This, this alone is the question here. – If he may be satisfied in this way, why could the writings of the evangelists and apostles not be lost without disadvantaging him? Be lost? Why could he not regard them as lost whenever he is confronted with objections to passages which make no essential difference to his religion? – If he may not do so, the main reason is doubtless that no complete and infallible set of doctrines has to this day been extracted from them, and that such a set of doctrines can perhaps never be extracted from them. For only then would it really be necessary for each individual to look at them through his own eyes, for each to become his own teacher and moral counsellor in the light of the Bible. But how I would pity you then, you poor innocent souls who were born in countries in whose language the Bible is not yet available, born into social classes which invariably still lack the basic foundation of a better education, namely the ability to read! You believe you are Christians because you were baptised. Unhappy wretches! Have you not heard that the *ability to read* is just as necessary to salvation as *baptism*!

He. – in appropriate conjunction with the writings of the Old Testament.

I. Now this to crown it all! – I fear, I fear, dear pious innocents, that you must also learn Hebrew if you wish to be sure of salvation.

He. I shall make no concessions here to his reason, although I always presuppose that the doctrines of that religion which is preached to me as the Christian religion must never contradict a general and undisputed principle of reason.

I. Herr Pastor! Herr Pastor! – Does the whole *rationality* of the Christian religion consist only in not being *irrational*? – Does your theological heart feel no shame at writing such a thing? – If you write it, you also preach it. And they allow you to preach such things in Hamburg?

He. We therefore recognise the truth of the Christian religion only if our concepts of it are the same as those which the written traditions, as contained in the Holy Scripture, *should* give rise to in our souls.

I. – *Should*! But to what concepts should they give rise? – Can you deny it, Herr Pastor, can you conceal from yourself the fact that only a few passages in the entire New Testament give rise to the same concepts in everyone? That by far the greater number give rise to some concepts in some people and other concepts in others? Which are the right concepts to which they *should* give rise? Who is to decide this? Hermeneutics? Everyone has his own hermeneutics. Which of them is true? Are they all true? Or is none of them true? And this thing, this wretched, irksome thing, is to be the test of inner truth? Then what would be the test of *it*?

He. Of course the written traditions cannot give the Christian religion inner truth if it does not have any.

I. It appears to me, Herr Pastor, that you were not so generous earlier when it seemed to you that a doctrine had enough inner truth if we had it before us in writing. Could the reason for your generosity perhaps be that you basically attach little value to the thing you are so generous with? That you are just as happy with a revealed truth which gives us nothing to think about as you are with one which does?

He. But it does not have to do so in any case.

I. How nice that it doesn't have to do what it cannot do! – But if the written tradition neither can nor should give the Christian religion inner truth, the Christian religion does not derive its inner truth from that source. But if it does not derive it from there, it cannot be dependent on it either. But if it does not depend on it, it can also survive without it. That's all I wished to say.

He. Its aim is therefore this: to discover and prove the inner truth of the Christian religion.

I. If 'discover' is supposed to mean 'make known for the first time', I have already shown that the Scriptures did not make the inner truth of the Christian religion known for the first time *to the world.* I shall only add here that they do so even less to individual people now. For we all come to it already equipped with the basic concepts of religion. – And as for 'prove', if it means no more than 'supply a written reference containing the words of the proposition that is to be proved', the Pastor has already admitted that such a reference cannot and should not be of any help to inner truth. But if 'prove' is to mean here what it really means, i.e. 'to demonstrate the link between a truth and other recognised and undoubted truths', any book can do this just as well as Scripture – especially after Scripture has done it beforehand. And so it is again unclear why the Christian religion cannot *now* survive without any Scripture.

He. It is consequently empty talk if one tries to set the inner truth of the Christian religion and the traditions – or more clearly the Holy Writ – *in opposition* to one another as two different things.

I. Opposition? Who wants to set these two things in opposition? I? But all I claim is that they *can now* be wholly independent of one another. Are any two things that are different also mutually opposed? Anyone who maintains that they are is welcome to indulge in empty talk; I shall certainly not do so. I have no wish to take the Scriptures away from the theologian who has learned to display his skills on them alone. I am too well aware of how greatly the learned study of Scripture has furthered all other branches of knowledge and science, and what barbarism we could easily relapse into if it were completely banished from the world. But the theologian should not seek to force his learned Biblical studies upon us

Christians in the guise of religion. He should not immediately denounce as unchristian any honest layman he encounters who is content with the doctrines which others have long ago extracted from the Bible for him, and who does not regard these doctrines as true because they were extracted from the Bible, but because he realises that they are more worthy of God and more beneficial to the human race than the doctrines of any other religion – and because he *feels* that these Christian doctrines give him comfort.

He. – It is just as futile as if one were to say that the laws of a legislator must be explained by his inner justice. Quite the reverse! The inner justice of a legislator must be recognised and judged on the evidence of his law.

I. The Pastor is uncommonly unfortunate in all his criticisms and explications. 'Quite the reverse!', I now reply in turn. And if truth is not a weathercock, I hope it will accept this command as final. What? The laws of a legislator should not be explained by his inner justice? If the letter of the law convicts someone whom the legislator cannot possibly have intended to convict, and if, according to the letter, punishment is prescribed for someone whose action, of a unique variety which could not have been foreseen by the legislator, ought rather to be rewarded than punished, does not the judge rightly abandon the letter and base his verdict on the inner justice which he assumes was present in the legislator? – What? The inner justice of a legislator must be recognised and explained on the evidence of his laws? Surely Solon was also a legislator? And Solon would have been very displeased if he had not been credited with a purer and more perfect justice than was evidenced by his laws. For when he was asked whether he had given his citizens the best laws, what did he reply? 'Well, of course, not the best possible ones, but the best they were capable of.'[18] Therefore: –

But I am heartily sick of talking any further with a deaf man. Otherwise I might not inappropriately recall an application of these words of Solon which would greatly annoy the Pastor if he did not happen to know already that it was a Church Father who made it.[19] And yet, what a drubbing the poor Church Fathers would receive, without exception, from our Lutheran pastors if they were to write today! This same Church Father

---

[18] Solon of Athens (c. 640–561 BC), whose words are cited from Plutarch's *Life of Solon* XV.2.
[19] Lessing probably alludes to Origen, who advocated different levels of religious instruction for Christians of different ability.

does not hesitate to recognise two kinds of Christian religion, one for the common man, and another, concealed beneath it, for the more refined and learned thinker. I do not go nearly so far as this. For me, the Christian religion remains one and the same – except that I wish to keep religion and the history of religion separate; except that I refuse to regard as indispensable a historical knowledge of its emergence and dissemination, and a conviction of this knowledge, which is absolutely impossible with any historical truth; except that I declare that the objections raised against the historical elements of religion are insignificant, whether or not they can be answered; except that I refuse to regard the weaknesses of the Bible as weaknesses of religion; except that I cannot stand the bragging of the theologian who would have the common man believe that all those objections have long since been answered; except that I despise the short–sighted interpreter who heaps possibilities upon possibilities in order to strengthen the possibility that these weaknesses might not be weaknesses at all, and who knows no other way of filling a small breach which the enemy has opened up in the rampart than by making another far greater hole with his own hands.

And does all this mean that I have sinned against the Christian religion? Because of this? Because I wrote: 'But what do this man's hypotheses, explanations, and proofs matter to the Christian? For him, Christianity is simply *there*, that same Christianity which he *feels* is so true and in which he feels himself so blessed. When the paralysed patient *experiences* the salutary shock of the electric spark, what does he care whether Nollet, or Franklin, or neither of the two is right?'

But the Pastor will no doubt refrain from mentioning to his newspaper readers that I have *also written this*. Nevertheless, it was only for the benefit of Christians *of this kind* that I added the whole passage on which he has seen fit to supply such an incomprehensible commentary. That was my sole intention in doing so – to assure the *feeling* Christian of a defensive position in which he might confidently take refuge if he no longer dared to hold the field along with his more courageous theologians. Who needs to be told that the theologians, including those of every sect, will be in no hurry to leave the battlefield, or have any need to do so – especially if they are merely skirmishing with others of their own kind? Have I not made this point sufficiently myself? Have I not explicitly acknowledged that every theologian will have answers enough in the spirit of the confession to which he subscribes? Did I not myself attempt to anticipate some of the answers they might give? If my attempt is of little value – as may well be the case – let anyone who can do so improve on it! That is my only wish. It was for that reason alone that I published the fragments. Or does anyone think that, since I wished and hoped for wholly satisfactory answers, I should rather have kept my consolations in reserve in case such answers were not forthcoming? But to what end? By offering this consolation, was I assuming in advance that all answers were superfluous? This consolation was offered only to the simple Christian, not to the theologian – or at least only to the theologian whose higher wisdom had not led him to forget how to be only a simple Christian too.

That the Pastor should describe this consolation, which I regard as the most invincible bulwark of Christianity, as a shield of straw is something which, for his sake, I much regret. He has not, I fear, remained uninfected in his theological wars by the heterodoxy of his enemy – more infected by it than he will wish to admit from a Hamburg pulpit, and perhaps more than he has himself realised. For he, too, must consequently deny any inner feeling for Christianity. And if we do not yet hear him declaim from the pulpit: 'Feeling! What feeling? Feeling is a shield of straw! Our hermeneutics, our articles of faith – these, these, are the all-protecting, impenetrable, adamantine shield of faith!', that is presumably only because even the articles of faith still rely on the shield of straw. So let it be made of straw, for there are other shields of straw there too. If only it were not at the same time so narrow! For there is room under it only for a single individual with religion in his heart. What use is it to the Pastor if he cannot also shelter his Bible, as well as his whole dear congregation, beneath it?

It is worth hearing in his own words how earnestly the Pastor proceeds to urge all his esteemed colleagues openly to flee the field of battle rather than make use of this shield. With a tremor in his voice, he declares:

> I would greatly pity the Christian who is also a theologian if, for lack of other reasons, he faced the sad necessity of holding up this shield of plaited straw against the fiery arrows unleashed by the fragments.

So would I, to some extent. At least I would shrug my shoulders at him for understanding his trade so imperfectly. But who spoke in the first place of the Christian who is also a theologian? Do all Christians also have to be theologians? I have always found the best Christians among those who knew least about theology. Why should those who do not have to face fiery arrows not have a shield of straw? If a shield of straw is no defence against fiery arrows, it does offer protection against blows. – The resolute Pastor continues: 'I would rather advise him (i.e. the Christian who is also a theologian) actually to flee.' – If he believes that he must at all costs retain the theologian of his own sect, may the flight be successful! It is enough that those who are *only* Christians will not desert the colours. – 'For by applying the principles laid down by the editor [of the fragments], he would *sacrifice the Bible* in order to *rescue religion*: but what religion?' – What religion? The same one which gave rise to the Bible. The same one which, in later ages, when it was thought to have lost its original purity, was again extracted from the Bible. Or has no religion yet been reliably extracted from it? Is the one which has been extracted from it only provisional, and not really Christian? This must be so, for the Pastor says quite decisively: 'Certainly not the Christian religion, which stands or falls with the Bible'. – I am so sorry! And the Bible stands or falls – presumably with its divine inspiration? He must in fact maintain that, if there is no Christianity without the Bible, there is no Bible without divine inspiration.

Let me make way at this point for another writer of whose comments I am reminded by the words 'stand or fall'. This man, whose services to the Bible are too considerable for his serious commitment to the Christian religion to be in any doubt, even by the Pastor's standards, declares:[20]

> The question of whether the books of the New Testament are in-spired by God is not nearly so important for the Christian religion as the previous question of whether they are genuine. *It does not stand or fall with this inspiration alone.* Supposing that God did not inspire any of the books of the New Testament, but simply left Matthew, Mark, Luke, John, and Paul to their own devices to record what they knew, and that the writings themselves were merely old, genuine, and credible, the Christian religion would still remain the true religion. The miracles by which it is confirmed would prove its truth just as well if those who witnessed them were not inspired, but purely human witnesses; for in examining the truth of these miracles, we do not in any case assume the divine authority of the writers, but regard them only as human witnesses. If the miracles reported by

---

[20] The following quotation is from Johann David Michaelis (cf. note 12 on p. 73 above), *Einleitung in die göttlichen Schriften des neuen Bundes* [*Introduction to the Holy Scriptures of the New Testament*] (1750).

the evangelist were true, the sayings of Christ which they confirm would also be the infallible word of God, albeit with the minor fear and exception that the narrator might perhaps have misunderstood something and not reported it to us entirely accurately. And even if the apostles were mistaken in minor matters, we would still be able to learn the main features of the Christian religion, which were so often reiterated and which Christ sent them out to preach, as reliably from their epistles as we learn Wolff's philosophical doctrines, for example, from Bilfinger's[21] synopsis. It would therefore be quite possible for someone to have doubts concerning the divine inspiration of the entire New Testament writings, or indeed to deny it altogether, and still sincerely believe the Christian religion; and there really are some people who think in this way, sometimes in private but sometimes also in public, and who must not immediately be classed as non-Christians. It may also be said – not in order to denigrate them but simply as a fact – that some ancient heretics who accepted the New Testament writings as genuine, but did not regard them as an infallible basis of knowledge and instead set themselves up as judges of the apostles, may well have thought along the same lines. –

How amply this passage would protect me if I needed to seek its protection! But I have no such need; and it was even less my intention to follow the custom of those villainous beggars whose only method of fending off vicious dogs is to set them on somebody else. For if I know Pastor Goeze, he is too concerned with his own advantage not to retain his grip on *me* rather than launch a new onslaught on someone like Michaelis.

---

[21] Georg Bernhard Bilfinger published a popular synopsis of Wolff's philosophy in 1725.

New hypothesis on the evangelists as merely human historians

Wolfenbüttel, 1778

1 Contents

Firstly, the hypothesis will be expounded in plain and simple language.
Next, the critical evidence in support of it, and all that led up to it, will
be presented.
After which its possible advantages in *resolving* various difficulties and
providing more precise explanations of disputed passages of Scripture
will be demonstrated, and finally submitted to closer examination.

2 Preface

These are the first outlines of a treatise on which I have been working for
many years. It was certainly not my intention to lay it before the world
until it was completely finished. But circumstances have intervened which
compel me to offer a foretaste of it.

For I have been rudely compelled to explain my position on certain
matters which are very closely connected with the present hypothesis. If
I have erred in my hypothesis, or in the matters referred to, or in both, it
will nevertheless be found that I did not go astray without a map, and that
I have used throughout one and the same map which is decried as more
inaccurate than careful checks and measurements are likely to confirm. –
To find the right path is often pure good luck; to endeavour to find the
right path is alone commendable.

Besides, since this discussion concerns only a hypothesis and I neither dispute nor deny the superior worth of the evangelists, this superior worth is entirely compatible with my hypothesis. I therefore hope that I shall cause no more offence or annoyance than is my intention.

It goes without saying, however, that I shall recognise as my assessors and judges only those theologians whose minds are as rich in cold, critical scholarship as they are free from prejudice; and I shall pay little heed to the judgements of all other members of their profession, however deserving of my respect they may be on other grounds.

§1

The first followers of Christ were exclusively Jews, and in accordance with Christ's example, they did not cease to live as Jews.* The other Jews gave them the name of *Nazarenes*, concerning which I need only refer to Acts 24.5.

> *For even if there were some Jewish proselytes among them, they were certainly not just proselytes of the *gate*, but proselytes of *righteousness* who, along with circumcision, had accepted the entire Mosaic law, as with Nicolas in Acts 6.5.

§2

The Jews may, of course, have given them this name out of contempt. But it was nevertheless very much in accord with the attitude of Christ's disciples not to repudiate a nickname which they shared in common with their master, but to transform the opprobrium which was thereby attached to them into an honour by freely accepting it.*

> *Epiphanius[1] says so explicitly: 'The disciples of Christ, called by others *Nazarenes*, did not reject this name (although they perceived the intention of those who gave it to them), because they were so designated on account of Christ.' (*Panarion*, xxix, 6.7)

---

[1] Epiphanius (c. 315–402), Church Father and author of *Panarion*, a history of Christian sects and heresies.

§3

Consequently, nothing could induce them to part readily with this name. On the contrary, we have reason to believe that, even after the name 'Christians' had arisen in Antioch and long since become universal,[2] the Jewish Christians* of Palestine must have greatly preferred their old name of *Nazarenes*, and retained it the more willingly because it served to distinguish them from the uncircumcised Christians towards whom they still entertained a certain aversion, many traces of which can be found in the New Testament.

> *At least in part. For how else could it have come about that, many centuries later, in the same region and under the same name, a variety of Christians survived who confessed the same principles and lived in complete isolation from the universal Church which consisted chiefly of Gentiles?

§4

Would it then be safe to assume that those original *Nazarenes*, very early on and soon after the death of Christ, had a written collection of re-ports concerning Christ's life and teachings which had grown out of the oral narratives of the apostles and of all those persons who had lived in association with Christ? – Why not?*

> *What I merely *postulate* here will be shown below to have been actually the case. Only those who are entirely ignorant of how curious the mass of people are about everything to do with a great man who has once gained their sympathy will challenge me on this postulate. And as a mass always seeks to increase its numbers, it is natural that everything that can be discovered about the great man is passed from hand to hand, and this must finally be done by written means when oral communication no longer suffices.

§5

And how, approximately, would this collection have looked? – Like a collection of reports whose beginnings are so insignificant that we feel able

---

[2] See Acts 11.26.

to forget their originators[3] without ingratitude; which are then enlarged from time to time by more than one person and copied by more than one person, with all the freedom which people allow themselves with such unattributable works – like any such collection, I say, might ever look. It is basically always the same, but every time it is copied, it is to some extent enlarged, to some extent abridged, or to some extent altered, just as the copyist or the owner of the copy might consider that he had accumulated more or better reports from the mouths of credible people who had lived with Christ.*

*If we now, in more recent times, have few examples – or none at all – of such historical reports which, like snowballs, grow at one moment and melt away at the next, this is because one or other of the first copies very soon acquires definitive form in its printed transcription. But anyone who has had frequent occasion to look through old manuscript chronicles of major cities or distinguished families will certainly know the extent to which each owner of each particular copy considered himself entitled to extend his proprietory right, as often as he liked, even to the text itself and to the length or brevity he wished to impose on it.

§6

And when the process of enlarging or altering this collection eventually had to stop – because those contemporaries on whose credible narratives everyone had seen fit to base such changes inevitably died out – what would the collection have been called? – Either, I imagine, it would have been called after the earliest authorities for the information it contained, or after the people for whose use the collection had primarily been made, or after this or that individual who had first given it an improved form or expressed it in more intelligible language.

§7

If it had been called after the original authorities, what would its title have been? – The original authorities were all people who had lived with Christ and had been more or less acquainted with him. They even included a

---

[3] See Luke 1.1–2.

number of women[4] whose little anecdotes of Christ were all the less deserving of contempt the more intimately some of them had been associated with him. But it was primarily from the mouths of his apostles that the most numerous and reliable reports were undoubtedly derived. Thus this collection would have been called *The Gospel of the Apostles* ('gospel' in the sense of a historical account of Christ's life and teachings).

§8

And if it were called after those for whose use it had expressly been made, what would its title have been? – What else but *The Gospel of the Nazarenes*? Or among those who did not wish to use the word 'Nazarenes', *The Gospel of the Hebrews*. For this name also belonged quite properly to the Nazarenes as Palestinian Jews.

§9

And finally, if it had been called after this or that individual who had first given it an improved form or translated it into a more intelligible language, what would its title have been? – What else but the gospel of this or that person who deserved the credit for so doing? –

§10

It will so far have seemed to my readers that I am intent on losing myself in empty conjectures, whereas they expect something quite different from me. – Let them be patient: for what they have hitherto taken for empty conjectures is no more and none other than what I have abstracted from credible historical evidence, which anyone else who wished to proceed less cautiously might well have used as direct proof of his assertions.

§11

For we do in fact find that the Nazarenes of the fourth century not only *claimed* to have, but *actually did* have, just such a collection of reports

---

[4] See Mark 15.40f.

concerning Christ and his teaching. They had their own distinct Chaldaic-Syriac gospel which the Church Fathers sometimes refer to as *The Gospel of the Apostles*, sometimes as *The Gospel of the Hebrews*, and sometimes as *The Gospel of Matthew*. It was given these three titles – in the third case *presumably* – for the reasons advanced respectively in §§7, 8, and 9 above.

§12

I say *presumably*, and this is the only supposition which I allow myself and build upon in my entire hypothesis. It also rests on so many grounds that no historical supposition in the world can have a greater claim to acceptance as historical truth.

§13

And yet I do not wish to conclude directly from this correspondence between the actual gospel of the later Nazarenes of the fourth century and a purely hypothetical gospel such as the very first Nazarenes must have had – if they did in fact have one – that the two were necessarily identical. For it may be said that the later Nazarenes were heretics, and the very first Nazarenes were simply Jewish Christians of weak faith, so that the former could well have put together something of which the latter were wholly ignorant.

§14

Let us therefore proceed as circumspectly as possible. – Did any Church Father who mentions the gospel of the later Nazarenes ever express such a suspicion, or utter the least word to suggest it? – Never; not one of them.

§15

Did not the most learned and perspicacious Church Fathers always speak of it rather with a certain respect – not indeed as a gospel inspired by the Holy Spirit, but nevertheless as an indubitably ancient work, written at or shortly after the time of the apostles? Certainly.

§16

Did not one of them, who was undoubtedly the only one of all the Church Fathers capable of using a Chaldaic-Syriac work, even believe on several occasions that he could use various passages from it to elucidate the Greek text of the existing evangelists? – Certainly: I refer to Jerome.[5]

§17

Did not this same Jerome consider it worthy of translation, and indeed of translation into two different languages? He says so himself.

§18

What reason is there therefore to deny that the gospel of the later Nazarenes originated with the first and earliest Nazarenes? Is it not rather wholly credible that the Syriac-Chaldaic gospel, which in Jerome's time was in the hands of the Nazarenes or Ebionites[6] of that period, must also have been in the hands of the Nazarenes at the time of the apostles? And that it must have been the written gospel which the apostles themselves first used?

§19

The later Nazarenes were, of course, *called* heretics. But basically, they *were* no more heretics than the early Nazarenes, who were not yet described as such (as we may conclude from the silence of Irenaeus).[7] For both groups believed themselves obliged to retain the ceremonial law of Moses along with Christianity.

§20

That the early Nazarenes were of no relevance whatsoever to the later Nazarenes was a figment of the *young* Mosheim when he brashly attacked

---

[5] Jerome: see note 1 to p. 89 above.
[6] A Jewish-Christian sect which used a version of St Matthew's Gospel.
[7] Irenaeus: see note 14 to p. 137 above.

one Church Father in order to hit out at the others as well; but the *older and wiser* Mosheim recanted this himself.[8]

§21

The small deviations [from the existing gospels], however, which can still be detected in the few surviving fragments of the Nazarene gospel which deal with the same topic, and from which some are inclined to extract the conclusion that the Ebionite and Nazarene gospels were entirely different, should rather be explained by their manner of origin (as I have assumed as probable in §6 above). For since it could not occur to any early Nazarene to regard a work gradually compiled from various reports as a divine book which admitted of no subtraction or addition, it was no wonder that the copies did not all agree.

§22

But if the Gospel of the Nazarenes was not some misconceived production substituted at a later date, it was also older than all our four gospels, the first of which was written at least thirty years after Christ's death.[9]

§23

And is it at all conceivable that, in these thirty years, there was no written record whatsoever of Christ and his teachings? that the first person who decided to compose one, after so long a time, sat down to write it simply from his own or others' memory? that he had nothing in front of him with which to justify himself if he were taken to task over this or that circumstance? This is simply incredible, even if he were inspired. For only he himself was aware of the inspiration, and people probably shrugged their shoulders even then at those who claimed to know historical facts by means of inspiration.

---

[8] Mosheim: see note 1 to p. 37 above; the works in question are two treatises on the Nazarenes and Ebionites (1719) and *De rebus Christianorum ante Constantinum Magnum commentarii* [*Commentaries on the History of Christianity before Constantine the Great*] (1753).

[9] According to today's scholarship, all of the lost versions referred to by Lessing are later than that of Matthew. Lessing's erroneous chronology is based on ambiguous designations of the works in question by Epiphanius and Jerome (see editor's comments in B VIII, 1092).

§24

There was, then, a written account of Christ older than that of Matthew, and for those thirty years it remained in the only language in which its authors could have written it. Or to put the matter less precisely but more accurately: it remained in the Hebrew language, or in the Syriac-Chaldaic dialect of this language, as long as Christianity was still largely confined to Palestine and to the Palestinian Jews.

§25

Only after Christianity was disseminated among the Gentiles, and so many people who knew no Hebrew or any modern dialect of it became anxious to acquire more precise information concerning Christ's person (which is unlikely to have happened in the earliest years of the Gentile mission, because the very first to be converted were content with the oral reports which their respective apostles gave them), was it considered necessary and useful to satisfy so pious a curiosity by turning to that Nazarene source and making extracts or translations from it in what was virtually the language of the entire civilised world.

§26

The first of these extracts, the first of these translations, was, in my opinion, made by Matthew. – And this, as already mentioned in §12 above, is the supposition which may be boldly included among the historical truths which we do possess concerning these matters. For not only is everything that we know, or can reasonably assume, concerning both Matthew as a person and his gospel wholly in accord with this supposition; it is also the case that a great deal which remains a mystery, despite the best efforts of innumerable scholars, can only be explained by this means.

§27

For *firstly*, Matthew is considered to be indisputably the first and earliest of our evangelists.[10] But this, as already stated, cannot possibly mean that

---

[10] Since the nineteenth century, the Gospel of Mark has generally been considered the earliest.

he was the very first to make any written record of Christ which the new converts possessed. It can only mean that he was the first to do so in the Greek language.

§28

Secondly, it is very likely that Matthew was the only one of the apostles who understood Greek without having to receive knowledge of this language directly from the Holy Spirit.

§29

Thirdly, this is confirmed by the circumstances under which Matthew is said to have composed his gospel. For Eusebius[11] writes: 'When Matthew, who preached the gospel to the Hebrews in Palestine for a number of years, finally decided to go to others with the same intention, he left his written gospel with the Hebrews in their mother tongue so that he might remain their teacher even during his absence.'* But only half of this statement is likely to be strictly true. Only the occasion on which Matthew wrote his gospel can be correct; but this occasion was not one on which he had to write a *Hebrew* gospel, but one on which he thought it necessary to compose a gospel in Greek. That is, after he had preached for long enough to the Hebrews, he did not leave his gospel behind for them in Hebrew (for various apostles still remained in Palestine, and the Hebrews could receive their oral instruction at any time); on the contrary, since he wished to preach the gospel to others who did not understand Hebrew, he now made extracts, for his future use, from the Hebrew *Gospel of the Apostles* in the language which a greater number of people understood.

> *This may be the place to correct a passage in Jerome. Jerome says in the introduction to his commentaries on Matthew: 'The first of them all [i.e. the evangelists] is Matthew, who edited a Gospel in the Hebrew language in Judaea, chiefly for the use of those among the Jews who believed in Jesus and *in no way* observed the shadow of the law, since they followed the truth of the Gospel.' They *in no way* (*nequaquam*) observed the shadow of the law? But the first

---

[11] Eusebius of Caesarea (c. 265–339), Church Father and author of the *Historia ecclesiastica* [*History of the Church*], from which Lessing's quotation is taken (III.24.6).

Jews in Judaea to become Christians certainly did remain stubbornly attached to the law. I therefore think that, for *nequaquam*, we should read *nequicquam*, [in the sense of] *incassum*, i.e. 'to no purpose' or 'in vain'.

And that Matthew really wrote for the Nazarenes – that is, for Jewish Christians who wished to associate Moses and Christ – can be seen from Matthew 5.17–20, where he has Jesus say something which no other evangelist reports him as saying, and which no doubt made the Nazarenes so stubborn – especially verse 17, where it is simply ridiculous to relate the reference not to the Mosaic law in general, but to the moral law alone. The interpretation in the Babylonian Talmud is undoubtedly the correct one. See the English Bible edition.[12]

We now, of course, have reason – indeed, we can claim the right – to interpret this passage differently. But could the first Jewish Christians be blamed for understanding it as they did?

In the same way, Mark and Luke have omitted the command which Matthew 10.5–6 has the Saviour give to those disciples whom he sent out to heal and perform miracles.

§30

Fourthly, this settles the dispute over the original language of Matthew in a manner satisfactory to both parties – both to those who, in accordance with the unanimous testimony of the Church Fathers, maintain that the original language of Matthew's Gospel was Hebrew, and to the Protestant dogmatic theologians of more recent times who have, and are bound to have, their reservations concerning this view.

§31

For the original of Matthew was certainly Hebrew, but Matthew himself was not the actual author of this original. It is true that various reports in the Hebrew original may have originated with him, as an apostle; but he himself had not put those reports down in writing. Others had recorded his oral reports in Hebrew and combined them with reports from the

---

[12] An eight-volume edition of the Bible in French, drawing on English anti-deistic apologetics, begun by Charles-Pierre Chais in 1742; a German edition appeared between 1749 and 1770.

rest of the apostles, and from this human collection he simply made, in due course, a coherent selection in Greek. But because his selection, his translation, followed so quickly upon the original, because he himself could just as well have written in Hebrew, and because it was more likely, given his personal circumstances, that he really did write in Hebrew, it was no wonder that the original was to some extent confused with the translation.

§32

And everyone will recognise how much those modern theologians stand to gain who, from the internal characteristics of Matthew and for not insignificant dogmatic reasons, believe they must conclude that Matthew cannot really have written in any language other than that in which we now have him. Matthew wrote what he wrote in Greek; but he drew it from a Hebrew source.

§33

If, then, he made this selection in a better-known language with all the diligence and all the caution which such an enterprise deserved, he was indeed assisted, even in purely human terms, by a good spirit. And no one can object if one calls this good spirit the Holy Spirit. And this must surely be how Matthew went to work; such a good spirit must indeed have guided and supported him. For not only did his selection or translation very soon acquire canonic status among the Christians in general; even among the Nazarenes themselves, the name of the Greek translator henceforth became attached to the Hebrew original, which was itself declared to be a work of Matthew. The Gospel *secundum Apostolos* [according to the apostles] was eventually called by most people *juxta Matthaeum* [according to Matthew], as Jerome expressly says.[13]

§34

That I have not picked up the wrong thread is shown by the long unbroken strand which it allows me to unwind from a very tangled ball.

---

[13] Jerome, *Dialogi contra Pelagianos* [*Dialogues against the Pelagians*] III.2.

That is, I am able to explain by this hypothesis of mine twenty things which remain insoluble problems if one accepts one or other of the usual propositions concerning the original language of Matthew. I shall cite the most important of them here, because it is common knowledge that, in critical matters, the new insights which a newly adopted opinion affords are so many proofs of its truth.

§35

When Epiphanius[14] says, for example, that the Nazarenes possessed the Gospel of Matthew 'in its most complete form in Hebrew', what comment can one make that is not open to some objection? – If Matthew himself wrote this complete Hebrew text, our Greek Matthew cannot be complete. – If Matthew originally wrote in Greek, then the Nazarenes have augmented it in their translation with human additions, which they would not have done if it had possessed the canonic status which it now enjoys. And how could Origen and Jerome take these additions so lightly? – Only in my interpretation do Epiphanius' words take on their correct sense. The Hebrew original of Matthew contained more than Matthew saw fit to include in his Greek selection. The extra material in the Hebrew Gospel of Matthew was not added by the later Nazarenes, but omitted by Matthew.

§36

Similarly, who can give answers to the following? – If Matthew originally wrote in Greek, how does it come about that the Church Fathers unanimously maintain that his gospel was written in Hebrew? – And if he originally wrote his gospel in Hebrew, how could this original Gospel be allowed to get lost? – Who, I ask, can answer these questions as satisfactorily as I can? – The Church Fathers found a Hebrew gospel which contained everything in Matthew and more besides, and they consequently regarded it as Matthew's own work. – But although this supposed Hebrew Matthew was indeed the source of the historical part of Matthew's Gospel, only the Greek selection was the actual work of an apostle who wrote under

---

[14] *Panarion* XXIX.9.4.

higher oversight. What, then, did it matter if the materials were lost after being put to the best and most credible use?

§37

Nothing, however, does more to confirm my opinion that Matthew did not write in Hebrew but merely translated and used a Hebrew original so faithfully and cautiously that the original itself was given his name – nothing, I say, does more to confirm this opinion than the fact that it renders intelligible a passage in Papias which has given so many commentators such thankless trouble. Papias says, as Eusebius tells us: 'Matthew wrote his Gospel in Hebrew; but each man translated it as best he could (ὡς ἠδύνατο ἕκαστος).'[15]

§38

The last words of this passage are, however, so problematic that people have seen fit to deny the good Papias all credibility with respect to the first part. They have not been able to accept that Papias really intended to say what his words so obviously do say. It is in particular very amusing to read what a drubbing Clericus gives him on this score,[16] and the schoolmasterly way in which he corrects the Greek words of the Greek writer, without considering that he is schoolmastering not so much Papias as Eusebius, or at any rate Eusebius as well as Papias (for every writer must also take responsibility for the words he quotes from someone else, in so far as they appear to contain nonsense which he accepts without the least word of censure).

§39

As I have said, there are certainly grounds for taking Papias to task and asking him whether he really knew what he meant by 'as best he could'. Was our Greek Matthew not as good a translation as could possibly be expected? Were there really several Greek translations of his Hebrew

---

[15] Papias (c. 60–120), Bishop of Hierapolis, quoted by Eusebius in *Historia ecclesiastica* III.39.16.

[16] Clericus: see note 10 to p. 72 above; the quotation is probably from his *Historia ecclesiastica duorum primorum . . . saeculorum* [*History of the Church in the First Two Centuries*] (1716).

Matthew in existence? And if so, how did it come about that there is not the slightest trace of these several translations anywhere? – It is impossible to tell what Papias might say in reply to these questions.

§40

But if my assumption is accepted that Papias was not referring to an original Hebrew Matthew, but to the Hebrew original of Matthew which, because Matthew was the first to make it generally known and accessible, henceforth circulated under his name, what is absurd about Papias' statement that several more people nevertheless set to work on the Hebrew original and produced further versions of it in Greek?

§41

Have we not already seen that Matthew was not a mere translator of everything and anything which he found in the Gospel of the Nazarenes? He left out much that was not known to him as entirely credible. There were accounts in it derived from all eleven apostles, many of which, though doubtless true, were not of sufficient use to Christian posterity. There were accounts derived solely from Christ's female acquaintances, and it was doubtful in some cases whether they had always properly understood the wonderful man whom they loved so much. There were accounts which could only have been derived from his mother, from people who had known him in his childhood in the house of his parents; and however reliable they were, of what help could they be to the world, which has enough to learn concerning what he did and said after he took up his office as a teacher?

§42

What, then, was more natural? – Since no infallible sign of divinity could be stamped on Matthew's translation, and since it could attain its canonic status only by examination and comparison and thereby have it confirmed by the Church – what was more natural than that several others who either did not know Matthew's work or did not wholly approve of it (because they would have preferred this or that to be added to it, or this or that

to be recounted differently) should have applied themselves to the same
task, each performing it to the best of his ability, i.e. 'as best he could' (ὡς
ἠδύνατο ἕκαστος)?

§43

And so we stand here at the source from which were derived both the better
gospels that are still extant and the inferior ones which, because they were
inferior, ceased to be used and eventually disappeared altogether.*

> *It is a complete misconception to imagine that the heretics invented
> false gospels. Quite the reverse: since there were so many kinds of
> gospel, all of which arose from the same Nazarene source, there were
> so many heretics, each of whom had as much evidence in his favour
> as the next.
>
> For example, it is not remotely credible that Cerinthus[17] made a
> gospel of his own. He possessed nothing more than his own transla-
> tion of the Hebrew original of Matthew.
>
> Jerome explicitly says so (in the preface to his commentary on
> Matthew): 'That there were several people who wrote gospels is also
> confirmed by the evangelist Luke, when he says: "Forasmuch as . . ."
> [Luke 1.1–4]; this is also shown by still extant writings which, pro-
> duced by different authors, became the source of various heresies.'
>
> Thus Epiphanius also says of the Sabellians[18] (*Panarion*, lxii, 2.4)
> that they derived their entire error from the false gospels: 'But they
> have derived all their confusion from certain apocryphal works, above
> all from the so-called Egyptian gospel.'

§44

On the evidence of Luke alone, we should have to accept that there were
many gospels of this second variety, even if we did not know it from
Church history. For Luke cannot really have been referring to the (wholly
fictitious) forged gospels and apostolic writings of the heretics,* but of
necessity to gospels whose basic contents were in fact unexceptionable,
even if their order, presentation, and intention was not entirely pure and

[17] Cerinthus: Gnostic heretic of the first century.
[18] Sabellians: followers of Sabellius, Unitarian heretic of the third century.

incorrupt, when he says that it was these which encouraged and entitled him to write his own history of the Lord.

> *'Epiphanius and Ambrose[19] believe that Luke was referring here to the gospels of the heretics Basilides,[20] Cerinthus, and others, as Daniel Heinsius[21] (*Sacrorum exercitationum ad Novum Testamentum libri xx*, Bk III, Ch. 1) has already noted.' (Masch, §30)[22]
>
> 'Basilides also dared to write a gospel under his own name', writes Origen (in his first sermon on Luke). Ambrose says the same (in his commentary on Luke), as does Jerome (in the preface to his commentary on Matthew). But Basilides lived in the second century, so how could Luke be referring to his gospel? – If, that is, Basilides really did write one, and Ambrose and Jerome are not just echoing Origen, who probably made this assertion without justification! (See Mosheim's *De rebus Christianorum ante Constantinum Magnum commentarii*, p. 357.)[23] But not one of them says that Luke was referring to it; they mention this gospel only in their comments on Luke; and that is a major lapse on the part of Herr Masch.
>
> As to Cerinthus, it is more likely that Luke was referring to him, and Epiphanius (*Panarion*, li, p. 428) seems to confirm this. But since Epiphanius says elsewhere that he only accepted the Gospel of Matthew, the gospel of Cerinthus will again have been simply his own translation of the Hebrew original.
>
> I do find in general that the heretics were accused of falsifying gospel history (though not as often as people imagine: for Origen says (*Contra Celsum*, ii, 27)[24] that this was done only by the pupils of Marcion[25] and Valentinos,[26] and, he adds, 'if I am not mistaken, of Lucanus').[27] But no evidence can be found that the heretics forged gospels wholly of their own invention. Their gospels were once again old narratives circulating under the names of the apostles or of apostolic men, except that they were not those which had been generally accepted by the Church. They did indeed come from the same source as these, except that those who drew from this source were less reliable.

---

[19] Ambrose (c. 339–97), Church Father and author of a commentary on Luke.
[20] Basilides: second-century Gnostic of Alexandria.
[21] Daniel Heinsius, Dutch philologist and author of the *Theological Studies of the New Testament* (1639), to which Lessing here refers by its Latin title.
[22] Andreas Gottlieb Masch, *Abhandlung von der Grundsprache des Evangelii Matthäi* [*Treatise on the Original Language of St Matthew's Gospel*] (1755).
[23] See note 8 above.   [24] See note 1 to p. 83 above.   [25] Marcion (c. 85–160), Gnostic heretic.
[26] Valentinos (c. 100–60), Egyptian Gnostic.   [27] Lucanus: follower of Marcion.

§45

I might even be inclined to think that, in the passage of Luke already mentioned, the Hebrew source is explicitly alluded to by its title, which could well have been (in Hebrew, of course) 'A narrative of the things which have been fulfilled among us' [Luke 1.1].* It may be that the subsequent words 'following the traditions handed down to us by the original eyewitnesses and ministers of the word' formed part of the title, or were simply added by Luke to give a clearer indication of that authentic collection.**

> *This title sounds quite Hebraic to me, although I cannot specify myself or with the help of others what it may have been called, for example, in Syriac or Chaldean. It is likely that it refers to the various prophecies which were fulfilled by the events associated with Christ and by his teachings and actions, as in the frequently occurring formula in Matthew: 'But all this happened so that what the Lord said through the prophet might be fulfilled.' (Matthew 1.22, 2.17, 4.14, 8.17, 12.17, 13.14)
>
> **In both cases, this confirms what I said in general in §§2–4 concerning the people who had a share, so to speak, in writing the Gospel of the Nazarenes. 'Ministers of the word' are the apostles, as the main contributors after whom the whole collection was called; and 'eyewitnesses' are all those, both male and female, who had personal knowledge of Christ.

§46

And if I were consequently to translate the whole first verse of Luke, namely Ἐπειδήπερ πολλοὶ ἐπεχείρησαν ἀνατάξασθαι διήγησιν περὶ τῶν πεπληροφορημένων ἐν ἡμῖν πραγμάτων, [into Latin] as: 'Quoniam quidem multi conati sunt, *iterum iterumque* in ordinem redigere narrationem *illam* de rebus quae in nobis completae sunt', what real objection could be raised against it?*

> *It seems to me, at any rate, that to translate ἀνατάξασθαι διήγησιν simply as 'litteris mandare' (i.e. 'to write' or 'to record') does not exhaust the meaning of these words. For ἀνα does seem to indicate here a frequent repetition, which goes very well with ἐπεχείρησαν, 'they have taken in hand'. I would consequently rather translate

it as 'Since many have *repeatedly* attempted to put into order that narrative of the things which have been fufilled among us, so...' (etc.). The task of 'putting into order' that old collection which had grown up from such varied accounts in so random a fashion was doubtless the more difficult part, and that of translating it, once the order had been decided, was undeniably easier. It is therefore not surprising that Luke refers only to the more difficult part in order to designate the entire work.

All this would, of course, be more plausible if τήν ['this'] came in front of διήγησιν ['narrative'].

§47

Indeed, although I offer this translation and interpretation only as a critical conjecture, which is far less bold and adventurous than critical conjectures generally are nowadays, it does seem to me that this is the only means of removing all the objections which can be raised against Luke's words.*

*For if he says, in line with the usual translation: 'Forasmuch as many have ventured to give an account of the events which have taken place among us, as handed down to us by those who from the beginning were eyewitnesses and ministers of the word', are we not justified in at once interrupting Luke to say: 'Then have those many written nothing but what the eyewitnesses and first ministers of the word reported it? And if so, my dear Luke, what need is there for your work which, despite all the care you have devoted to it, cannot do any better? You have always investigated everything yourself from the beginning: then were you able to investigate it more fully than "as it was handed down to us by those who from the beginning were eyewitnesses and ministers of the word"?' Only if these last words are either part of the title of the first Hebrew document, or were added to by Luke to describe it more closely and accurately so that they apply to the Hebrew document itself and not to the ordering and translating undertaken by many, was Luke justified in undertaking a similar task after he had investigated everything from the beginning – i.e. after he had examined and confirmed everything contained in the Hebrew document in the light of the oral explanations of those apostles to whom he had occasion to speak.

§48

But be that as it may, it is enough that this much is certain: Luke himself had before him the Hebrew document, the Gospel of the Nazarenes, and he transferred if not all, at least most of it, into his gospel, only in a somewhat different order and in somewhat better language.

§49

It is even more certain that Mark, who is commonly held to be only an epitomiser of Matthew, gives this impression simply because he drew on the same Hebrew document, but presumably had a less complete copy before him.*

> *That he did in fact draw directly on the Hebrew document is shown by Mark 5.41, which quotes the actual Chaldaic words spoken by Christ when he raised the daughter of Jairus, words not found in either Matthew or Luke. See also 'Corban' in Mark 7.11.
>
> Mark is supposed to have been the interpreter and trusted disciple of Peter. This is doubtless why he came to omit what Matthew 14.28–31 relates concerning Peter. On the other hand, it is all the more incomprehensible why he also omitted what Matthew relates of Peter in 16.17, even though he (Mark) retains 8.33.

§50

In short, Matthew, Mark, and Luke are simply different yet not different translations of the so-called Hebrew Gospel of Matthew, which each translator accomplished as best he could: ὡς ἠδύνατο ἕκαστος.

§51

And St John? – John most certainly knew and read that Hebrew document and used it in his gospel. Nevertheless, his gospel should not be grouped together with the others as belonging to the Nazarene class: on the contrary, it is in a class of its own.

§52

The view that John merely wished to write a supplement to the other three gospels is certainly without foundation.* One only needs to read him to gain quite a different impression.**28

§53

That John consequently had no knowledge of the other three gospels is, however, both unprovable and incredible.

§54

Instead, he felt himself called upon to write his gospel precisely because he had read the other three, as well as several others derived from the Nazarene document, and because he saw what kind of effect these gospels had.

§55

For we need only recall who the authors of the Gospel of the Nazarenes actually were. They were all people who had personal associations with Christ, and who must therefore have been thoroughly convinced of Christ as a man; and apart from Christ's own words, which they had impressed on their memory more faithfully than they had grasped them clearly through their understanding, they could not relate anything about him which could not also have been true of a mere human being, albeit one who performed miracles and was furnished with powers from on high.

§56

Was it therefore any wonder that not just the Jewish Christians of Palestine to whom the name 'Nazarenes' was particularly applied, but all and sundry Jews and Gentiles who had derived their knowledge of Christ directly or indirectly from the Nazarene document, did not pay sufficient reverence to Christ from the point of view of his divinity?

28 The asterisks in this paragraph indicate footnotes which Lessing planned to add.

§57

The Nazarenes, given their original background, could not possibly have wished to retain the Mosaic law in addition [to the Christian faith] if they had regarded Christ as more than an extraordinary prophet. Indeed, even if they also regarded him as the true promised Messiah, and called him, as the Messiah, the Son of God, it still cannot be denied that they did not mean by this a Son of God who was of the same essence as God.

§58

Anyone who is reluctant to admit this with regard to the first Jewish Christians must at least concede that the Ebionites – that is, those Jewish Christians who, before the destruction of Jerusalem, settled beyond the Jordan in Pella, and even in the fourth century recognised no other gospel than the Hebrew original of Matthew – that the Ebionites, I say, according to Origen's testimony, had a very inadequate conception of Christ, even if it is not true that their very name was derived from this impoverished way of thinking.[29]

§59

Similarly Cerinthus, who was certainly a Jew (but scarcely a Palestinian Jew, because he is classed among the Gnostics), regarded Christ as merely the legitimate son of Joseph and Mary, born in the normal course of nature, because – or in consequence of which – he considered either the Hebrew original of Matthew or the Greek Matthew as the only gospel.*

*Given the evidence I cited in my note to §44 above, it even seems credible to me that he made his own translation of the Hebrew original, and consequently himself belonged to those who, according to Papias, translated Matthew 'as best they could'.

§60

The same is true of Carpocrates,[30] who likewise either could have no higher idea of Christ because he accepted only Matthew, or could accept

[29] The reference is to Origen, *Against Celsus* II.I.   [30] Carpocrates: second-century Gnostic.

only Matthew because he believed he should have no higher idea of Christ.

§61

In a word: both orthodox and sectarians either had no conception at all of the divine person of Christ or a completely false conception, as long as no other gospel was available except the Hebrew document of Matthew or the Greek gospels derived from it.

§62

Thus, if Christianity was not to become dormant again and disappear among the Jews as a mere Jewish sect, and if it was to survive among the Gentiles as a distinct and independent religion, John had to intervene and write his gospel.

§63

His gospel alone gave the Christian religion its true identity. We have only his gospel to thank if the Christian religion, despite all attacks, still survives in this definitive form and will presumably last as long as there are human beings who think they require a mediator between themselves and the deity – that is, *for ever.*

§64

That we accordingly have only two gospels, Matthew and John – the gospel of the flesh and the gospel of the spirit – was recognised even by the early Church Fathers, and this has not yet been denied by any modern orthodox theologian.[31]

§65

And now I would only have to explain how it came about that the gospel of the flesh was preached by three evangelists – if I have not already done

---

[31] Lessing refers here to Lutheran orthodoxy.

so. For to be more precise, I would only have to explain why, out of many other Greek gospels derived from the Nazarene document, the Church retained, apart from Matthew, only Mark and Luke; for the reason which Augustine gives for this is hardly satisfactory.[32]

§66

I will state my opinion briefly. Mark and Luke were retained by the Church along with Matthew because they in many respects filled the gap, as it were, between Matthew and John, and because one was a pupil of Peter and the other a pupil of Paul.

§67

That, I say, is my opinion, which provides an adequate reason why the four evangelists were arranged together as they are, and in no other order, in nearly all the ancient copies. For it has not been demonstrated that they were written chronologically in this same order.

§68

But I cannot provide a proof for this opinion here, because it must be done inductively, and I cannot put together enough examples to turn such an induction into a kind of demonstration.

---

[32] Augustine (354–430), Church Father; Lessing's reference is to his *De consensu Evangelistarum* [*On the Unanimity of the Evangelists*] 1.2.4 and 1.3.6.

Necessary answer to a very unnecessary question of Herr Hauptpastor Goeze of Hamburg[1]

Wolfenbüttel, 1778

At last Hauptpastor Goeze, after such lengthy and tiresome preliminaries as only the worst kind of exhibition fencers employ, seems ready to take up his blade and concentrate on the fight.

At least he now declares that he will give immediate and proper attention to the point which he disputes with me, namely *whether the Christian religion could survive even if the Bible were lost completely, if it had been lost long ago, or if it had never existed*, as soon as I have given a definite statement concerning *what kind of religion I understand by the Christian religion*.

If I knew that my conscience were less clear than it is, who could hold it against me if I rejected this demand, which contains a genuine calumny, on the same grounds as those on which he sees fit to decline a far less offensive demand of mine? For he declares that 'the Librarian of Wolfenbüttel cannot give orders to the Hauptpastor in Hamburg'. Very true! But what authority does the Hauptpastor in Hamburg have over the Librarian in Wolfenbüttel that allows him to serve the latter with a public summons to answer a question which assumes that he cannot answer it satisfactorily?

But the Librarian will not insist on his rights. For the Librarian, as already mentioned, knows that his conscience is clear, and must laugh heartily when the Hauptpastor claims to be convinced 'that if I had known in advance that the controversy would take this course, I would have taken

---

[1] The work by Goeze to which Lessing here replies is reproduced in B IX, 357–94.

care not to give my position away so soon and to reveal the true sentiments of my heart'.

I wished for nothing more than that; and it will soon become apparent which one of us, the Hauptpastor or the Librarian, will leave the contest with his nose in one piece.

For in short, I shall answer the question before me as definitely as anyone can possibly require of me, by declaring that I understand by the Christian religion all those articles of faith which are contained in the creeds of the first four centuries of the Christian Church.

Lest the Hauptpastor should imagine that I might fall into the same trap as Whiston,[2] I shall add that I will even include among them the so-called Apostles' Creed and the Athanasian Creed, despite the fact that we know they do not belong to the period in question.

I could well let matters rest with this explanation, and wait to see how the Hauptpastor will choose to continue his campaign. For it is now up to him to prove:

(1) why the doctrines contained in those creeds must necessarily be lost if the Bible were lost;
(2) why these doctrines must have been lost long ago if the Bible had been lost; and
(3) why we would know nothing of these doctrines if the Bible had never existed.

But I do not wish to be responsible for prolonging our controversy unnecessarily, and I therefore append the following short sentences on which the Hauptpastor can take me to task at any time. But he must not try to take me to task on any of them until he has delivered his proof, otherwise our learned dispute will plainly turn into an inquisition. It is enough that he can gain from them a rough idea of what I have in reserve, and what he will have to face up to.

§1

The essential content of those confessions of faith was known among the earliest Church Fathers as the *regula fidei*.

---

[2] William Whiston (1667–1752), mathematician and theologian, denied that the doctrine of the Trinity was part of the early Christian faith and rejected as inauthentic those later creeds which refer to it.

§2

This *regula fidei* is not drawn from the writings of the New Testament.

§3

This *regula fidei* was in existence before a single book of the New Testament existed.

§4

This *regula fidei* is even older than the *Church*. For the intention for which, and the rules under which, a congregation is brought together must certainly be prior to the congregation itself.

§5

Not only the first Christians, in the lifetime of the apostles, were content with this *regula fidei*; the subsequent Christians of the entire first four centuries also regarded it as perfectly sufficient for Christianity.

§6

Thus this *regula fidei*, and *not the Scriptures*, is the rock on which the Church of Christ was built.

§7

This *regula fidei*, and *not Peter and his successors*, is the rock on which the Church of Christ was built.

§8

The writings of the New Testament, as contained in our present canon, were unknown to the first Christians, and the individual items which they did happen to know were never held by them in that esteem which they have enjoyed among some of us *since* the time of Luther.

§9

The laity of the early Church were not even allowed to read these individual items – not, at least, without the permission of the presbyter who was in charge of them.

§10

It was even considered no small offence if the laity of the early Church put more faith in the written word of an apostle than in the living word of their bishop.

§11

Even the writings of the apostles were judged in accordance with the *regula fidei*. The selection from these writings was made according to their degree of conformity to the *regula fidei*, and writings which conformed to it less closely were rejected, even if their authors were, or were alleged to be, apostles.

§12

In the first four centuries, the Christian religion was never proved by means of the New Testament writings, but at most elucidated and confirmed by them as the occasion arose.

§13

The proof that the apostles and evangelists wrote their works with the intention that the Christian religion should be wholly and completely extracted and demonstrated from them cannot be sustained.

§14

The proof that the Holy Spirit so ordered and arranged it by its guidance, even without the intention of the writers, is even less sustainable.

§15

The authenticity of the *regula fidei* can be demonstrated much more easily and correctly than the authenticity of the New Testament writings.

§16

The divine nature of the *regula fidei* can also be inferred with much greater certainty from its incontrovertibly demonstrated authenticity than, as is now supposed, the inspiration of the New Testament writings can be inferred from their authenticity. This, incidentally, is the *new and daring step* which makes the Librarian so dissatisfied with all newfangled demonstrations of the truth of the Christian religion.

§17

The writings of the apostles were not even regarded, in the first centuries, as an authentic commentary on the entire *regula fidei*.

§18

And that was precisely why the earliest Church would never allow the heretics to appeal to Scripture. That was precisely why they would on no account dispute with a heretic on the basis of Scripture.

§19

The whole true worth of the apostolic writings with regard to the articles of faith is simply that they occupy the highest position among the writings of the Christian teachers, and that, in so far as they agree with the *regula fidei*, they are its earliest attestations, but not its sources.

§20

The additional material which they contain over and above the *regula fidei* is not, in the opinion of the first four centuries, necessary to salvation; it may be true or false, and it can be interpreted in one way or another.

* * *

I have collected these propositions from my own careful and repeated reading of the Church Fathers of the first four centuries, and I am in a position to undertake the most rigorous scrutiny of the matter with the most learned patristic scholar. The best-read scholar has had no more sources to draw on than I. The best-read scholar can therefore know no more than I do, and it is by no means the case that such profound and extensive knowledge is required to get to the bottom of all these matters as some no doubt imagine, and as some would have the world believe.

I ought perhaps to add something more on the innocuous character of this system of mine, and at the same time to indicate the particular use and advantage which the Christian religion can expect from it in relation to its present enemies. But the further course of the controversy will afford me sufficient opportunity to do so, especially if the Hauptpastor is willing to keep it separate from the rest of our squabbles and to address it without bringing in new slanders.

To give him further encouragement to do so, I have carefully abstained in this pamphlet from all similes, all images, and all allusions,[3] and I am prepared to continue in this vein if he will employ the same precision and simplicity in his counter-propositions.

[3] Lessing refers here to those features of his own style to which Goeze had taken particular exception.

The religion of Christ

For the Father also seeketh those who thus worship him.

John 4. 23

§1

Whether Christ was more than a human being is a problem. That he was a true human being – if he was a human being at all – and that he never ceased to be a human being is not in dispute.

§2

Consequently, the religion of Christ and the Christian religion are two quite different things.

§3

The former, the religion of Christ, is that religion which he himself recognised and practised as a human being; which every human being can share with him; and which every human being must be all the more eager to share with him, the more exalted and amiable a character he ascribes to Christ as merely human.

§4

The latter, the Christian religion, is that religion which takes it as true that he was more than a human being, and makes Christ himself, as such, an object of its worship.

§5

How these two religions, the religion of Christ and the Christian religion, can exist in Christ as one and the same person is inconceivable.

§6

The doctrines and principles of both can scarcely be found in one and the same book. It is evident at least that the former, namely the religion of Christ, is contained in the evangelists quite differently from the Christian religion.

§7

The religion of Christ is contained in them in the most clear and distinct language.

§8

The Christian religion, on the other hand, is so uncertain and ambiguous that there is scarcely a single passage which any two individuals, throughout the history of the world, have thought of in the same way.

That more than five senses are possible for human beings

(1) The soul is a simple entity which is capable of infinite representations [*Vorstellungen*].

(2) Since, however, it is a finite entity, it is not capable of having these infinite representations all at once, but attains them gradually in an infinite temporal sequence.

(3) If it attains its representations gradually, there must be an order in which, and a measure according to which, it attains them.

(4) This order and this measure are the *senses*.

(5) It has at present five such senses. But nothing can persuade us to believe that it at once began to have representations with these five senses.

(6) If nature nowhere makes a leap, the soul will also have progressed through all the lower stages before it reached the stage at which it is at present. It will first have had each of these five senses singly, then all ten combinations of two, all ten combinations of three, and all five combinations of four before it acquired all five together.

(7) This is the route it has already covered, and there can have been very few stops along the way if it is true that the way which it still has to cover in its present condition continues to be so uniform – that is, if it is true that no other senses are possible beyond the present five, and that the soul will retain only these five senses for all eternity, so that the wealth of its representations can grow only through an increase in the perfection of its present senses.

(8) But how greatly this way which it has hitherto covered is extended if we contemplate, in a manner worthy of the creator, the way which still lies before it – that is, if we assume that far more senses are possible, all of which the soul has already possessed singly and in their simple groupings (i.e. every combination of two, three, or four) before it arrived at its present combination of five senses.

(9) That which has limits is called matter.

(10) The senses determine the limits of the soul's representations (cf. §4); the senses are therefore material.

(11) As soon as the soul began to have representations, it had a sense and was consequently conjoined with matter.

(12) But it was not at once conjoined with an organic body. For an *organic body* is a combination of several senses.

(13) Every particle of matter can serve as a sense for the soul. That is, the whole material world is animated down to its smallest parts.

(14) Particles which serve as a single sense for the soul constitute homogeneous elements.

(15) If we knew how many homogeneous masses the material world contains, we would also know how many senses are possible.

(16) But what is the need? It is enough that we know for sure that there are more than five homogeneous masses such as those which correspond to our present five senses.

(17) Thus, just as the sense of sight corresponds to the homogeneous mass through which bodies attain a condition of visibility (i.e. light), so also is it certain that particular senses can and will correspond, e.g., to electrical matter or organic matter, senses through which we shall immediately recognise whether bodies are in an electrical or magnetic state. We can at present attain this knowledge only by conducting experiments. All that we now know – or can know in our present human condition – about electricity or magnetism is no more than what Saunderson[1] knew

---

[1] Nicholas Saunderson (1682–1739), English mathematician who lost his sight at the age of one.

of optics. – But as soon as we ourselves have the sense of electricity or the sense of magnetism, we shall experience what Saunderson would have experienced if he had suddenly gained his sight. A whole new world will suddenly emerge for us, full of the most splendid phenomena, of which we can as little form a conception now as he could of light and colours.

(18) And just as we can now be assured of the existence of magnetic and electrical forces, or of the homogeneous elements (masses) in which these forces are active, despite the fact that little or nothing was known about them at one time, so also can we be confident that a hundred or a thousand other forces exist in their respective masses, although we do not yet know anything about them. For each of these, a corresponding sense will exist.

(19) Nothing can be said concerning the number of these as yet unknown senses. It cannot be infinite, but must be *determinate*, even though it *cannot be determined* by us.

(20) For if it were infinite, the soul would not have been able to gain possession of even two senses simultaneously throughout all eternity.

(21) Similarly, nothing can be said concerning the phenomena among which the soul will find itself when it is in possession of each individual sense.

(22) If we had only four senses and lacked the sense of sight, we would be as little able to form a conception of the latter as we can of a sixth sense. And so we can as little doubt the possibility of a sixth sense, and of further senses, as we could doubt the possibility of the fifth sense if we had only four. The sense of sight serves to make us sensible of the matter of light, and of all its relations to other bodies. How many other materials of this kind may there as yet be, diffused no less universally throughout creation!

* * *

This system of mine is surely the oldest of all philosophical systems. For it is in fact none other than the system of the soul's pre-existence and of metempsychosis, which not only Pythagoras and Plato, but the Egyptians and Chaldeans and Persians – in short, all the wise men of the East – thought of before them.

And this alone must predispose us in its favour. The first and oldest opinion in speculative matters is always the most probable one, because common sense immediately lit upon it.

But two things stood in the way of this oldest, and in my opinion uniquely probable, system. Firstly, –

Ernst and Falk: dialogues for Freemasons
To His Grace Duke Ferdinand[1]

Wolfenbüttel, 1778[2]

Most Gracious Duke,

I, too, was at the well of truth and have drawn from it. How deeply I have drawn, only he can judge from whom I await permission to draw more deeply. – The people have long craved refreshment and are dying of thirst. –

Your Grace's
most humble servant

– –

Preface by a third party[3]

If the following pages do not contain the true *ontology* of Freemasonry, I would very much like to know in which of the countless writings inspired by it a more precise definition of its *essential nature* is provided.

But if all Freemasons, whatever their stamp, will readily concede that the point of view indicated here is the only one from which healthy eyes can distinguish a true image (rather than a mere phantom as it appears

---

[1] Duke Ferdinand of Brunswick-Lüneburg, brother of the reigning duke and Grand Master (from 1772) of the 'Strict Observance' order of Freemasons in Germany; this is the only dedication in all of Lessing's works.

[2] The date of publication, like the dedication, applies only to the first three dialogues, which Lessing himself published in 1778 – not in Wolfenbüttel, as stated, but in Göttingen.

[3] Another of Lessing's subterfuges (perhaps occasioned by the ban of July 1778 on his publishing further writings on religion without advance approval by the Brunswick censorship); the preface is undoubtedly by him.

to defective eyesight), the only question which remains to be answered is this: why has no one spoken out so clearly long ago?

This question could be answered in many different ways. But it would be difficult to find another question which resembled it more closely than this: why did the systematic textbooks of Christianity arise at so late a stage? why have there been so many good Christians who neither could nor would define their faith in an intelligible manner?

And this might still have come too soon for Christianity – for the faith has perhaps derived little benefit from it – even if Christians had not taken it into their heads to define their faith in a completely absurd manner.

Readers may make the application for themselves.

First dialogue

Ernst. What are you thinking about, my friend?
Falk. Nothing.
Ernst. But you're so quiet.
Falk. For the same reason. Who thinks when he's enjoying himself? And I'm enjoying the refreshing morning.
Ernst. You're right; and you could well have given me back my question.
Falk. If I were thinking of something, I would talk about it. There's nothing better than *thinking aloud* with a friend.
Ernst. Certainly.
Falk. If *you*'ve had enough enjoyment from the fine morning and something occurs to you, then speak *yourself*. Nothing occurs to me.
Ernst. Well said! – It occurs to me that I've long been meaning to ask you something.
Falk. Then ask me it.
Ernst. Is it true, my friend, that you're a Freemason?
Falk. The question is that of one who isn't.
Ernst. Of course! – But give me a more direct answer. – Are you a Freemason?
Falk. I think I am.
Ernst. The answer is that of one who isn't exactly sure where he stands.
Falk. Not at all! I'm fairly sure where I stand.
Ernst. For you will surely know whether and when and where and by whom you were initiated.
Falk. I do indeed know that; but that wouldn't mean very much.

Ernst. No?

Falk. Who doesn't initiate, and who isn't initiated?

Ernst. Explain yourself.

Falk. I think I'm a Freemason; not so much because I was initiated by senior Masons in a properly constituted lodge, but because I understand and recognise what Freemasonry is and why it exists, when and where it has existed, and how and by what means it is helped or hindered.

Ernst. And yet you express yourself so equivocally? 'I think I am'!

Falk. It's just an expression I regularly use. It's not because I lack convictions of my own, but because I don't like to stand in anyone else's way.

Ernst. You answer me as if I were a stranger.

Falk. Stranger or friend!

Ernst. You've been initiated, and you know everything – –

Falk. Others have been initiated, and they think they know.

Ernst. Then could you be admitted without knowing what you know?

Falk. Unfortunately, yes.

Ernst. How so?

Falk. Because many who initiate others don't know themselves; but the few who do know *cannot* say so.

Ernst. And could you know what you know without being initiated?

Falk. Why not? – Freemasonry is not something arbitrary or dispensable, but something necessary, which is grounded in human nature and in civil society. So it must be possible to arrive at it just as easily through personal reflection as through external guidance.

Ernst. Freemasonry is not something arbitrary? – Doesn't it have words and signs and customs which could all be other than they are, and which are therefore arbitrary?

Falk. It does have these. But these words and these signs and these customs are not Freemasonry.

Ernst. Freemasonry is not something dispensable? – Then what did people do before Freemasonry existed?

Falk. Freemasonry has always existed.

Ernst. Then what exactly is it, this necessary, this indispensable Freemasonry?

Falk. As I've already told you, it's something which even those who know cannot say.

Ernst. Then it's an absurdity.

Falk. Don't jump to conclusions.

Ernst. If I have a conception of something, I can also express it in words.

Falk. Not always; and at least often not in such a way that others derive exactly the same conception from the words as what I have in mind.

Ernst. If not exactly the same, then at least an approximation!

Falk. An approximate conception would in this case be useless or dangerous. Useless if it didn't contain enough, and dangerous if it contained the slightest amount too much.

Ernst. How strange! – So if the Freemasons, who know the secret of their order, cannot communicate it in words, how do they still manage to disseminate their order?

Falk. Through deeds. – They allow good men and youths whom they consider worthy of their company to divine and guess at their deeds – to see them, in so far as they can be seen. These others find them to their liking, and perform similar deeds.

Ernst. Deeds? Deeds of Freemasons? – I know of none except their speeches and songs, which are usually printed more impressively than they are conceived and spoken.

Falk. They share this quality with many other speeches and songs.

Ernst. Or am I to take as their deeds what they boast about in these speeches and songs?

Falk. So long as they don't just boast about them.

Ernst. And what exactly do they boast about? – Only such things as one expects of every good person and every good citizen. – They are so friendly, so beneficent, so obedient, so full of patriotism!

Falk. Does that mean nothing?

Ernst. Nothing! – nothing to distinguish them from other people. – Shouldn't everyone be all of these things?

Falk. Should!

Ernst. Who doesn't have sufficient motive and opportunity to be all of these things even without Freemasonry?

Falk. But in it, and through it, they have an additional motive.

Ernst. Don't tell me about the number of motives! It's better to lend as much strength and intensity as possible to a single motive! – The number of such motives is like the number of wheels in a machine: the more wheels, the more unreliable it is.

Falk. That I cannot deny.

Ernst. And what kind of additional motive? – One which devalues all other motives and renders them suspect! One which claims to be the strongest and best!

Falk. Be reasonable, my friend. – Exaggeration! On a par with those empty speeches and songs! Amateurism! Beginners' work!

Ernst. In other words: Brother Orator is a mere prattler.

Falk. All it means is that what Brother Orator praises in the Freemasons is certainly not their deeds. For at least Brother Orator is no idle gossip, and deeds speak for themselves.

Ernst. Yes, now I see what you're getting at. Why didn't I think of them at once, those speaking deeds! I'm tempted to call them shouting deeds! It's not enough for the Freemasons to give each other the strongest possible support – for that would only be a necessary precondition of any organised group. What don't they do for the public at large in every state of which they are members!

Falk. For example? – so that I can see whether you're on the right track.

Ernst. For example, the Freemasons in Stockholm! – Didn't they establish a large orphanage?

Falk. So long as the Freemasons in Stockholm acted appropriately on another occasion too!

Ernst. On what other occasion?

Falk. On other occasions, I mean.

Ernst. And the Freemasons in Dresden! who put poor young girls to work making lace and embroidery – to keep down the size of the orphanage.

Falk. Ernst! Need I remind you of your name?

Ernst. No gratuitous comments, then. – And the Freemasons in Brunswick! who give drawing lessons to gifted boys from poor backgrounds![4]

Falk. Why not?

Ernst. And the Freemasons in Berlin, who support Basedow's Philanthropic Institute![5]

Falk. What do you say? The Freemasons? The Philanthropic Institute? Support? – Who told you that story?

Ernst. It was all over the newspaper.

---

[4] An initiative supported by Duke Ferdinand, to whom these dialogues are dedicated.

[5] Johann Bernhard Basedow, founder of the 'Philanthropin' in Dessau (1774), an 'enlightened' educational institution designed to further the all-round development of its pupils.

Falk. The newspaper! – I'd have to see Basedow's handwritten receipt first. And I'd have to be certain that the receipt was addressed not to the Freemasons in Berlin, but to *all* Freemasons.

Ernst. What does that mean? – Don't you approve of Basedow's Institute?

Falk. Not approve of it? Who could approve of it more!

Ernst. Then you surely won't begrudge him this support?

Falk. Begrudge him it? – Who could have greater goodwill for him than I do?

Ernst. Well, then! – I cease to follow you.

Falk. I can well believe it. And the fault is mine. – For even *the* Freemasons can do something which they don't do *as* Freemasons.

Ernst. And does that apply to all their other good deeds too?

Falk. Perhaps! – Perhaps all the good deeds you've just mentioned are only – to use a scholastic expression for the sake of brevity – their deeds *ad extra*.[6]

Ernst. What do you mean by that?

Falk. Only those deeds which people notice; – only the deeds which they do simply in order to be noticed.

Ernst. So that they may be respected and tolerated?

Falk. That might well be so.

Ernst. But what about their true deeds? – You don't answer?

Falk. Didn't I answer you already? – Their true deeds are their secret.

Ernst. Aha! So they can't be explained in words either?

Falk. Probably not! – I can and may tell you only this much: the true deeds of the Freemasons are so great, and so far-reaching, that whole centuries may elapse before one can say 'This was their doing!' They have nevertheless done all the good that has so far existed in the world – mark my words: in the *world*! – And they continue to work on all the good that has yet to come in the world – mark my words – in the *world*.

Ernst. Be off with you! You're having me on.

Falk. I truly am not. – But look! There's a butterfly I must have. It's the one from the wolf's milk caterpillar. – Let me just say quickly that the true deeds of the Freemasons are aimed at making all that are commonly described as good deeds for the most part superfluous.

---

[6] Outward (i.e. externally observable) deeds.

Ernst. And yet they are good deeds too?

Falk. There can be none better. – Think about it for a moment. I'll be back shortly.

Ernst. Good deeds aimed at making good deeds superfluous? – That's a riddle. And I refuse to think about riddles. – I'd rather lie down under this tree and observe the ants.

Second dialogue

Ernst. Well? What held you up? And you didn't get the butterfly after all?

Falk. It lured me on from one bush to the next, right down to the stream. – And suddenly it crossed over.

Ernst. Oh, yes. There are such lurers!

Falk. Have you thought about it?

Ernst. About what? About your riddle? – I won't catch it either, that fine butterfly! But nor will I let it trouble me any further. – I've talked with you once about Freemasonry, but never again. For I can see very well that you're just like all the rest.

Falk. Like all the rest? But they don't all say what I said.

Ernst. No? So there are heretics among Freemasons too, are there? And maybe you're one of them. – But all the heretics still have something in common with the orthodox, and that's what I was talking about.

Falk. What were you talking about?

Ernst. Orthodox or heretical Freemasons – they all play with words, and invite questions, and answer without answering.

Falk. Do you think so? – Very well, let's talk about something else, now that you've roused me out of a relaxed state of silent wonderment.

Ernst. Nothing could be easier than to return you to that state – just sit down beside me and look!

Falk. What is it, then?

Ernst. The life and movement on and in and around this anthill. What activity, and yet how much order! They're all carrying and pulling and pushing, yet none of them hinders the other. Just look! They're even helping each other.

Falk. The ants live in society, just like the bees.

Ernst. And in an even more remarkable society than the bees. For they have no one among them to keep them together and govern them.

Falk. So it must be possible for order to exist without a government.

Ernst. If every individual knows how to govern himself, why not?

Falk. I wonder whether human beings will ever reach that stage.

Ernst. That's hardly likely!

Falk. A pity!

Ernst. Yes, indeed!

Falk. Stand up and let's move on. For the ants will crawl all over you. And I've also just thought of something that I must ask you while I have the chance. – I've no idea what your views on it are.

Ernst. On what?

Falk. On the civil society of human beings in general. – What do you think it is?

Ernst. A very good thing.

Falk. Undeniably. – But do you see it as an end or a means?

Ernst. I don't understand you.

Falk. Do you think that human beings were created for states? Or that states exist for human beings?

Ernst. Some people seem to claim the former. But the latter may well be truer.

Falk. I think so too. – States unite human beings so that each individual may enjoy his share of happiness better and more securely through and within this union. – The sum of the individual happiness of all its members is the happiness of the state. There is none at all apart from this. Every other happiness of the state whereby even the smallest number of individual members suffer, and *must* suffer, is a cloak for tyranny. Nothing else!

Ernst. I wouldn't say that so loudly.

Falk. Why not?

Ernst. A truth which everyone judges according to his own situation can easily be abused.

Falk. Do you know, my friend, that you're already half a Freemason?

Ernst. Me?

Falk. You. For you already recognise truths which are better left unsaid.

Ernst. Although they *could* be said.

Falk. The wise man *cannot* say what is better left unsaid.

Ernst. Well, just as you like! – Let's not go back to the Freemasons again. I really don't want to hear anything more about them.

Falk. Forgive me! – you can at least see that I'm willing to tell you more about them.

Ernst. You're making fun of me. – Very well! The civil society of human beings, and all political constitutions, are nothing but means to human happiness. What then?

Falk. Nothing but means! And means invented by man; although I won't deny that nature has so arranged everything that man was bound to hit upon this invention very soon.

Ernst. And this is no doubt why some people have regarded civil society as an end of nature. Since everything leads to it, including our passions and our needs, it follows that it is the ultimate goal of nature. So they have argued. As if nature didn't also have to produce the means in a purposive manner! As if the happiness of an abstract concept – such as the state, the fatherland, and the like – had been nature's intention, rather than the happiness of every actual individual human being!

Falk. Very good! You're well on the way to agreeing with me. For just tell me: if political constitutions are means, means invented by man – can they alone be exempt from the fate of human means?

Ernst. What do you mean by the fate of human means?

Falk. I mean what is inseparably associated with human means, what distinguishes them from infallible divine means.

Ernst. And what is that?

Falk. That they are not infallible. That they not only frequently fail to match their intention, but may well achieve the exact opposite.

Ernst. An example! – if you can think of one.

Falk. For example, ships and navigation are means of travelling to distant countries, yet they become the cause of many people never reaching them.

Ernst. Because they are shipwrecked and drown. I think I understand you now. – But we know very well why it is that so many individual people gain no extra happiness from the constitution of their state. There are many political constitutions; therefore one is better than the other; some are very defective and obviously at odds with their intention; and the best one has perhaps still to be invented.

Falk. We can leave that aside! Let's assume that the best conceivable constitution has already been invented, and that all human beings throughout the world have accepted this best constitution: don't you think that even then, even this best constitution must give rise to things which are highly detrimental to human happiness, and of which human beings in the state of nature would have been totally ignorant?

Ernst. In my opinion, if such things were to arise out of the best constitution, it would no longer be the best one.

Falk. And a better one would be possible? – Then I'll assume that this better one is the *best* one, and repeat my question.

Ernst. It seems to me that all your reasoning here is based on the assumption that every means invented by man, in which you include each and every political constitution, cannot be anything other than defective.

Falk. Not just that.

Ernst. And you would find it difficult to name one of those detrimental things –

Falk. – to which even the best constitution must necessarily give rise? Oh, I'll give you ten if you like!

Ernst. One will do for now.

Falk. Then let us assume that the best constitution has been invented, and that everyone in the world lives under this constitution. Would everyone in the world therefore constitute only a single state?

Ernst. Well, hardly. Such an enormous state would be impossible to administer. It would have to divide itself up into several little states, and all of them would be administered according to the same laws.

Falk. In other words, people would then continue to be Germans and French, Dutch and Spanish, Russians and Swedes, or whatever else they might be called.

Ernst. Most certainly!

Falk. Then we've agreed on at least one thing. For isn't it the case that each of these little states would have its own interest? And every member of these states would share his own state's interest?

Ernst. What else?

Falk. These diverse interests would often come into collision, just as they do now; and two citizens of two different states would no more be able to meet each other in an unbiassed frame of mind than a German is now when he meets a Frenchman or a Frenchman when he meets an Englishman.

Ernst. That's very likely!

Falk. In other words: when a German at present meets a Frenchman, or a Frenchman an Englishman (or vice versa), it is no longer a meeting between a *mere* human being and another *mere* human being who are attracted to one another by virtue of their common nature, but a meeting between *such* a human being and *such* a human being who are conscious of their differing tendencies. This makes them cold, reserved, and distrustful towards one another, even before they have had the least mutual interaction or shared experience as individuals.

Ernst. That is unfortunately true.

Falk. So it is then also true that the means which unites people in order to assure them of their happiness through this union simultaneously creates a division between them.

Ernst. If that's the way you look at it.

Falk. Take one step further. Many of the smaller states would have quite different climates, therefore quite different needs and satisfactions, therefore quite different habits and customs, therefore quite different moral doctrines, therefore quite different religions. Don't you agree?

Ernst. That's an enormous step!

Falk. People would then still be Jews and Christians and Turks and the like.

Ernst. I wouldn't venture to deny it.

Falk. And if that were the case, they would still behave towards one another – no matter what they called themselves – no differently from the way in which our Christians and Jews and Turks have behaved towards each other since time immemorial: not as *mere* human beings towards *mere* human beings, but as *such* human beings towards *such* human beings who make competing claims to some spiritual advantage on which they base rights which would never occur to natural man.

Ernst. That is very sad – but unfortunately very probable.

Falk. Only probable?

Ernst. For I should in any case think that, just as you have assumed that all states might have the same kind of constitution, they could equally well have the same kind of religion. In fact, I don't understand how the same kind of constitution is even possible without the same kind of religion.

Falk. Nor do I. – Besides, I only made that assumption to head off your counter-argument. The one is surely just as impossible as the other. One state: several states. Several states: several constitutions. Several constitutions: several religions.

Ernst. Yes, yes: so it seems.

Falk. So it is! – Now you see the second evil which civil society causes, quite contrary to its intentions. It cannot unite people without dividing them; and it cannot divide them without placing gulfs between them, without constructing dividing walls through their midst.

Ernst. And how dreadful those gulfs are! How insurmountable those dividing walls often are!

Falk. Let me add my third example. – It's not enough for civil society to divide people up into different nations and religions. – Such a division into a few large parts, each of which formed a whole in itself, would still be preferable to no whole at all. – No; civil society also continues to make divisions within each of these parts, so to speak ad infinitum.

Ernst. How so?

Falk. Or do you believe that a state is conceivable without class differences? Whether it is good or bad, or more or less near to perfection, it is impossible for all its members to have the same relationship to each other. – Even if they all have a share in the legislation, they cannot have an equal share in it, or at least not an equally direct share. There will therefore be higher-ranking and lower-ranking members. – Even if all the property of the state is initially distributed equally among them, this equal distribution cannot last for more than two generations. One man will know how to make better use of his property than another. One will nevertheless have to distribute his less well-managed property among more descendants than the other. There will therefore be richer and poorer members.

Ernst. That goes without saying.

Falk. Now just consider how much evil there is in the world which is not occasioned by this difference between classes.

Ernst. If only I could contradict you! – But why should I contradict you in any case? – All right, people can only be united through division! and only through incessant division can they remain united! That's just the way things are. And they cannot possibly be otherwise.

Falk. That's just what I'm saying!

Ernst. Then why are you saying it? To turn me against living in society? To make me wish that people had never had the idea of uniting into states?

Falk. Do you misjudge me to that extent? – If the only benefit of civil society were that it is the sole context in which human reason can be cultivated, I would bless it even if it contained far greater evils.

Ernst. He who enjoys the fire – as the proverb has it – must also put up with the smoke.

Falk. Certainly! – But since smoke is an inevitable part of fire, was that a reason for not inventing the chimney? And was the person who invented the chimney necessarily an enemy of fire? – That, you see, is what I was getting at.

Ernst. At what? – I don't understand you.

Falk. But the image was highly appropriate. – If people cannot be united into states other than through such divisions, do such divisions therefore become good?

Ernst. Hardly so.

Falk. Do they therefore become sacred, these divisions?

Ernst. What do you mean by sacred?

Falk. So that it might be forbidden to lay hands on them?

Ernst. With what intention?

Falk. With the intention of not letting them become any more firmly entrenched than is strictly necessary. With the intention of rendering their consequences as harmless as possible.

Ernst. How could that be forbidden?

Falk. But it cannot be required either, not by civil laws! – For civil laws never extend beyond the boundaries of the state which made them. And this would in fact transcend the boundaries of each and every state. – Consequently, it can only be an *opus supererogatum*;[7] and one can only wish that the wisest and best members of every state might voluntarily undertake this *opus supererogatum*.

Ernst. One can only wish; but it is most desirable!

Falk. I should think so! It is most desirable that there should be men in every state who have got beyond national prejudices and know exactly where patriotism ceases to be a virtue.

Ernst. Most desirable!

Falk. It is most desirable that there should be men in every state who are not susceptible to the prejudice of their native religion and do not believe that everything must necessarily be good and true which they accept as good and true.

Ernst. Most desirable!

Falk. It is most desirable that there should be men in every state who are not overawed by exalted rank or repelled by social inferiority; men in whose company the exalted willingly cease to stand on their dignity and those of inferior rank boldly assert themselves.

Ernst. Most desirable!

Falk. And what if these wishes were fulfilled?

---

[7] A work of supererogation, i.e. a work performed beyond the call of duty.

Ernst. Fulfilled? – Such a man can no doubt be found here and there and from time to time.

Falk. Not just here and there; and not just from time to time.

Ernst. At certain times and in certain countries, there may even be more than one of them.

Falk. What if such men were to be found everywhere now? And if they must continue to exist at all times?

Ernst. Would to God it were so!

Falk. And if these men did not live in ineffectual isolation, and not always in an invisible church?

Ernst. A fine dream!

Falk. Let me be brief. – And what if these men were the Freemasons?

Ernst. What do you say?

Falk. What if it were the Freemasons who had made it *part* of their business to reduce as far as possible the divisions which so much alienate people from one another?

Ernst. The Freemasons?

Falk. I say *part* of their business.

Ernst. The Freemasons?

Falk. Ah! Forgive me! – I had forgotten again that you don't want to hear anything more about the Freemasons – Look, they're just calling us to breakfast. Come along!

Ernst. Not yet! – Just a moment! – The Freemasons, you say –

Falk. The conversation brought me back to them against my will. Pardon me! – Come! We'll soon find material for a more suitable discussion in the larger company there. Come along!

Third dialogue

Ernst. You've been eluding me all day in the crowds of people. But I've tracked you down to your bedroom.

Falk. Do you have something of such importance to tell me? I've had enough of mere conversation for today.

Ernst. You're mocking my curiosity.

Falk. Your curiosity?

Ernst. Which you managed to arouse in such a masterly fashion this morning.

Falk. What were we talking about this morning?

Ernst. About the Freemasons.

Falk. Well? Surely I didn't betray the secret under the influence of the Pyrmont water?[8]

Ernst. The secret which, as you put it, cannot be betrayed.

Falk. But of course; that puts my mind at rest.

Ernst. But you did tell me something about the Freemasons which I didn't expect – it caught my attention and made me think.

Falk. And what was that?

Ernst. Oh, don't torment me! – You surely remember it.

Falk. Yes, it's gradually coming back to me. – And that's what made you so distracted all day among your friends of both sexes?

Ernst. That was it! – And I won't get to sleep unless you answer me at least one more question.

Falk. That depends on what the question is.

Ernst. But how can you give me proof, or at least plausible evidence, that the Freemasons really do have those great and worthy intentions?

Falk. Did I say anything about intentions? Not that I'm aware of. – On the contrary, since you couldn't form any conception of the true deeds of the Freemasons, I just wanted to draw your attention to an area in which so much could yet happen and of which our political experts don't have the least inkling. – Perhaps the Freemasons are at work in this area. – Perhaps! in this area! – Just to relieve you of your prejudice that all the sites which need building on have already been discovered and occupied, and that all the necessary work has been put in the appropriate hands.

Ernst. You can turn whichever way you like now. – I shall only say that I imagine the Freemasons, from what you have said, as people who have freely taken it upon themselves to counteract the unavoidable evils of the state.

Falk. This interpretation can at least do them no discredit. – Hold on to it! – But be sure you understand it correctly. Don't add anything which doesn't belong there. – The unavoidable evils of the state! – Not of this or that state. Not the unavoidable evils which, if we assume a particular political constitution, necessarily follow from that assumption. With evils

---

[8] Mineral water from Bad Pyrmont, a fashionable spa near Hamelin, where Lessing discussed his theories of the origin of Freemasonry with the historian Justus Möser in 1766.

of this kind, the Freemason will never have any truck – not, at least, as a Freemason. He leaves the alleviation and cure of such evils to the citizen, who may tackle them according to his own insight and courage, and at his own risk. Evils of an altogether different kind, of an altogether higher order, are the object of the Freemason's activity.

Ernst. I have fully grasped that point. – Not evils which make the citizen discontented, but evils which even the happiest citizen cannot do without.

Falk. Correct! To counter – how did you put it? – to counteract these evils?

Ernst. Yes!

Falk. That term says rather a lot. – To counteract! – In order to remove them completely? – That cannot be. For one would simultaneously destroy the state itself along with them. – They mustn't even be shown all at once to those who are not yet aware of them. 'To counteract' can here mean at most to activate this awareness in them from afar, to encourage it to germinate, to transplant the seedlings and remove the weeds and superfluous leaves. – Do you understand now why I suggested that, although the Freemasons may always have been active, centuries might pass without our being able to say 'this was their doing'?

Ernst. And now I understand the second part of the riddle too: 'good deeds aimed at making good deeds superfluous'.

Falk. Very well! – Now go and study those evils, and get to know them all, and weigh up all their mutual effects, and be assured that this study will enable you to grasp things which, in days of depression, may strike you as the most devastating and insoluble objections to providence and virtue. This insight, this illumination will make you calm and happy – even if you are not *called* a Freemason.

Ernst. You put so much emphasis on 'called'.

Falk. Because one can *be* something without being called it.

Ernst. Very good! I understand. – But to return to my question – although I must formulate it a little differently. Since I now know those evils which Freemasonry addresses – –

Falk. You know them?

Ernst. Didn't you name them to me yourself?

Falk. I named only a few of them as examples. Only a few of those which are evident to even the most short-sighted observer: only a few of the most incontestable and comprehensive ones. – But how many still remain which, even if they are not so evident, not so incontestable, and not so comprehensive, are nevertheless just as certain and just as necessary!

Ernst. Then let me confine my question to those instances which you yourself mentioned explicitly. – How can you prove to me that, even in those instances alone, the Freemasons really do have them in view? – You say nothing? – Are you reflecting?

Falk. Certainly not about how to answer your question! – But I can't think what reasons you can have for asking it.

Ernst. And will you answer my question if I tell you the reasons?

Falk. I promise you I will.

Ernst. I know and fear your acuteness.

Falk. My acuteness?

Ernst. I fear that you are passing off your own speculation as fact.

Falk. I'm much obliged to you!

Ernst. Does that offend you?

Falk. No, I should thank you instead for describing as acuteness something to which you could have given a very different name.

Ernst. Certainly not. On the contrary, I know how easily an acute individual can delude himself; how easily he lends and attributes to other people plans and intentions which had never occurred to them.

Falk. But what does one deduce people's plans and intentions from? Surely from their particular actions?

Ernst. From what else? – And here I come back to my question: from what particular and incontestable actions of the Freemasons can it be concluded that it is even just *part* of their aim to redress, through itself and in itself, that division between people which you mentioned as a necessary consequence of the state and of states in general?

Falk. And without detriment to this state or these states.

Ernst. So much the better! – Perhaps this conclusion doesn't even have to be based on actions, so long as there are certain peculiarities or special features which point to it or result from it. – Even your own speculation must have started out from something of this kind – assuming that your system is only hypothetical.

Falk. Your distrust is still apparent. – But I hope that it will vanish if I draw your attention to a basic law of the Freemasons.

Ernst. Which one?

Falk. One of which they have never made a secret, and by which their actions have always been governed for all the world to see.

Ernst. That is?

Falk. That is, to admit to their order every worthy man of the right disposition, irrespective of nationality, irrespective of religion, and irrespective of social class.

Ernst. Really!

Falk. This basic law seems, of course, rather to presuppose the kind of men who have already transcended those divisions than to indicate any intention of educating them. But the sodium nitrate must doubtless be present in the air before it can settle on walls as saltpetre.

Ernst. Oh, yes!

Falk. And why shouldn't the Freemasons have made use of a common stratagem here? – By pursuing part of their secret intentions quite openly, in order to deflect suspicion, which always expects to find something quite different from what it sees.

Ernst. Why not?

Falk. Why should the artist who can *make* silver not deal in old scrap silver, so as to arouse less suspicion that he can make it?

Ernst. Why not?

Falk. Ernst! – Do you hear me? – You seem to answer as if in a dream.

Ernst. No, my friend! But I've had enough. Enough for tonight. Tomorrow, first thing, I'll go back to the city.

Falk. Already? And why so soon?

Ernst. You know me, and ask such a question? For how much longer will you be taking the waters?

Falk. I only began the treatment two days ago.

Ernst. Then I'll see you again before it's finished. – Goodbye! Goodnight!

Falk. Goodnight! Goodbye!

To the reader

The spark had ignited: Ernst went off and became a Freemason. What he meanwhile discovered is the subject of a fourth and fifth conversation, at which point – the ways part.

* * *

Preface by a third party[9]

The author of the first three dialogues is known to have had the manuscript of this sequel ready for press when he received a request from a *higher instance*[10] not to publish it.

But he had previously shown these fourth and fifth dialogues to several friends who, presumably without his permission, had made copies of them. By a curious chance, one of these copies came into the hands of the present editor. He regretted that so many splendid truths were destined to be suppressed, and resolved to have the manuscript printed without authority.

If the desire to cast more general light on such important matters does not sufficiently excuse this liberty, nothing further can be said in its defence except that the editor is not an accepted Mason.

It will, however, also be noticed that, out of caution and respect for a certain branch of this society,[11] the editor has omitted in the printed version certain names which were given in full in the manuscript.[12]

Fourth dialogue

Falk. Ernst! Welcome! You're back again at last! I've long since finished taking the waters.

Ernst. And you're the better for it? I'm glad.

Falk. What's this? No one has ever said 'I'm glad' with more annoyance!

Ernst. I am indeed annoyed, and I'm not far short of being annoyed with you.

Falk. With me?

Ernst. You misled me into taking a foolish step – Look at this – Give me your hand![13] – What do you say? – You shrug your shoulders? That's all I needed!

---

[9] This preface is by A. F. von Knigge, who published the fourth and fifth dialogues (Frankfurt-on-Main, 1780) without Lessing's permission.

[10] That is, from Duke Ferdinand, who nevertheless circulated these dialogues in manuscript among his Masonic associates in support of his own plans to reform some of the abuses to which Lessing refers (see editor's commentary in B x, 713).

[11] Namely the 'Strict Observance', which, like the so-called 'Scottish system' of Freemasonry, claimed descent from the medieval Knights Templar.

[12] The names in question, all relating to the Templars, are restored, in square brackets, in the present edition.

[13] Ernst gives Falk the Masonic handshake.

Falk. Misled you?

Ernst. It may be that you didn't intend to.

Falk. Yet I'm supposed to be at fault.

Ernst. The man of God tells the people of a land where milk and honey flow, and the people are not supposed to long for it? Or to complain about the man of God if he leads them not into this promised land, but into arid deserts?

Falk. Well, well! The damage can't be all that great – Besides, I see that you have already worked *at the graves of our forefathers.*[14]

Ernst. But they weren't enveloped in *flames*, but in smoke.

Falk. Then wait until the smoke clears, and the flame will give light and warmth.

Ernst. The smoke will suffocate me before the flame gives me light, and I can see very well that others who can better endure the smoke will warm themselves at it.

Falk. You're surely not referring to people who don't mind putting up with the smoke so long as it comes from someone else's well-stocked kitchen?

Ernst. So you *do* know them?

Falk. I've heard about them.

Ernst. And for that very reason, what can have induced you to send me on such a fool's errand? And to hold out prospects to me which you knew very well were baseless?

Falk. Your anger makes you very unjust – Did I really tell you about Freemasonry without indicating in more than one way how pointless it is for every honest man to become a Freemason? – Not just pointless, but harmful too!

Ernst. That may well be so.

Falk. Did I not tell you that one can fulfil the highest duties of Masonry without being called a Freemason?

Ernst. I do indeed remember that – But you know very well that, once my imagination spreads its wings and takes off – am I able to stop it? – My only reproach is that you offered me such a tempting bait. –

Falk. Which you very soon grew tired of pursuing – And why didn't you tell me what you were planning?

[14] Symbols used in the 'Scottish system' of Freemasonry, along with its 'higher degrees' of initiation and the Templar legend.

Ernst. Would you have advised me against it?

Falk. Most certainly! – *Who would encourage a bold child to return to a walking frame just because he sometimes falls down?* I'm not just flattering you; you had already progressed too far to go back to that stage. All the same, you couldn't be given exceptional treatment. Everyone must go down that road.

Ernst. Nor would I have regretted going down it if I could expect more from the rest of the journey. But all I get are promises, more promises, and nothing but promises!

Falk. Well, at least that's something! And what exactly do they promise you?

Ernst. You'll know already – Scottish Masonry, the Scottish Knights.[15]

Falk. That's all very well – But what can the Scottish Knight promise himself?

Ernst. Goodness only knows!

Falk. And people like you, the other recent initiates to the order, don't they know anything either?

Ernst. Oh, them! They know so much! They expect so much! – One wants to make gold, another wants to raise spirits, a third wants to restore the [Templars] – You smile – And you *only* smile? –

Falk. What else can I do?

Ernst. Show your indignation at such idiots!

Falk. Except that *one* thing does reconcile me to them.

Ernst. And what is that?

Falk. That I see in all these fantasies a quest for reality, and that one can still deduce from all these false directions where the true path leads to.

Ernst. Even from alchemy?

Falk. Even from alchemy. Whether gold really can be made or not is a matter of indifference to me. But I am very confident that rational people will only wish to be able to make it in the interests of Freemasonry. And whoever happens to discover the philosopher's stone will at that same instant become a Freemason – and it is really strange that all the reports that circulate about real or reputed alchemists confirm this.

Ernst. And those who call up spirits?

Falk. Much the same is true of them – It is impossible for spirits to heed the voice of anyone but a Freemason.

---

[15] See notes 11 and 14 above.

Ernst. How can you say such things so seriously! –

Falk. By all that is sacred – no more seriously than they deserve!

Ernst. If only that were true! – But finally, what about the – God permitting – new [Templars]?

Falk. What next!

Ernst. There, you see! You have nothing to say about them. And there really were [Templars] at one time, but makers of gold and conjurers of spirits may never have existed; and it is no doubt easier to say how the Freemasons relate to such imaginary beings than to real ones.

Falk. I can indeed only express myself in a dilemma: Either, or –

Ernst. That's fine! Then we know at least that one out of two propositions is true. So! Either these would-be [Templars] –

Falk. Ernst! Before you come out with another facetious remark! On my conscience! – These – these same people are either certainly on the right track, or they are so far away from it that they no longer have even a hope of ever finding it.

Ernst. I can only listen to what you say. For to ask you for a fuller explanation –

Falk. Why not? Mystifications have been passed off as the secret for quite long enough.

Ernst. What do you mean by that?

Falk. The secret of Freemasonry, as I've already told you, is something which the Freemason *cannot* put into words, even if it were possible for him to *want* to do so. But mystifications are things which could very well be said, and which, at certain times and in certain countries, have simply been concealed out of jealousy, suppressed out of fear, or kept quiet for reasons of prudence.

Ernst. For example?

Falk. For example, this very relationship between [Templars] and Freemasons. It may well be that it was at one time necessary and desirable not to give anything of this away – But now – now, on the contrary, it may be extremely harmful to make a secret of this relationship any longer. It should rather be stated openly, so long as one defines the specific point which made the [Templars] the Freemasons of their time.

Ernst. May I be told what this point is?

Falk. Read the history of the [Templars] carefully! You must guess what it is. Besides, you're bound to guess correctly, and that was precisely why you had no need to become a Freemason.

Ernst. If only I had my books to hand! – And if I guess what it is, will you confirm that I've guessed correctly?

Falk. You will immediately find that you don't need this confirmation – But to return to my dilemma, it is this very point which alone holds the solution to it! If all the Freemasons who are currently captivated by the [Templars] can see and feel this essential point: happy are they, and happy is the world at large! Blessings on all that they do, and all that they leave undone! – But if they do not recognise and feel this point, if they have been misled by a mere similarity of words, if it is only the *Freemason who works in the [Temple]* who has made them think of the [Templars], if they have simply fallen for the [red cross] on the [white cloak],[16] if they would just like to obtain lucrative [commanderies] and wealthy benefices for themselves and their friends – then may heaven fill us with compassion, so that we may refrain from laughing.

Ernst. See, you can still become heated and bitter after all!

Falk. Unfortunately so! – I'm grateful for your comment, and I'm as cold as ice again.

Ernst. And which of the two cases do you think applies to these gentlemen?

Falk. I fear the latter. – I hope I'm mistaken! – For if the former were the case, how could they have such a strange objective? – to revive the [Templars]! – That great point which marked the [Templars] out as Freemasons is no longer present. Europe, at least, has long progressed beyond it, and in this respect no longer requires any special encouragement – So what do they want? Do they want to become a saturated sponge to be squeezed dry some day by the powers that be? But to whom should this question be directed? And against whom? For did you tell me – or were you able to tell me – that others apart from the novices in the order are afflicted with these fads for alchemy, exorcism, and the [Templars]? Others apart from children or people who have no qualms about leading children astray? – But children do become men – Just leave them to it! – It's enough, as I said, that I can already discern in their toys the weapons which the men will one day wield with a steady hand.

Ernst. But basically, my friend, it isn't these childish antics which upset me. Without suspecting that there could be anything serious behind them, I simply disregarded them – they are casks, I thought, thrown overboard

[16] Costume adopted by the 'Strict Observance' in imitation of the Knights Templar.

for the young whales! – But what bothers me is that I can nowhere see and hear anything but these childish antics, and that nobody wants to know anything about what *you* led me to expect. I can sound this note as often as I like and with whom I like, but no one will take me up on it, and there is always the profoundest silence everywhere.

Falk. You mean –

Ernst. That equality which you told me was the basic law of the order, that equality which filled my entire soul with such unforeseen hope – to be able to breathe it at last in the company of people who know how to think beyond all social gradations without abusing one of these to someone else's detriment –

Falk. Well?

Ernst. Does it still exist? If it ever did exist! – Let an enlightened Jew come and present himself! 'Yes', they say, 'a Jew? A Freemason must, of course, at least be a Christian. *It doesn't matter what kind of Christian.* "Irrespective of religion" merely means "belonging to any one of the three confessions publicly tolerated in the Holy Roman Empire"'.[17] – Do you agree with this?

Falk. I should think not.

Ernst. Let an honest cobbler – even the likes of Jakob Böhme[18] or Hans Sachs[19] – who has enough idle moments at his last to have some good ideas, let him come and present himself! 'Yes', they say, 'a cobbler! He is, of course, a cobbler.' – Let a loyal, experienced, and tested servant come and present himself – 'Yes', they say, 'such people, of course, don't choose the colour of their own livery – and we are in such good company among ourselves' –

Falk. And how good a company are they?

Ernst. Well, then! I don't really have anything to criticise about them, except that they are *only* the kind of good company one grows so tired of in the world at large – princes, counts, gentry, officers, councillors of every description, merchants, artists, who do indeed mill around together in the lodge irrespective of social class. But they all in fact belong to *one* class, and that is unfortunately –

Falk. That certainly wasn't so in my time – But wait! – I don't know, I can only guess – it's so long since I had any contact with lodges of any

---

[17] Namely Catholic, Lutheran, and Reformed (i.e. Calvinist).
[18] Jakob Böhme (1575–1624), cobbler and Protestant mystic.
[19] Hans Sachs (1494–1576), cobbler, poet, and Mastersinger of Nuremberg.

kind – Not to be admitted *to a lodge for the moment*, for a given time, and *to be excluded from Freemasonry*, are surely two different things?

Ernst. How so?

Falk. Because a lodge is to Freemasonry what the Church is to religious faith. No conclusions whatsoever can be drawn from the external prosperity of the Church as to the faith of its members. On the contrary, there is a certain kind of outward prosperity which could only by a miracle co-exist with genuine faith. Besides, the two have never got along together; instead, the one has always destroyed the other, as history confirms. And so, I fear, I fear –

Ernst. What?

Falk. In short, I simply can't comprehend the business of the lodges as I'm told it is at present conducted. To have financial resources, to accumulate capital, to invest this capital, to seek the best possible yield from it, to try to purchase land, to solicit privileges from kings and princes, to use the power and standing conferred by these to suppress those brothers who follow an observance other than that which one wishes to present as definitive – can this be beneficial in the long term? – How glad I would be if my prophecies were mistaken!

Ernst. Well, then, what can be done about it? The state no longer interferes so much these days; and besides, there are probably too many Freemasons by now among the very people who make or administer its laws –

Falk. Good! So if they also have nothing to fear from the state, what sort of an influence do you think such a constitution will have on the Masons themselves? Does it not mean that they are back in the position they wished to break away from? Will they not cease to be what they intend to be? – I don't know if you quite understand me –

Ernst. Please continue!

Falk. Admittedly – yes, indeed – nothing lasts for ever. – Perhaps this is the very route which providence has chosen to put an end to the whole present scheme of Freemasonry –

Ernst. The scheme of Freemasonry? What do you mean by that? The scheme?

Falk. Well – scheme, guise, outward garb.

Ernst. I don't yet know –

Falk. You surely don't think that Freemasonry always played the part of Freemasonry?

Ernst. What does this mean? Freemasonry didn't always play the part of Freemasonry?

Falk. In other words: do you think that what Freemasonry is was always called Freemasonry? – But look! It's past noon now! There are my guests arriving already! You'll stay, won't you?

Ernst. I didn't intend to, but I suppose I must. For I expect a double satisfaction.

Falk. But please, not a word of this at table!

Fifth dialogue

Ernst. At last they've gone! – Oh, what prattlers! – And didn't you notice, or didn't you want to notice, that the one with the wart on his chin – whatever his name is – is a Freemason? He kept giving those knocks.[20]

Falk. I heard him all right. I even noticed something in his conversation which you may have overlooked – He is one of those people who defend the American cause in Europe –

Ernst. That wouldn't be the worst thing about him.

Falk. And he has got it into his head that Congress is a lodge, and that it is *there* that the Freemasons are at last establishing their empire by force of arms.

Ernst. Are there really such *fantasists* as this?

Falk. I suppose there must be.

Ernst. And how did you get this idea out of him?

Falk. From a feature you will eventually become more familiar with.

Ernst. My God! If I thought that I had been as badly mistaken as *this* about the Freemasons!

Falk. Don't worry, the Freemason calmly waits for the sunrise, and lets the candles burn as long as they will and can. – To extinguish the candles and not realise until after they are out that the stumps must be relit, or indeed replaced by other candles – that is not the Freemason's way.

Ernst. I think so too – And whatever costs blood is certainly not worth shedding blood for.[21]

---

[20] Knocks: Masonic signs of recognition.

[21] Saying attributed by the world traveller Georg Forster, who visited Lessing in 1779, to Benjamin Franklin.

Falk. Excellent! – Now ask whatever questions you like, and I must give you an answer.

Ernst. Then there will be no end to my questions.

Falk. Except that you can't find the beginning.

Ernst. Did I understand you correctly or not when we were interrupted? Did you or did you not contradict yourself? – For when you told me that *Freemasonry has always existed*, I did understand you to mean that not only its essential being, but also its present constitution, dates from time immemorial.

Falk. If the two were one and the same thing! – Essentially, Freemasonry is just as old as civil society. The two necessarily arose *together* – if, indeed, civil society is not simply an offshoot of Freemasonry. For the flame at the focus [of the burning glass] is also a product of the sun.

Ernst. I think I see what you mean –

Falk. But whether their relationship is that of mother and daughter or that of two sisters, their respective destinies have always influenced one another. Wherever civil society was present, Freemasonry was present too, and vice versa. It was always the surest sign of a healthy and vigorous constitution if it allowed Freemasonry to flourish alongside it, just as it is even now an infallible indication of a weak and apprehensive state if it is unwilling to tolerate publicly what it must tolerate covertly, whether it likes it or not.

Ernst. In other words, Freemasonry!

Falk. Of course! – For it depends basically not on *external associations*, which can so easily degenerate into *civil regulations*, but on the shared sentiments of kindred spirits.

Ernst. And who would venture to make these compulsory?

Falk. Meanwhile, of course, Freemasonry has at all times and places had to adapt and conform to civil society, which was invariably the stronger of the two. And however many forms civil society has assumed, Freemasonry has had no option but to assume them too, and every new form naturally had a new name. How can you believe that the name 'Freemasonry' is older than that dominant way of thinking among states to which Freemasonry was precisely adjusted?

Ernst. And what is this dominant way of thinking?

Falk. That must be left to your own researches. – Suffice it to say that the name 'Freemason', as the designation for a member of our secret fraternity, was unheard of before the beginning of the present century.

You can depend on it that it does not occur in any printed book before this time, and I'd like to meet the person who could show me it even in a written document of an earlier date.

Ernst. You mean the German name?

Falk. No, no! Also the original 'Free Mason', as well as all equivalent terms in any language whatsoever.

Ernst. Surely not! – Just think for a moment – In no printed book before the beginning of the present century? In none at all?

Falk. In none at all.

Ernst. I have nevertheless myself –

Falk. So? – Have you got some of that dust in your eyes which they continue to stir up?

Ernst. But there is a passage in –

Falk. In *Londinopolis*,²² you mean? – Dust!

Ernst. And the Act of Parliament under Henry VI?²³

Falk. Dust!

Ernst. And the grand privileges which Charles XI, King of Sweden, granted to the Gothenburg lodge?²⁴

Falk. Dust!

Ernst. And Locke?

Falk. What kind of lock?

Ernst. The philosopher. – His letter to the Earl of Pembroke; his notes on an interrogation recorded in Henry VI's own hand?²⁵

Falk. That must surely be a new discovery, for I don't know about it – But Henry VI again? – Dust, and nothing but dust!

Ernst. Surely not!

Falk. Do you know any milder expression for the manipulation of words and the forgery of documents?

Ernst. And you think they could have got away with this for so long, before the eyes of the world?

Falk. Why not? There are too few sensible people to contradict every stupidity the moment it arises. It's enough that these stupidities don't change their character with the passage of time. – Of course it would

---

²² *Londinopolis* (1657), by James Howell; Howell's reference to 'Free-Masons' is to the builders or 'operative' masons of the Middle Ages.

²³ This, too, refers to 'operative' masons.

²⁴ An apocryphal claim made by some eighteenth-century Freemasons.

²⁵ Another apocryphal legend, referred to in various Masonic publications of the eighteenth century.

be better if no stupidities whatsoever were inflicted on the public. For even the most contemptible nonsense can in the course of time acquire the appearance of something very serious and sacred, simply because it is contemptible nonsense which no one has taken the trouble to refute. Then it is said a thousand years later: 'Would anyone have got away with writing this for all the world to read if it hadn't been true? No one contradicted these trustworthy men at the time, and you propose to contradict them now?'

Ernst. Oh history, history! What are you?

Falk. Anderson's threadbare rhapsody,[26] which substituted the history of architecture for the history of the order, was all very well! At one time, and at his time, it may have been acceptable – and besides, the deception was so blatant! – But to continue today to build on this unstable ground, to continue to assert *in print* what one would be ashamed to say *aloud* to any serious man, to permit oneself, for the sake of prolonging a joke which ought to have been abandoned long ago, a *forgery* which, if it concerned some trifling civil interest, would be punishable by the *pillory*[27] –

Ernst. But what if it were after all true that something more were at stake here than a play on words? If it were after all true that the secret of the order had been preserved from long ago by the very craft which goes by the same name? –

Falk. If it were true?

Ernst. And must it not be true? – For how would the order otherwise have come to borrow the symbols of this very craft? This very one? And why not any other?

Falk. That is certainly a tricky question.

Ernst. Such a circumstance must surely have a cause?

Falk. It does have one.

Ernst. It does have one? And a different one from what is usually supposed?

Falk. A completely different one.

Ernst. Shall I guess, or may I ask?

Falk. If you had earlier asked me another question which I had long expected, you wouldn't find it hard to guess now.

Ernst. Another question which you had long expected?

---

[26] James Anderson, *The Constitutions of the Free-Masons* (1723; revised edition, 1767).
[27] Lessing uses the English words 'forgery' and 'pillory' here.

Falk. For when I told you that what Freemasonry is was not always called Freemasonry, what was more natural and obvious –

Ernst. Than to ask what it was previously called? – yes, indeed! – So I ask it now.

Falk. You ask what Freemasonry was known as before it was called Freemasonry? – *massoney* [28] –

Ernst. Why, yes, of course! *masonry* in English –

Falk. In English, not *masonry* but *masony*. – Not from *mason* or builder, but from *mase*, a table.

Ernst. *Mase*, a table? In what language?

Falk. In the language of the Anglo-Saxons, though not only in this, but also in the language of the Goths and Franks, for it was an original Germanic word, of which so many derivatives are still current today – or were at least until recently – such as *maskopie, masleidig, masgenosse*. [29] Even *masoney* was still in regular use in Luther's time, although it had by then acquired a somewhat more negative meaning.

Ernst. I know nothing of either its positive or its more negative meaning.

Falk. But you surely do know of our forefathers' custom of deliberating even the most important matters at table? – So *mase* was a table, and *masoney* was a closed and intimate company at table. And you can easily appreciate how a closed and intimate company at table became a drunken gathering, which is what Agricola[30] understood by the word *masoney*.

Ernst. Has the word 'lodge' fared any better in recent times?

Falk. But previously, before some of the *masoney*s degenerated in this manner and forfeited the esteem of the public, their reputation was correspondingly greater. There was no court in Germany, either small or large, which did not have its *masoney*. The old songbooks and histories bear witness to it. Special buildings connected with or close to the castles and palaces of the rulers took their name from them, a name which has so often been misinterpreted in more recent times. – And what more need I say to you in their defence than that the society of the *Round Table* was the first and oldest *masoney*, from which all the rest are descended?

Ernst. The Round Table? That takes us back to a very fabulous antiquity –

[28] From Old French *masnie* or *maisnie* ('household' or 'domestic community').
[29] 'Commercial company', 'averse to eating', and 'table companion'.
[30] Johann Agricola (c. 1492–1566), Protestant theologian and anthologist of proverbs.

Falk. However fabulous the story of King *Arthur* may be, the *Round Table* is much less so.

Ernst. But Arthur is supposed to have founded it.

Falk. Not at all! Not even according to the legend – Arthur, or his father, had taken it over from the Anglo-Saxons, as the very name *masoney* indicates. And what is more self-evident than that the Anglo-Saxons brought no customs over to England that they did not also leave behind them in their native land? It can also be seen from several Germanic peoples of those times that the tendency to form smaller, intimate societies within and alongside the larger civil society was characteristic of them.

Ernst. What do you mean by that? –

Falk. I declare that, the next time I am with you in town among my books, I will demonstrate in black and white everything that I have just told you in passing and perhaps without the necessary precision – Hear me now simply as one hears the first rumour of some major event: it stimulates one's curiosity more than it satisfies it.

Ernst. Where were we then?

Falk. The *masoney* was consequently a Germanic custom which the Saxons transplanted to England. Scholars disagree over who the *mase-thanes* among them were. They were by all appearances the noble members of the *masoney*, which took such deep root in this new soil that it survived under all the subsequent political changes and blossomed from time to time in the most impressive manner. The *masoney*s of the [Templars] in the twelfth and thirteenth centuries had a particularly high reputation. And it was a [Templar] *masoney* of this kind which, despite the abolition of the order, survived in the middle of London until the end of the seventeenth century – This is the start of a period in which the signposts of written history are, of course, absent; but a carefully preserved tradition, which displays so many internal hallmarks of truth, is available to make good this deficiency.

Ernst. And what prevents this tradition from finally being recorded in writing and raised to the rank of history?

Falk. Prevents? Nothing prevents it! On the contrary, everything recommends it – At least I feel – I feel entitled, indeed obliged, no longer to make any secret of it to you or anyone else in your position.

Ernst. Well, then! – I am full of expectation!

Falk. That [Templar] *masoney*, then, which still existed in London at the end of the last century – albeit in the utmost secrecy – had its meeting place quite near St Paul's Cathedral,[31] which was just being rebuilt. The architect of this second greatest church in the world was

Ernst. Christopher Wren –

Falk. And you have named the creator of the whole of present-day Freemasonry –

Ernst. Him?

Falk. In short – Wren, the architect of St Paul's Cathedral, near which an ancient *masoney* had met since time immemorial, was a member of this *masoney*, which he visited all the more often in the thirty years during which the building work lasted.

Ernst. I begin to suspect a misunderstanding.

Falk. Quite so! The true meaning of the word *masoney* was forgotten and lost by the English people. A *masony* which lay close to so important a building, and which the architect of this building visited so assiduously – what else could it be but a *masonry*, a society of building experts with whom Wren discussed the difficulties he encountered?

Ernst. That's natural enough!

Falk. The progress of the building, and of such a church, interested the whole of London. To obtain first-hand reports of this work, everyone who thought he knew something about architecture applied for admission to the supposed *masonry* – and applied in vain. And finally – you know Christopher Wren not just by name, but also realise how inventive and active a thinker he was. He had previously helped to draft the plan for a scientific society[32] *designed to make speculative truths more widely accessible and more useful to civil life.* He suddenly hit on the idea of an alternative society *which would move up from the practice of civil life to the level of speculation.* 'The one', he thought, 'would investigate what is useful in the realm of truth; and the other would investigate what is true in the realm of utility. What if I were to make some of the principles of the *masoney* exoteric? What if I were to conceal those things which cannot be made exoteric in the hieroglyphs and symbols of that craft which people are now determined to discover in the word *masony*? What if I were to expand the *masony* into a *Free-Masonry* in which a greater number of people could participate?' – Such were Wren's thoughts, and Freemasonry came into being. – Ernst! Are you feeling well?

---

[31] Lessing alludes to the Temple, south of Fleet Street.
[32] The Royal Society, of which Wren was President in 1681–2.

Ernst. I feel as if I'd been blinded.

Falk. Do you see any light now?

Ernst. Any? Too much all at once!

Falk. Do you now understand –

Ernst. No more, I beg you, my friend! – But don't you have business in town soon?

Falk. Do you want me to be there?

Ernst. Want? After you promised me –

Falk. Then I do have enough business there – To repeat: I have no doubt expressed myself too imprecisely and unsatisfactorily through speaking from memory – Among my books, you will be able to see and grasp – But the sun is setting, and you have to go into town. Goodbye! –

Ernst. Another sun has risen for me. Goodbye!

* * *

Note

A sixth dialogue which took place between these friends cannot be reproduced in the same manner. But the essential elements will be incorporated in critical notes to the fifth conversation, which are for the moment withheld.[33]

---

[33] No such continuation has ever come to light.

The education of the human race

All these things are in certain respects true for the same reason that they are in certain respects false.

Augustine[1]

Berlin, 1780

Editor's preface[2]

I published the first half of this essay in my *Contributions*.[3] I am now in a position to add the rest.

The author has placed himself on a hill, from which he believes he can see rather more than the prescribed course of his present day's journey.

But he does not call on any hasty traveller, who wishes only to reach his overnight lodging, to deviate from his path. He does not expect that the view which delights him should also delight every other eye.

And so, I should think, we could very well leave him to stand and wonder where he stands and wonders!

But what if he were to bring back from that immeasurable distance, which a soft evening glow neither wholly conceals nor wholly reveals, a pointer I have often felt in need of!

---

[1] Augustine, *Soliloquies* II.10; Augustine refers here to art, but taken out of context, his words apply to the content of the present work.

[2] Lessing never abandoned the pretence that he was merely the editor, not the author, of this work.

[3] See p. 79 above; the *Contributions* are the periodical referred to in note 1 on p. 61 above.

I mean this. – Why should we not see in all the positive religions simply the process whereby the human understanding in all places can alone develop, and will develop further still, instead of reacting with either mockery or anger to one of them? If nothing in the best of worlds deserves this scorn, this indignation on our part, why should the religions alone deserve it? Can God's hand be at work in everything except in our errors?

The education of the human race

§1

What education is to the individual human being, revelation is to the whole human race.

§2

Education is revelation imparted to the individual; and revelation is education which has been, and still is, imparted to the human race.

§3

I shall not consider here whether it is pedagogically useful to view education in this light. But in theology, it may certainly be of very great use, and may remove many difficulties, if one conceives of revelation as an education of the human race.

§4

Education gives the individual nothing which he could not also acquire by himself; it merely gives him what he could acquire by himself, but more quickly and more easily. Thus revelation likewise gives the human race nothing which human reason, left to itself, could not also arrive at; it merely gave it, and gives it, the most important of these things sooner.

§5

And just as education is not indifferent to the order in which it develops the human faculties, and just as it cannot impart everything to an individual at once, so also has God had to observe a certain order, a certain measure, in his revelation.

§6

Even if the first human being was immediately equipped with a concept of the one and only God, this concept, being imparted and not independently acquired, could not possibly retain its purity for long. As soon as human reason, left to its own devices, began to work on it, it divided the one immeasurable being into several more measurable parts, giving each of these a separate designation.

§7

Thus polytheism and idolatry arose by a natural process. And who knows for how many millions of years human reason would have drifted aimlessly among those errors – despite the fact that some individuals at all times and places recognised them as such – had it not pleased God to give it a better direction by means of a new impulse.

§8

But as he no longer could or would reveal himself to each *individual human being*, he chose an *individual people* for his special education; and he chose precisely the most uncultivated and barbarous people, in order to start with it from the very beginning.

§9

This was the people of Israel, of whom we do not even know what kind of worship it had in Egypt. For such despised slaves were not allowed to participate in the cult of the Egyptians, and the God of their fathers had become completely unknown to them.

§10

Perhaps the Egyptians had expressly forbidden them to have any god or gods, plunging them into the belief that they had no god or gods whatsoever, and that to have a god or gods was the exclusive right of the superior Egyptians – merely in order to tyrannise them with a greater semblance of justice. – Do Christians treat their slaves very differently even now? –

§11

To this uncouth people, God first let himself be made known as the God of its fathers, simply in order to acquaint and familiarise it with the idea that it, too, had a God of its own.

§12

Soon afterwards, through the miracles with which he led it out of Egypt and settled it in Canaan, he showed himself to it as a God more powerful than any other God.

§13

And by continuing to show himself to it as the most powerful of all – and this can only be *one* – he gradually accustomed it to the concept of the *One*.

§14

But how far did this concept of the One still fall short of the true transcendental concept of the One which reason learned at so late a stage to deduce with certainty from the concept of the infinite!

§15

But even if the superior members of the people were already drawing more or less close to the true concept of the One, the people at large were long unable to raise themselves to it; and this was the only true reason why they so often abandoned their one God and imagined they could find the One, i.e. the most powerful one, in some other god of another people.

§16

But what kind of *moral* education was so uncouth a people capable of, a people ill equipped for abstract thoughts and still so completely immersed in its childhood? – Of none other than that which is appropriate to the age of childhood, namely an education through immediate punishments and rewards of a sensuous kind.

§17

Thus here again, education and revelation coincide. God still could not give his people any other religion, any other law, than one through whose observance or non-observance it hoped or feared that it might become happy or unhappy here on earth. For its vision did not yet extend beyond this life. It knew of no immortality of the soul; it did not long for a life to come. But if God had revealed to it these things for which its reason was so little prepared, what else would this have been but the error of a vain pedagogue who prefers to push the child too far and boast of its progress instead of giving it thorough instruction?

§18

But what was the point, one may ask, of this education of so uncouth a people, a people with whom God had to make so completely new a beginning? My answer is this: so as to be able, in the course of time, to use individual members of this people with greater assurance as educators of all other peoples. In this people, he was educating the future educators of the human race. It was Jews who became these educators; and Jews alone, as men from a people educated in this way, were able to do so.

§19

To continue: for when the child had grown up with beatings and caresses and now reached the age of understanding, the father promptly thrust it out into foreign lands; and here it promptly recognised the good which it had enjoyed but failed to recognise in its father's house.

§20

While God led his chosen people through all the stages of a child's education, the other peoples of the earth had continued on their path by the light of reason. Most of them had lagged far behind the chosen people; only a few had advanced beyond it. And this is likewise the case with children who are allowed to grow up on their own: many remain completely backward, while some develop to an astonishing degree by themselves.

§21

But just as these more fortunate few do not disprove the use and necessity of education, neither do the few heathen peoples who up to now seemed to be ahead of the chosen people, even in their knowledge of God, do anything to disprove revelation. The child of education begins with slow but sure steps; it is late in overtaking the more fortunately organised child of nature; but it does overtake it, and then it can never again be overtaken by it.

§22

In the same way – leaving aside the doctrine of the unity of God, which is both present and absent in the books of the Old Testament – the fact that at least the doctrine of the soul's immortality and the related doctrine of reward and punishment in a future life are completely foreign to them does just as little to disprove the divine origin of these books. All the miracles and prophecies contained in them may nevertheless be perfectly genuine. For let us suppose that those doctrines were not only *absent* from it, but also *not* even *true* ; let us suppose that everything really comes to an end for human beings in this life: would the existence of God therefore be any the less demonstrated? Would God therefore be any the less free, and would it therefore befit him less, to take direct control of the temporal fate of any people among this transitory race? For the miracles he performed for the Jews, and the prophecies which he led them to record, were not just for the few mortal Jews in whose times they took place and were recorded: what he thereby intended concerned the entire Jewish people and the entire human race, which are perhaps destined to last eternally here on earth, even if each individual Jew and each individual human being dies and departs for ever.

§23

Once again: the lack of those doctrines in the Old Testament writings does nothing to disprove their divinity. Moses was indeed sent by God, although the sanction of his law extended only to this life. For why should it extend further? He was sent only to the people of *Israel*, to the Israelites *of that time*; and his assignment was perfectly appropriate to the knowledge, capacities, and inclinations of the Israelites *of that time*, as well as to their *future* destiny. And that is sufficient.

§24

This is as far as *Warburton*[4] should have gone, and no further. But this learned man overstretched his bow. Not content that the lack of those doctrines did not detract from Moses' divine mission, he even saw their absence as proof of it. If only he had tried to base this proof on the suitability of such a law for such a people! But he took refuge instead in a miracle extending without interruption from Moses to Christ, by means of which God supposedly made each individual Jew just as happy or unhappy as his obedience or disobedience to the law deserved. This miracle, he claimed, made up for the lack of those doctrines, without which no state can subsist; and this substitution, he claimed, proves precisely what that lack seems at first sight to deny.

§25

How fortunate it was that *Warburton* could not find anything to substantiate or lend credibility to this continuous miracle, which he saw as the essential element of the Israelites' theocracy. For had he been able to do so, he would thereby have rendered the difficulty truly insuperable – for me at least. – For what was supposed to corroborate the divine nature of Moses' mission would have cast doubts on the very matter [i.e. the

---

4 William Warburton, Bishop of Gloucester and author of *The Divine Legation of Moses* (1737–41).

immortality of the soul] which, while God did not wish to reveal it at this time, he certainly did not wish to make less comprehensible either.

§26

I shall explain myself by means of the counter-image to revelation. A primer for children may very well pass over in silence this or that important part of the science or art which it expounds, if the teacher judges that it is not yet appropriate to the capacities of the children for whom he is writing. But it must contain absolutely nothing which might block the children's way to the important items hitherto withheld, or point them in the wrong direction. Instead, all the avenues to these items must be carefully left open; and to direct the children away from even one of these avenues, or to delay their entry to it, would in itself be enough to turn the incomplete state of the primer into a fundamental fault.

§27

Thus, the doctrine of the soul's immortality and future retribution could also perfectly well be omitted from the writings of the Old Testament, those primers for the uncouth people of Israel who had so little practice in thinking; but they could on no account contain anything which might even delay the people for whom they were written on their way to this great truth. And what, to say the least, would have *delayed* them more than a promise of that miraculous retribution in this life, coming from him who makes no promises which he does not keep?

§28

For even if the unequal distribution of goods in this life, which seems to take so little account of virtue and vice, scarcely furnishes the strongest proof of the soul's immortality and of an afterlife in which this problem might be resolved, it is at least certain that, without this problem, the human understanding would still be far from discovering better and more rigorous proofs, and perhaps might never have discovered them at all. For what incentive would it have to look for these better proofs? Mere curiosity?

§29

This or that Israelite might well, of course, have extended to each individual member of the state those divine promises and threats which applied to the state as a whole, and have firmly believed that anyone who is pious must also be happy and that anyone who is, or becomes, unhappy must be paying the penalty for his misdeeds – a penalty which would at once be transformed into a blessing as soon as he desisted from the latter. Such a person seems to have written the Book of Job, for its plan is entirely in this spirit. –

§30

But daily experience could not possibly confirm this belief, otherwise a people with such experience would have lost *for ever* the opportunity to recognise and assimilate a truth with which it was not yet familiar. For if the pious man were absolutely happy, and if it were also an essential part of his happiness that his contentment should not be disturbed by terrible thoughts of death, and that he should die old and 'full of days',[5] how could he then long for another life? and how could he reflect on something which he did not long for? But if the pious man did not reflect on it, who else would do so? The villain? someone who felt the punishment of his misdeeds and, if he cursed this life, would so willingly have renounced any other?

§31

It was far less important that this or that Israelite directly and explicitly denied the immortality of the soul and future retribution on the grounds that the law made no mention of them. Denial by an individual – even if that individual were a Solomon[6] – did not retard the progress of the common understanding, and was already a proof in itself that the people had now moved a great step nearer to the truth. For the individual only denies what several are contemplating; and to contemplate something about which no one had previously been in the least concerned is half way to knowledge.

---

[5] Genesis 35.29.   [6] Ecclesiastes 3.19–22.

§32

Let us also admit that it is a heroic [kind of] obedience to obey the laws of God merely because they are God's laws, and not because he has promised to reward those who observe them here and in the hereafter – to observe them even if one already despairs utterly of any future reward and is not entirely certain of a temporal reward either.

§33

If a people has been educated in this heroic obedience towards God, must it not be destined, and more able than any others, to execute God's quite specific intentions? – Let the soldier who shows blind obedience to his leader also be convinced of his leader's sagacity, and then say what this leader may not dare to execute with his help! –

§34

In its Jehovah, the Jewish people had as yet venerated rather the mightiest than the wisest of all gods; it had as yet feared him as a jealous God rather than loved him: this, too, is a proof that the concepts it had of its One supreme God were not exactly the right concepts we should have of God. But the time had now come for these concepts to be expanded, refined, and corrected, for which purpose God employed a perfectly natural means, a better and more accurate yardstick against which the Jewish people now had occasion to assess him.

§35

Instead of assessing him, as before, only against the wretched idols of the small and uncouth tribes of the neighbourhood, with whom they lived in constant rivalry, they began, in their captivity under the wise Persian,[7] to measure him against the being of all beings as recognised and venerated by a more practised reason.

§36

Revelation had guided their reason, and now reason suddenly illuminated their revelation.

---

[7] Cyrus II (the Great), ruler of Persia 550–529 BC.

§37

That was the first reciprocal service which the two performed for one another; and such a reciprocal influence is so far from unbefitting to the author of both that without it, one of the two would be superfluous.

§38

The child sent into foreign lands saw other children who knew more and lived with greater propriety, and asked itself in shame: why do I not know this too? why do I not live in this way too? should I not have been taught this and urged to behave in this way in my father's house? Then it once again consults its primers, with which it had long since lost patience, in order to put the blame on them. But lo and behold! It realises that it is not the books which are to blame, but that it is itself entirely to blame for not having long since acquired precisely this knowledge and lived in precisely this way.

§39

Now that the Jews, on the strength of the purer Persian doctrine, recognised their Jehovah not just as the greatest of all national deities but as God; now that they could the more readily find him as such and show him to others in their sacred writings, which they now consulted once more, because he really was present in them; and now that they expressed – or were at least enjoined in these writings to feel – as great an aversion to all sensuous representations of God as the Persians had ever felt: was it any wonder that they found favour in the eyes of Cyrus with a divine worship which, though he perceived it as far inferior to pure Sabaism,[8] he also recognised as far superior to the crude idolatries which had replaced it in the land which the Jews had left?

§40

Thus enlightened [*erleuchtet*] with regard to their own unrecognised treasures, they came home and became a quite different people, whose first concern was to make this enlightenment [*Erleuchtung*] permanent among

---

[8] Ancient Semitic cult of the heavenly bodies.

themselves. Soon, there could be no further thought of apostasy and idolatry among them. For one may well become unfaithful to a national god, but never to God once he has been recognised as such.

§41

The theologians have tried to explain this complete change in the Jewish people in various ways, and one of them, who has shown very well how inadequate all these various explanations are, finally claimed that the true reason for this change was 'the manifest fulfilment of the proclaimed and recorded prophecies concerning the Babylonian captivity and the release therefrom'.[9] But even this reason can only be true in so far as it presupposes those refined concepts of God which had only now been attained. The Jews must only now have realised that working miracles and prophesying the future are the prerogative of God alone, whereas previously, they had also ascribed such powers to false idols, which is precisely why miracles and prophecies had hitherto made only a weak and transitory impression on them.

§42

No doubt the Jews had also learned more about the doctrine of the soul's immortality among the Chaldeans and Persians. They became more familiar with it in the schools of the Greek philosophers in Egypt.

§43

But since this doctrine did not have the same relevance to their Holy Scriptures as did the doctrine of God's unity and attributes; since the latter had been crassly overlooked in them by this sensual people, whereas the doctrine of immortality still had to be looked for; and since the doctrine of immortality also required *preparatory exercises*, whereas only *allusions* and *pointers* had been available – for all these reasons, the belief in immortality

---

[9] The source of this quotation has not been identified.

could naturally never be shared by the entire people. It was and remained the belief only of a particular sect[10] within them.

§44

What I call a *preparatory exercise* for the doctrine of immortality might include, for example, the divine threat to punish the misdeeds of the father upon the children down to the third and fourth generation.[11] This accustomed the fathers to live in thought with their most distant progeny, and to feel in advance the misfortune which they had brought upon these innocent people.

§45

What I call an *allusion* is something which should merely arouse curiosity and elicit a question – as, for example, the frequently used expression 'to be gathered to one's fathers'[12] to denote death.

§46

What I call a *pointer* is something which contains some kind of germ from which a truth hitherto withheld may be developed. Christ's inference from the description of God as 'the God of Abraham, Isaac, and Jacob'[13] was of this kind. This pointer does, however, seem to me capable of development into a rigorous proof.

§47

Such preparatory exercises, allusions, and pointers constitute the *positive* perfection of a primer, just as the above-mentioned quality of not blocking or rendering more difficult the way to those truths which are still withheld was its *negative* perfection.

§48

Add to all this the figures of speech and the style:

[10] The Pharisees.   [11] Exodus 20.5.   [12] See Genesis 49.29.   [13] Matthew 22.31–32.

(1) Those abstract truths which could not readily be omitted are represented by means of allegories and instructive individual examples related as real occurrences. Of this kind are the image of creation as the dawn of day; the origin of moral evil in the tale of the forbidden tree; the origin of linguistic diversity in the story of the tower of Babel, etc.

§49

(2) The style is sometimes plain and simple, sometimes poetic, full of tautologies throughout, but of the kind which exercise one's acumen by appearing at one moment to say something different while yet saying the same thing, and at another to say the same thing while basically meaning (or possibly meaning) something different –

§50

– and you have all the good qualities of a primer, for children as well as for a childlike people.

§51

But every primer is only for a certain age. To continue using it for longer than intended with a child who has outgrown it is harmful. For in order to do this in at all useful a way, one must read more into it than is present and introduce more than it can hold. One must look for and invent too many allusions and pointers, extract too much from the allegories, interpret the examples too circumstantially, and press the words too hard. This gives the child a petty, warped, and hairsplitting understanding; it makes the child secretive, superstitious, and full of contempt for everything comprehensible and straightforward.

§52

The very way in which the rabbis treated their sacred books! The very character which they thereby imparted to the spirit of their people!

§53

A better instructor must come and snatch the exhausted primer from the child's grasp. Christ came.[14]

§54

That portion of the human race which God had wished to include in *one* educational plan was now ready for the second great step in its education. But he had only wished to include in this plan that portion of humanity which by its language, activities, government, and other natural and political circumstances was already united in itself.

§55

That is, this portion of the human race had come so far in the exercise of its reason that it required, and could make use of, nobler and worthier motives for moral action than the temporal rewards and punishments which had hitherto been its guide. The child becomes a boy. Sweets and playthings give way to a burgeoning desire to become as free, as honoured, and as happy as its elder siblings.

§56

The better members of that portion of the human race had already long been accustomed to let themselves be governed by a *shadow* of such nobler motives. The Greek or Roman would do anything to live on after this life, if only in the memory of his fellow-citizens.

§57

It was time for the expectation of another *true* life after this life to gain an influence on their actions.

§58

And so Christ became the first *reliable* and *practical* teacher of the immortality of the soul.

---

[14] The first section of the work, as published in 1777, ends here; Lessing published the complete work, including the remaining forty-seven paragraphs, in 1780.

§59

The first *reliable* teacher. – Reliable through the prophecies which seemed fulfilled in him; reliable through the miracles he performed; reliable through his own revival after a death by which he had set the seal on his own doctrine. Whether we can still prove this revival and these miracles now is a question which I leave open – just as I leave it open who the person of this Christ was. All this may have been important then for the *acceptance* of his doctrine; but it is no longer so important now for the recognition of its truth.

§60

The first *practical* teacher. – For it is one thing to conjecture, desire, and believe in the immortality of the soul as a philosophical speculation, and another to direct one's inner and outer actions accordingly.

§61

And the first to teach this, at least, was Christ. For although the belief that evil actions will eventually be punished in the afterlife had already been introduced among many peoples before his time, this referred only to such actions as were prejudicial to civil society and were therefore already subject to civil penalties as well. To recommend an inner purity of the heart with a view to another life was reserved for him alone.

§62

His disciples faithfully propagated this doctrine. And if they had no other merit than that of having given more general currency among various peoples to a truth which Christ seemed to have destined only for the Jews, they would on this count alone have to be reckoned among the supporters and benefactors of the human race.

§63

If, however, they combined this one great doctrine with other doctrines whose truth was less evident and whose utility was less considerable, how could this be otherwise? Let us not blame them for this, but rather seriously investigate whether even these additional doctrines have not become a new *guiding impulse* for human reason.

§64

It is, at least, already clear from experience that the New Testament Scriptures in which these doctrines were eventually recorded have served, and continue to serve, as the second, better primer for the human race.

§65

For seventeen hundred years, they have exercised the human understanding more than any other books and illuminated it more than any other books, if only through the light which the human understanding itself brought into them.

§66

No other book could possibly have become so universally known among such diverse peoples; and the fact that such utterly disparate mentalities occupied themselves with this same book has unquestionably done more to further the progress of the human understanding than if each people had had a primer for its own specific use.

§67

It was also imperative that each people should regard this book for a time as the *non plus ultra* of its knowledge. For that is also how a boy should see his primer in the first instance, lest his impatience to be done with it should rush him on to things for which he has not yet laid the foundations.

§68

And what is still of the utmost importance now: – take care, you more able individual who stamp and fret on the last page of this primer, take care not to let your weaker classmates detect what you scent, or already begin to see!

§69

– Until they have caught up with you, those weaker classmates! Rather go back again to this primer yourself, and consider whether what you regard as procedural formulas or pedagogical expedients are not in fact something more.

§70

In the childhood of the human race, you have seen from the doctrine of God's unity that God also reveals purely rational truths directly – or permits and encourages purely rational truths to be taught for a time as directly revealed truths – in order to disseminate them more quickly and establish them more firmly.

§71

In the boyhood of the human race, you find it is the same with the doctrine of the soul's immortality. It is *preached* in the second, better primer, rather than *taught* as the result of human reasoning.

§72

Just as we are now able to dispense with the Old Testament for the doctrine of God's unity, and just as we are also gradually beginning to be able to dispense with the New Testament for the doctrine of the soul's immortality, might there not also be further truths of this kind adumbrated in the latter which we must wonder at as revelations until human reason has learned to deduce them from its other established truths, and to link them with these?

§73

For example, the doctrine of the Trinity. – What if this doctrine were at last to lead the human understanding, after endless vagaries to one side and the other, on to the right path to recognise that God cannot possibly be *one* in the sense that finite things are *one*, and that his unity must also be a transcendental unity which does not exclude a kind of plurality? – Must God not at least have the most complete representation of himself, i.e. a representation which contains everything which is present within him? But would it include everything within him if it contained only a representation, only a possibility of his *necessary reality*, as well as of his other qualities? This possibility exhausts the essence of his other qualities. But does it also exhaust that of his necessary reality? I think not. – Consequently, God can either have no complete representation of himself, or this complete representation is just as necessarily real as he himself is, etc. – Admittedly, my own image in a mirror is only an empty representation of me, because it contains only as much of me as is present in the rays of light which fall on its surface. But if this image contained *everything*, everything without exception which I myself possess, would it then still be an empty representation, or not rather a true duplication of myself? – If I believe that I can recognise a similar duplication in God, I am perhaps not so much in error as that language is inadequate for my concepts; and this much at least remains forever indisputable, that those who wished to popularise the idea could scarcely have expressed themselves more comprehensibly and fittingly than by describing it as a *Son* whom God begets from eternity.

§74

And the doctrine of original sin. – What if everything should finally convince us that man, at the *first and lowest* stage of his humanity, is quite simply not sufficiently in control of his actions to be able to follow moral laws?

§75

And the doctrine of the Son's satisfaction. – What if everything should finally compel us to assume that God, despite that original incapacity of man, nevertheless chose rather to give him moral laws and to forgive him all transgressions in consideration of his *Son* – i.e. in consideration of the independently existing sum of his own perfections, in comparison with which and in which every imperfection of the individual disappears – than not to give him them and thereby to exclude him from all moral happiness, which is inconceivable without moral laws?

§76

Let it not be objected that such rational speculations on the mysteries of religion are forbidden. – The word 'mystery', in early Christian times, meant something quite different from what we understand by it now; and the development of revealed truths into truths of reason is absolutely necessary if they are to be of any help to the human race. When they were revealed, of course, they were not yet truths of reason; but they were revealed in order to become such truths. They were, so to speak, the result of the calculation which the mathematics teacher announces in advance, in order to give his pupils some idea of what they are working towards. If the pupils were satisfied with knowing the result in advance, they would never learn to calculate, and would frustrate the intention with which the good master gave them a guideline to help them with their work.

§77

And why should we not nevertheless be guided by a religion whose historical truth, one may think, looks so dubious, to better and more precise conceptions of the divine being, of our own nature, and of our relations with God, which human reason would never have arrived at on its own?

§78

It is not true that speculations on these things have ever done damage and been disadvantageous to civil society. – This reproach should be aimed not at these speculations, but at the folly and tyranny of suppressing them and begrudging them to those who pursued them on their own initiative.

§79

On the contrary, such speculations – whatever individual results they may lead to – are unquestionably the *most fitting* exercises of all for the human understanding, so long as the human heart is at all capable of loving virtue for its everlasting salutary consequences.

§80

For given this selfishness of the human heart, to exercise the understanding only on what concerns our bodily needs would in effect be to blunt it rather than to sharpen it. It must at all costs be exercised on spiritual objects if it is to attain complete enlightenment [*Aufklärung*] and generate that purity of heart which enables us to love virtue for its own sake.

§81

Or shall the human race never arrive at these ultimate stages of enlightenment [*Aufklärung*] and purity? Never?

§82

Never? – Let me not contemplate this blasphemy, all-bountiful One! – Education has its *goal*, for the race no less than for the individual. Whatever is educated is educated for a purpose.

§83

The flattering prospects which are held out to the youth, the honour and prosperity which are dangled before him: what are they but means of educating him to be a man who, even when these prospects of honour and prosperity vanish away, will still be able to do his duty?

§84

If this is the aim of human education, can divine education fall short of it? Can nature fail to achieve with the whole what art achieves with the individual? Blasphemy! Blasphemy!

§85

No – it will certainly come, the time of fulfilment, when man, the more convinced his understanding feels of an ever better future, will nevertheless have no need to borrow the motives for his actions from this future; when he will do good because it is good, not because it brings arbitrary rewards which previously served only to fix and fortify his capricious gaze so that he might recognise the inner and better rewards of such action.

§86

It will certainly come, the time of a *new, eternal gospel*,[15] which is promised to us even in the primers of the New Covenant.

§87

Perhaps even certain enthusiasts [*Schwärmer*] of the thirteenth and four-teenth centuries[16] caught a glimpse of this new eternal gospel, and erred only in proclaiming that its coming was so close at hand.

§88

Perhaps their *three ages of the world* were not just an empty fancy; and they certainly had no ill intentions when they taught that the New Covenant must become just as *antiquated* as the Old has become. For them too, it was still the same economy of the same God. It was still – to put it in my terms – the same plan of the universal education of the human race.

§89

– Except that they were in too much of a hurry, and believed that, without enlightenment [*Aufklärung*] or preparation, they could at one stroke turn their contemporaries, who had scarcely emerged from their childhood, into men worthy of their *third age*.

§90

And that was precisely what made them enthusiasts. The enthusiast often has very accurate insights into the future – but he cannot wait for this future to come. He wishes it to come more quickly, and to do so through his agency. What nature takes thousands of years to prepare is expected to

[15] Cf. Revelation 14.6.
[16] Lessing alludes here to the ideas of Joachim of Flora or Fiore (c. 1132–1202) and his followers.

come to fruition at the precise moment of his existence. For what use is it to him if what he perceives as better does not become better in his lifetime? Will he come back [to life]? Does he expect to do so? – It is strange that this enthusiasm alone remains out of fashion among the enthusiasts!

§91

Go your inscrutable way, eternal providence! But let me not despair of you because of this inscrutability. – Let me not despair of you, even if your steps should seem to me to go backward! – It is not true that the shortest line is always the straight one.

§92

You have so much to take with you on your eternal way! So many diversions to make! And what if it were as good as certain that the great, slow-moving wheel which brings the [human] race closer to its perfection is only set in motion by smaller, faster wheels, each of which makes its own contribution to this end?

§93

Exactly so! Every individual – one sooner, another later – must first have traversed the same route whereby the race attains its perfection. But can he have traversed it in one and the same lifetime? Can he, in this life, have been both a sensual Jew and a spiritual Christian? Can he have overtaken both of them in this same life?

§94

Well, surely not! – But why should every individual not have been present more than once in this world?

§95

Is this hypothesis so ridiculous just because it is the oldest one? Because the human understanding hit upon it at once, before it was distracted and weakened by the sophistry of the schools?

§96

Why should I not likewise have already taken all the steps here towards my perfection which merely temporal rewards and punishments can lead mankind to take?

§97

And why should I not, on another occasion, have taken all those steps which the prospects of eternal rewards give us so strong an incentive to take?

§98

Why should I not come back as often as I am able to acquire new knowledge and new accomplishments? Do I take away so much on one occasion that it may not be worth the trouble coming back?

§99

Should I not come back because of this? – Or because I forget that I have been here before? It is as well that I should forget. The memory of my previous states would only permit me to make poor use of the present one. And does what I *must* forget for the present have to be forgotten for ever?

§100

Or am I not to return because too much time would be lost in so doing? – Lost? – And what exactly do I have to lose? Is not the whole of eternity mine?

[Friedrich Heinrich Jacobi, Recollections of conversations with Lessing in July and August 1780]

I had always revered the great man; but my desire to make his closer acquaintance had only become more intense since his theological controversies, and after I had read his *Parable*. It was my good fortune that *Allwill*[1] aroused his interest, that he sent me some friendly messages, at first through travellers, and finally, that he wrote to me in 1779. I replied that I was planning a journey in the following spring which would take me through Wolfenbüttel, where I longed to conjure up through him the spirits of several wise men whose views on certain things I was unable to determine.

My journey duly took place, and on the afternoon of 5 July [1780] I first held Lessing in my arms.

On that same day, we discussed many important matters; we also discussed people – moral and immoral, atheists, deists, and Christians.

On the following morning, Lessing came into my room before I had finished some letters I was writing. I gave him various items from my note-case to occupy him until I was ready. As he handed them back, he asked me whether I had anything else for him to read. 'Yes!', I said as I sealed the letters. 'There's another poem here. – Since you have given offence on various occasions, you might as well be offended for once yourself.' . . .[2]

---

[1] Jacobi's novel *Eduard Allwills Papiere* [*Edward Allwill's Papers*] (1775–6).

[2] These and other series of dots denoting ellipses are in Jacobi's original text (cf. note a on p. 245 below).

Prometheus[3]

Cover your heaven, Zeus,
With cloudy vapours
And like a boy
Beheading thistles
Practise on oaks and mountain peaks –
Still you must leave
My earth intact
And my small hovel, which you did not build,
And this my hearth
Whose glowing heat
You envy me.

I know of nothing more wretched
Under the sun than you gods!
Meagerly you nourish
Your majesty
On dues of sacrifice
And breath of prayer
And would suffer want
But for children and beggars,
Poor hopeful fools.

Once too, a child,
Not knowing where to turn,
I raised bewildered eyes
Up to the sun, as if above there were
An ear to hear my complaint,
A heart like mine
To take pity on the oppressed.

Who helped me
Against the Titans' arrogance?
Who rescued me from death,
From slavery?
Did not my holy and glowing heart,
Unaided, accomplish all?
And did it not, young and good,

---

[3] This famous poem by Goethe, given here in Michael Hamburger's translation, had not previously been published.

Cheated, glow thankfulness
For its safety to him, to the sleeper above?

I pay homage to you? For what?
Have you ever relieved
The burdened man's anguish?
Have you ever assuaged
The frightened man's tears?
Was it not omnipotent Time
That forged me into manhood,
And eternal Fate,
My masters and yours?

Or did you think perhaps
That I should hate this life,
Flee into deserts
Because not all
The blossoms of dream grew ripe?

Here I sit, forming men
In my image,
A race to resemble me:
To suffer, to weep,
To enjoy, to be glad –
And never to heed you, Like me!

Lessing. (after reading the poem and handing it back to me). I haven't taken offence; I've had all this long ago at first hand.
I. You know the poem?
Lessing. I've never read the poem before; but I think it's good.
I. Of its kind, I agree; otherwise I wouldn't have shown it to you.
Lessing. That's not what I meant . . . The point of view from which the poem is written is my own point of view . . . I have no more use for the orthodox concepts of the deity; they give me no satisfaction. Ἕν καὶ Πᾶν!⁴ I know nothing else. That's also the sense of this poem; and I must confess that I like it very much.
I. Then you would be pretty much in agreement with Spinoza.
Lessing. If I must call myself after anyone, I know of no one else.
I. Spinoza will do; but his name will hardly lead us to salvation!

---

⁴ 'One and all' (i.e. God is one, and all things are God).

Lessing. Yes, if you say so!... And yet... Do you know of anything better?...

Director Wolke of Dessau[5] had meanwhile arrived, and we went to the library together.

The following morning, I had returned to my room to dress after breakfast, and Lessing joined me a little later. As soon as we were alone, he began to speak.

Lessing. I have come to discuss my Ἓν καὶ Πᾶν with you. You seemed shocked yesterday.

I. You took me by surprise, and I was confused. I wasn't shocked. Of course I wasn't prepared to find that you were a Spinozist or pantheist, and even less for you to announce it to me in such plain and forthright terms. My main reason for coming here was to seek your help against Spinoza.

Lessing. So you do know him?

I. I think I know him as very few can have known him.

Lessing. Then there's no help for you. You should rather make friends with him properly. There is no other philosophy than that of Spinoza.

I. That may be true. For the determinist, if he wants to be consistent, must become a fatalist: and then all the rest follows.

Lessing. I see that we understand one another. I'm all the more eager to hear from you what you think the *spirit* of Spinozism was – I mean the spirit by which Spinoza himself was driven.

I. That was surely none other than the old 'nothing arises out of nothing', which Spinoza considered in more abstract terms than the philosophical cabbalists[6] and others before him. Viewing it in these more abstract terms, he found that whenever anything arose within the infinite, no matter what images or words were used to describe it, and whenever any change took place within it, the emergence of *something out of nothing* was posited. So he rejected any *transition* from the infinite to the finite, and all transitory causes in general, whether secondary or remote; and he replaced the emanating En Sof[7] with a purely *immanent* one, an indwelling cause of

---

[5] Christian Wolke, Director of Basedow's 'Philanthropic Institute' (cf. note 5 to p. 188 above) in Dessau.

[6] Adherents of Jewish mysticism, as expounded in the Cabbala.

[7] The archetypal light from which, according to the Cabbala, all being emanates.

the universe, eternally unchanging *in itself*, which, taken together with all its consequences – is one and the same.

. . . . . .ª

This indwelling, infinite cause has, as such, no explicit understanding or will, for given its transcendental *unity* and constant absolute infinity, it can have no object of thought or volition; and an ability to generate a concept *before the concept*, or a concept which existed before its object and served as *its own comprehensive cause*, or equally, a will which exercised volition and determined itself *completely*, are all absurdities . . .

. . . The objection that an infinite series of effects is impossible (and they are not *merely* effects, because the indwelling cause is always and everywhere present) is self-refuting, because every series, if it is not to arise out of *nothing*, must be absolutely infinite. And from this it follows in turn that, since each individual concept must arise out of another individual concept and relate *directly to an actually present object*, neither individual thoughts nor individual determinations of the will are to be found in the first cause, whose nature is infinite, but only their inner, elementary, and universal substance [*Urstoff*] . . . The first cause can just as little act in accordance with intentions or final causes as it can itself be the result of a particular intention or final cause; and it can just as little have an *initial* reason or *final cause* for doing something as it can have a *beginning* or *end* within itself . . . But basically, what we call succession or continuity is merely an illusion; for since a *real effect* is simultaneous with its *real and comprehensive* cause, and differs from it only in our conception [*Vorstellung*] of it, succession and continuity are *in truth* only a particular way of looking at the diversity within the infinite.

Lessing. . . . . . . Then we shall not fall out over our personal creed.

I. Let's not do that on any account. But my creed is not to be found in Spinoza.

Lessing. I hope it's not to be found in any book.

I. Not just that. – *I believe in an intelligent and personal cause of the universe.*

ª As I continue this description, I shall condense my account as far as possible by omitting the intervening remarks, thereby avoiding excessive wordiness. What now follows was occasioned by Lessing's observation that the most obscure aspect of Spinoza was that which Leibniz also found most obscure and had not fully understood (*Theodicy*, §173). I make this point here once and for all, and I shall not repeat it when I take similar liberties with the rest of the account.

Lessing. Oh, so much the better! Then I'm sure to hear something quite new.

I. Don't build up too many hopes. I get out of the difficulty by a *salto mortale*,[8] and you don't much care for *somersaults*.

Lessing. Don't say that! So long as I don't have to do one myself. And you will soon land on your feet again. So – if it's not a secret – tell me more!

I. You can watch me do it any time. The whole operation consists in my drawing from fatalism conclusions directly opposed to fatalism and all that is connected with it. – If there are only efficient causes and no final causes, the only role for our thinking capacity in the whole of nature is that of an onlooker; its sole function is to accompany the mechanism of active forces. The conversation we are at present having is merely a disposition of our bodies; and the whole content of this conversation, reduced to its elements, consists of extension, movement, and degrees of velocity, together with the concepts of these and the concepts of these concepts. The inventor of the clock did not basically invent it; he merely watched it emerging from blindly developing forces. The same was true of Raphael when he devised 'The School of Athens', and of Lessing when he composed his *Nathan* [*the Wise*]. The same applies to all philosophies, arts, forms of government, and wars on land and at sea – in short, to everything possible. For even the emotions and passions do not operate in so far as they are sensations and thoughts – or more precisely, in so far as they *are accompanied by* sensations and thoughts. We only *believe* we are acting out of anger, love, generosity, or rational decisions. A complete illusion! In all of these cases, what moves us is basically *a something* which *knows nothing* of all this, and which, *to that extent*, is absolutely devoid of sensation and thought. These, however (i.e. sensation and thought), are only concepts of extension, movement, degrees of velocity, etc. – I am unable to refute the opinion of anyone who can accept these conclusions. But anyone who cannot accept them must be diametrically opposed to Spinoza.

Lessing. I see that you would like to have a free will. I have no desire for a free will. In fact, what you have just said doesn't alarm me in the least. It is one of our human prejudices to regard thought as the first and foremost factor and to try to derive everything from it, whereas everything,

---

[8] 'mortal leap'.

including our own conceptions [*Vorstellungen*], depends on higher principles. Extension, movement, and thought are obviously based on a higher power which they do not remotely exhaust. It must be infinitely superior to this or that effect; and so it may experience a kind of pleasure which not only transcends all concepts, but lies completely *beyond* conceptuality. The fact that we cannot conceive of it does not rule out its possibility.

I. You go further than Spinoza does; for him, *understanding* [*Einsicht*] was everything.

Lessing. For *human beings*! But he was far from presenting our miserable manner of acting according to intentions as the highest method, and from putting thought above all else.

I. For Spinoza, understanding is the best aspect of *all finite* natures, because it is the one respect in which each finite nature transcends its finitude. One could in a sense say that he, too, ascribed two souls to every being: one which relates only to the present individual thing, and another which relates to the whole. He also invests this second soul with immortality. But as for the one infinite substance of Spinoza, it has, in itself, no particular existence of its own distinct from individual things. If it did have its own particular individual reality for itself as a unit (if I may so put it), if it had a personality and life of its own, understanding would be its best feature too.

Lessing. Good. But what sort of conceptions do you have of your personal, extramundane deity? Those of Leibniz, perhaps? I fear that he was himself a Spinozist at heart.

I. Do you really mean that?

Lessing. Do you really doubt it? – Leibniz's conceptions of truth were such that he could not bear to have too narrow limits imposed on it. Many of his assertions are a product of this way of thinking, and it is often very difficult, even with the keenest perception, to discover what he really means. It is for that very reason that I value him so highly – for this grand manner of thinking, and not for this or that opinion which he only appeared to have, or may have had in reality.

I. Quite correct. Leibniz liked to 'strike fire from every stone'.[9] But you did say of a certain opinion, i.e. Spinozism, that Leibniz *was at heart attached to it*.

---

[9] Jacobi quotes here from Lessing's essay *Leibniz on Eternal Punishment*: see p. 46 above.

Lessing. Do you recall a passage in Leibniz where it is said of God that he exists in a constant state of expansion and contraction, and that this is the creation and continued existence of the world?

I. I know about his fulgurations,[10] but I don't know the passage you refer to.

Lessing. I shall look it up, and you must then tell me what a man like Leibniz could or *must* have meant by it.

I. Show me the passage. But I must tell you in advance that, when I call to mind so many other passages of this same Leibniz, so many of his letters, treatises, his *Theodicy* and *Nouveaux Essais*, and his philosophical career in general, my mind reels at the hypothesis that this man may not have believed in an extramundane cause of the world, but only an intramundane one.

Lessing. In this respect I must defer to you. This will also remain the dominant view, and I admit that I went rather too far. Nevertheless, the passage I had in mind, and some others too, do remain extraordinary. – But we must not forget: what ideas induce you to believe in the opposite of Spinozism? Do you think that Leibniz's *Principles*[11] put an end to it?

I. How could I, when I was firmly convinced that a consistent determinist is no different from a fatalist? . . . The monads, together with their connections [*vinculis*],[12] leave me with as little understanding of extension and thought, and *reality* in general, as I had before, and I don't know which way to turn . . . Besides, I know of no philosophical system which corresponds so closely to Spinozism as that of Leibniz; and it is hard to say which of their originators deluded us and himself more completely – albeit in good faith! . . . Mendelssohn showed in a published work that pre-established harmony is present in Spinoza.[13] It follows from this alone that much more of Leibniz's basic doctrines must be present in Spinoza, or else Leibniz and Spinoza (who would hardly have taken to Wolff's teachings) cannot have been the astute thinkers they undoubtedly were. I am confident that I could expound the whole of Leibniz's psychology on the basis of Spinoza . . . They both have basically the same doctrine on freedom, and the difference between their theories is purely illusory. Whereas Spinoza elucidates our feeling of freedom by the example of a stone which

---

[10] See Leibniz, *Monadology*, §47.

[11] *Principles of Nature and Grace, Founded on Reason* (1714).

[12] See *Monadology*, §56.

[13] See note 1 to p. 32 above, and Lessing's own fragment on this same topic (pp. 32–4 above).

can think and knows that it is endeavouring to continue its movement to the best of its ability (Letter LXII, *Opera posthuma*, pp. 584f.),[14] Leibniz elucidates it by the example of a magnetic needle which desires to point north and believes that it turns independently of any other cause, being unaware of the imperceptible movement of the magnetic matter (*Theodicy*, Pt I, §50). – . . . Leibniz explains final causes by an appetite or immanent endeavour (endowed with self-consciousness).[15] So also Spinoza, who could fully accept them in this sense, and for whom *desire and represen-tation of external things constitute the essence of the soul*, just as they do for Leibniz. – In short, if we pursue the matter to its conclusion, we discover that, for Leibniz as well as for Spinoza, every final cause presupposes an efficient cause . . . Thought is not the source of substance, but substance is the source of thought. Thus something which does not think must be assumed as pre-existing thought, something which, if not necessarily in reality, at least in our conception [*Vorstellung*] of it, in its essence and inner nature, must be considered primary. Leibniz was therefore honest enough to call souls 'spiritual automata'.[16] But how (I speak here in accordance with Leibniz's most basic and fullest sense, so far as I understand it) the principle of all souls can *exist* and *act* on its own . . . , spirit before matter, thought before its object – he left this great knot, which he would have had to unravel if he were really going to resolve our difficulties, as convoluted as it was before . . .

Lessing. . . . . . . I will give you no peace until you acknowledge this par-allelism openly . . . For people still speak of Spinoza as if he were a dead dog . . .

I. They will always speak of him thus. To grasp Spinoza properly requires too long and too persistent an intellectual effort. And no one to whom a single line of the *Ethics* remains obscure has grasped him properly – no one who does not comprehend how this great man could have that firm and profound conviction of his philosophy which he expresses so often and so emphatically. Even at the end of his life, he wrote: . . . 'I do not presume to have *discovered* the best philosophy, *but I know that I understand the true one.*'[17] – Few can have tasted such peace of mind, or such an intellectual heaven, as this pure, clear thinker achieved.

Lessing. And you are not a Spinozist, Jacobi!

---

[14] Letter to G. H. Schuller, 1674.   [15] See *Monadology*, §§15–19.   [16] *Theodicy*, Pt I, §52.
[17] To Albert de Burgh, end of 1675.

I. No, on my honour!

Lessing. Then with *your* philosophy, you must, on your honour, turn your back on all philosophy.

I. Why should I turn my back on all philosophy?

Lessing. In that case, you are a complete sceptic.

I. On the contrary, I withdraw from a philosophy which makes complete scepticism necessary.

Lessing. And where do you go from there?

I. Towards that light of which Spinoza says that it illuminates itself as well as the darkness. – I love Spinoza because, more than any other philosopher, he has led me to the complete conviction that certain things cannot be further explained, and that we must not therefore close our eyes to them, but take them as we find them. I have no concept that is closer to my heart than that of final causes; no more lively conviction than *that I do what I think* rather than *that I can only think what I do*. Of course this means that I must assume a source of thought and action which remains wholly inexplicable to me. But if I insist absolutely on explaining it, I must arrive at that second proposition which, considered in its full extent and applied to individual instances, a human mind can scarcely find bearable.

Lessing. You express yourself almost as bluntly as the Imperial Diet at Augsburg;[18] but I remain an honest Lutheran and retain 'the more bestial than human error and blasphemy that there is no free will', a conclusion which the *pure, clear* mind of your Spinoza was also able to accept.

I. But Spinoza also had to go to considerable lengths to conceal his fatalism in its application to human behaviour, especially in Parts Four and Five,[19] where I might say that he sometimes stoops to sophistry. – And that was just the point I was making: that even the greatest thinker must end up in absurdities if he insists absolutely on explaining everything, on making sense of it by means of clear concepts and refusing to accept anything else.

Lessing. And what of those who don't try to explain it?

I. I believe that anyone who doesn't try to explain what is incomprehensible, but wishes only to know the limit beyond which it begins and

---

[18] At this Diet, whose resolution Lessing proceeds to quote, Luther's teachings were condemned as heretical.

[19] Of his *Ethics*.

to recognise that it is there, will achieve the greatest scope for genuine human truth within himself.

Lessing. Words, dear Jacobi; words! The limit you wish to impose is impossible to define. And beyond it, you give unlimited scope to dreams, nonsense, and blindness.

I. I believe that this limit could be defined. I don't want to *impose* a limit, but only to find the limit which is imposed already, and to leave it where it is. And as far as nonsense, dreams, and blindness are concerned...

Lessing. They are at home wherever confused concepts prevail.

I. And even more so where *fallacious* concepts prevail. Even the blindest and most senseless belief – if not the most foolish one – will in that case rule supreme. For once someone has become enamoured of certain explanations, he will blindly accept every consequence drawn from them by a deduction which he cannot refute, even if it told him that he was standing on his head.

... In my judgement, the greatest service an enquirer can perform is to uncover and reveal *existence* [*Dasein*]... Explanation will be a means he employs, a path towards his goal – his proximate but never his ultimate end. His ultimate end is what cannot be explained: it is irreducible, immediate, and simple.

... A boundless obsession with explanation makes us look so feverishly for common factors that we overlook the differences; we constantly seek to make connections when we might often, with vastly greater benefit, make distinctions... Besides, if we simply *put* or *hang* together the explicable aspects of things, a certain light will shine within our soul which blinds it more than it illuminates it. We then sacrifice what Spinoza, profoundly and sublimely, calls 'knowledge of the supreme kind'[20] to inferior kinds of knowledge; we close the eye through which the soul perceives God and itself, in order to look with less distraction through what are only the eyes of the body...

Lessing. Good, very good! I have a use for all of that too; but I cannot do the same thing with it. At any rate, I rather like your *salto mortale*; and I can see how a thinking head might perform this kind of headstand just to get out of the bit. Take me with you, if you can!

I. If you will just step on the springboard which lifts me off, the rest will take care of itself.

[20] *Ethics*, Pt V, Props. 25–7.

Lessing. But even that would mean taking a leap which I can no longer impose on my old legs and heavy head.

* * *

This conversation, of which I have supplied only the essentials here, was followed by others which led us, by more than one route, back to the same topics.

Lessing once said, half smiling, that he himself was perhaps the supreme being, and at present in the state of extreme contraction. – I begged for my own existence. – He replied that that was certainly not what he meant, and he explained himself in a manner which reminded me of Henry More[21] and van Helmont.[22] He then explained himself more clearly, but in such a way that I was again able to accuse him of something approaching cabbalism. This greatly delighted him, so I took the opportunity to speak out in favour of the Cabbala, *in the strictest sense, from the point of view* that it is inherently impossible to derive the infinite from the finite as it presents itself to us, and then to comprehend their mutual relation and express it through any kind of formula. Consequently, if one wished to say anything about it, one would have to rely on revelation. Lessing continued to maintain that he '*required a natural account of everything*'; and I maintained that there could be no natural philosophy of the supernatural, although both (the natural and the supernatural) were obviously present.

* * *

If Lessing wished to imagine a *personal* deity, he conceived of it as the soul of the universe; and he conceived of the whole by analogy with an organic body. This soul of the universe, *as a soul*, would therefore – like all other souls, according to all possible systems – be only an effect. But its organic extent could not be conceived by analogy with the organic *parts* of this extent, inasmuch as it could not relate to anything existing outside itself or take anything from it or give anything back to it. Thus, in order to sustain its life, it would have to withdraw from time to time into itself, so

[21] Henry More (1614–87), philosophical mystic and one of the Cambridge Platonists.
[22] Johann Baptist van Helmont (1579–1644), Flemish scientist and mystic – or possibly his son, Franciscus Mercurius van Helmont (1618–99), who worked within the same neo-Platonic tradition.

to speak, and combine death and resurrection, together with life, within itself. One could, however, conceive of the inner economy of such a being in various different ways.

Lessing was very attached to this idea, and he applied it – sometimes seriously and sometimes in jest – to all kinds of instances. – When he accompanied me, after my second visit to him, to see Gleim[23] at Halberstadt, we were sitting at table and it unexpectedly began to rain. Gleim expressed regret at this, for we had planned to go into his garden after the meal. Lessing, who was sitting next to me, said: 'Jacobi, you realise that this is *my* doing.' I replied: 'Or *mine*, perhaps'. Gleim looked at us with some astonishment, but did not pursue the matter further.

* * *

Lessing could not come to terms with the idea of a personal and absolutely infinite being in the unchanging enjoyment of its supreme perfection. He associated it with such an impression of *infinite boredom* that it caused him pain and apprehension.

He considered it not unlikely that human beings might experience a continued personal existence after death. He told me that, in the work by Bonnet which he was currently rereading, he had come across ideas which were very close to his own on this subject, and to his own system in general.[24] The turn the conversation took and my own intimate knowledge of Bonnet (whose collected works I used to know almost by heart) were responsible for my failure to question him on this; and since I no longer found anything obscure or doubtful about Lessing's system, I never consulted Bonnet again with this in mind until the present occasion finally led me to do so today. The work by Bonnet which Lessing was then rereading is surely none other than his *Palingenesis*,[25] with which you are doubtless familiar; and the seventh section of the first part of that work, together with the thirteenth chapter of the fourth section of the *Contemplation de la nature*,[26] to which Bonnet himself refers in the former work, probably contains the ideas which Lessing had in mind. One passage in

---

[23] Johann Wilhelm Ludwig Gleim (1719–1803), poet and friend of Lessing.

[24] Charles Bonnet (1720–93), Swiss naturalist and philosopher; by 'his own system', Lessing means his own ideas concerning metempsychosis.

[25] *Palingénésie philosophique* (1769); this work almost certainly inspired Lessing's fragment *That More than Five Senses Are Possible for Human Beings* (pp. 180–3 above).

[26] Another of Bonnet's works, published in 1764.

particular struck me, in which Bonnet says (p. 246 of the first edition): 'Could anyone imagine that the universe is less *harmonious* – I almost said less organic – than an *animal*?'

* * *

On the day on which I parted from Lessing to continue my journey to Hamburg, we again talked seriously and at length about all these subjects. Very little separated us in our philosophies, and we differed only in our faith. I gave Lessing three works by the philosopher Hemsterhuis,[27] of whose writings he knew nothing apart from the *Lettre sur la sculpture*: these were the *Lettre sur l'homme et ses rapports*, *Sophyle ou la philosophie*, and *Aristée ou la divinité*. I was reluctant to leave *Aristée* with him, for I had only just received it on my way through Münster, and I had not yet read it myself; but Lessing's desire to read it was too great.

On my return, I found him so enraptured with *Aristée* that he had resolved to translate it himself. – It was manifestly Spinozism, said Lessing, in such a fine exoteric garb that the garb itself also helped to amplify and elucidate the inner doctrine. – I assured him that Hemsterhuis, to the best of my knowledge (I did not yet know him personally) was not a Spinozist: I even had confirmation from Diderot that this was the case. – 'Read the book', Lessing replied, 'and you will no longer be in any doubt. In his *Lettre sur l'homme et ses rapports*, it's still rather inconclusive, and it may be that Hemsterhuis had not at that time fully recognised his Spinozism himself; but now, he is quite certainly clear about it.'

This judgement may seem paradoxical to anyone who is less familiar with Spinozism than Lessing was. What he described as the exoteric garb of *Aristée* can quite properly be seen merely as an extension of the doctrine of the inseparable, intimate, and eternal connection of the infinite with the finite, of the universal (and in that respect indeterminate) power with the determinate, individual power, and of their necessarily opposite directions. The rest of *Aristée* can scarcely be seen as incompatible with Spinozism either. – Nevertheless, I must also solemnly testify that Hemsterhuis is certainly not a Spinozist, but is completely opposed to that doctrine in its essential points.

---

[27] François Hemsterhuis (1721–90), Dutch philosopher.

Lessing had not yet read Hemsterhuis's *Lettre sur les désirs*. It arrived, in a parcel addressed to me, just after I left.[b] He wrote to me that his impatient curiosity had given him no peace until he opened the package and sent the remaining contents on to me at Kassel. He added: 'As for the work itself, which gives me uncommon pleasure, I shall have more to say shortly.'

Not long before he died, he wrote to me (on the fourth of December [1780]): 'It occurs to me on reading *Woldemar*[28] that I had promised to inform you of my thoughts concerning Hemsterhuis's system of love. And you won't believe how closely these thoughts are connected with that system, which, in my opinion, does not really explain anything and seems to me, as the mathematicians would say, merely to substitute one formula for another, so that it is more likely to lead me into new errors than to bring me any closer to solving the problem. – But am I now in a position to write what I want to write? – I cannot even write what I have to write (etc.).'

* * *

Until I got to know Lessing's opinions in the manner described above, I was firmly of the belief, which was also supported by *evidence*, that Lessing was an orthodox theist, so that certain passages in his *Education of the Human Race* – especially §73 – were completely incomprehensible to me. I wonder whether anyone can make sense of this passage other than in terms of Spinozism. But in this light, it is very easy to interpret it. The God of Spinoza is the pure principle of reality in all that is real, of *being* in all existence, devoid of individuality and absolutely infinite. The unity of this God is based on the identity of the indistinguishable, so that it does not exclude a kind of plurality. Viewed *solely* in this transcendental unity, however, the deity must be absolutely devoid of reality, which can only find expression in determinate individuality. The latter – i.e. *reality* together with its concept – is therefore based on *natura naturata* (the Son from all eternity), just as the former – i.e. *potentiality, the essence,*

---

[b] During my first stay in Wolfenbüttel, I had been obliged to send away for it in order to satisfy Lessing's great desire to read this work.

[28] Novel by Jacobi, published in 1779.

the substantial being of the infinite together with its concept – is based on *natura naturans* (the Father).[29]

Since I have already tried to convey something of the spirit of Spinozism, I see no need for me to enlarge further on it here.

You know as well as I do how many more or less confused forms these same notions have assumed among human beings since the earliest antiquity. – Language is indeed inadequate to our concepts here, just as one concept is inadequate to the other.

Several people can testify that Lessing cited his Ἓν καὶ Πᾶν, frequently and emphatically, as the essence of his theology and philosophy. He stated and wrote it on various occasions as his definitive motto. Thus it can also be seen in Gleim's summerhouse, written in his own hand beneath a motto of mine.

Further information on this might be obtainable from the Marchese Lucchesini,[30] who was in Wolfenbüttel not long before I was. Lessing praised him highly to me as a very lucid thinker.

* * *

What I have reported is not a tenth of what I could have reported if my memory were sufficiently reliable with regard to formulations and expression.[31] For this very reason, I have cited Lessing's own words as sparingly as possible in what I have actually related. After whole days of conversation on very many different things, one's memory of detail is inevitably lost. And a further factor is involved. Once I knew quite definitely that *Lessing does not believe in any cause of things distinct from the world itself*, or that *Lessing is a Spinozist*, what he subsequently said about it in this or that new formulation did not impress itself on me more profoundly than any other matters. It could not occur to me that I ought to keep a record of his words, and it seemed to me very understandable that Lessing was a Spinozist. If he had said the opposite of what my curiosity expected, I would very probably still be able to give an account of every significant word that he uttered.

---

[29] *Natura naturata* and *natura naturans*: passive and active principles within Spinoza's universe (*Ethics*, Pt I, Prop. 29).
[30] Girolamo Lucchesini (1751–1825), appointed Librarian to Frederick the Great in 1780.
[31] See also notes 2 and a above.

Index

Index

Cambridge texts in the history of philosophy

Titles published in the series thus far

Aristotle *Nicomachean Ethics* (edited by Roger Crisp)

Arnauld and Nicole *Logic or the Art of Thinking* (edited by Jill Vance Buroker)

Augustine *On the Trinity* (edited by Gareth Matthews)

Bacon *The New Organon* (edited by Lisa Jardine and Michael Silverthorne)

Boyle *A Free Enquiry into the Vulgarly Received Notion of Nature* (edited by Edward B. Davis and Michael Hunter)

Bruno *Cause, Principle and Unity* and *Essays on Magic* (edited by Richard Blackwell and Robert de Lucca with an introduction by Alfonso Ingegno)

Cavendish *Observations upon Experimental Philosophy* (edited by Eileen O'Neill)

Cicero *On Moral Ends* (edited by Julia Annas, translated by Raphael Woolf)

Clarke *A Demonstration of the Being and Attributes of God and Other Writings* (edited by Ezio Vailati)

Classic and Romantic German Aesthetics (edited by J. M. Bernstein)

Condillac *Essay on the Origin of Human Knowledge* (edited by Hans Aarsleff)

Conway *The Principles of the Most Ancient and Modern Philosophy* (edited by Allison P. Coudert and Taylor Corse)

Cudworth *A Treatise Concerning Eternal and Immutable Morality* with *A Treatise of Freewill* (edited by Sarah Hutton)

Descartes *Meditations on First Philosophy,* with selections from the *Objections and Replies* (edited by John Cottingham)

Descartes *The World and Other Writings* (edited by Stephen Gaukroger)

Fichte *Foundations of Natural Right* (edited by Frederick Neuhouser, translated by Michael Baur)

Herder *Philosophical Writings* (edited by Michael Forster)

Hobbes and Bramhall on Liberty and Necessity (edited by Vere Chappell)

Humboldt *On Language* (edited by Michael Losonsky, translated by Peter Heath)

Kant *Critique of Practical Reason* (edited by Mary Gregor with an introduction by Andrews Reath)

Kant *Groundwork of the Metaphysics of Morals* (edited by Mary Gregor with an introduction by Christine M. Korsgaard)

Kant *The Metaphysics of Morals* (edited by Mary Gregor with an introduction by Roger Sullivan)

Kant *Prolegomena to any Future Metaphysics* (edited by Gary Hatfield)

Kant *Religion within the Boundaries of Mere Reason and Other Writings* (edited by Allen Wood and George di Giovanni with an introduction by Robert Merrihew Adams)

La Mettrie *Machine Man and Other Writings* (edited by Ann Thomson)

Leibniz *New Essays on Human Understanding* (edited by Peter Remnant and Jonathan Bennett)

Lessing *Philosophical and Theological Writings* (edited by H. B. Nisbet)

Malebranche *Dialogues on Metaphysics and on Religion* (edited by Nicholas Jolley and David Scott)

Malebranche *The Search after Truth* (edited by Thomas M. Lennon and Paul J. Olscamp)

Medieval Islamic Philosophical Writings (edited by Muhammad Ali Khalidi)

Melanchthon *Orations on Philosophy and Education* (edited by Sachiko Kusukawa, translated by Christine Salazar)

Mendelssohn *Philosophical Writings* (edited by Daniel O. Dahlstrom)

Newton *Philosophical Writings* (edited by Andrew Janiak)

Nietzsche *Beyond Good and Evil* (edited by Rolf-Peter Horstmann and Judith Norman)

Nietzsche *The Birth of Tragedy and Other Writings* (edited by Raymond Geuss and Ronald Speirs)

Nietzsche *Daybreak* (edited by Maudemarie Clark and Brian Leiter, translated by R. J. Hollingdale)

Nietzsche *The Gay Science* (edited by Bernard Williams, translated by Josefine Nauckhoff)

Nietzsche *Human, All Too Human* (translated by R. J. Hollingdale with an introduction by Richard Schacht)

Nietzsche *Untimely Meditations* (edited by Daniel Breazeale, translated by R. J. Hollingdale)

Nietzsche *Writings from the Late Notebooks* (edited by Rüdiger Bittner, translated by Kate Sturge)

Novalis *Fichte Studies* (edited by Jane Kneller)

Schleiermacher *Hermeneutics and Criticism* (edited by Andrew Bowie)

Schleiermacher *Lectures on Philosophical Ethics* (edited by Robert Louden, translated by Louise Adey Huish)

Schleiermacher *On Religion: Speeches to its Cultured Despisers* (edited by Richard Crouter)

Schopenhauer *Prize Essay on the Freedom of the Will* (edited by Günter Zöller)

Sextus Empiricus *Outlines of Scepticism* (edited by Julia Annas and Jonathan Barnes)

Shaftesbury, *Characteristics of Men, Manners, Opinions, Times* (edited by Lawrence Klein)

Adam Smith, *The Theory of Moral Sentiments* (edited by Knud Haakonssen)

Voltaire *Treatise on Tolerance and Other Writings* (edited by Simon Harvey)